Mary Archer

Mary Archer
For Richer, For Poorer

MARGARET CRICK

SIMON &
SCHUSTER

London · New York · Sydney · Toronto

A VIACOM COMPANY

First published in Great Britain by Simon & Schuster UK Ltd, 2005
A Viacom company

1 3 5 7 9 10 8 6 4 2

Simon & Schuster UK Ltd
Africa House
64–78 Kingsway
London WC2B 6AH

www.simonsays.co.uk

Simon & Schuster Australia
Sydney

A CIP catalogue record for this book
is available from the British Library

ISBN 0-7432-5962-9
EAN 9780743259620

Typeset by M Rules
Printed and bound in Great Britain
by The Bath Press, Bath

Photo credits: Section one – pic 1 © Cheltenham Ladies College; pic 2 © Newsquest,
Oxfordshire; pic 3 © Ronald Fortune/*Daily Mail*; pic 4 © *Oxford Times*; pic 5 © Rex USA; pic 6
originally published in the *Louth Standard*; pic 7 © Jimmy Jones/Associated Newspapers; pic 8 ©
Daily Mail; pic 9 © *News of the World*; pic 10 © PA/Empics; pic 11, 12 & 13 © *Daily Mail*; pic
14 © *News of the World*; pic 15 & 16 © *Daily Mail*; pic 17 © *Sun*; pic 18 © Alan Davidson; pic
19 © Brian Moody/Scope Features; pic 20 © *The Times*. **Section two** – pic 21 © Eleanor
Bentall/*Daily Telegraph*; pic 22, 23 and 24 © Sven Arnstein/Stay Still Ltd; pic 25 © PA/Empics;
pic 26 © *Daily Mail*; pic 27 © Mark St George/Rex USA; pic 28 © Richard Phole/*The Times*; pic
29 © Tony Kyriacou/Rex USA; pic 30 © Steve Hill/Rex USA; pic 31 © Andre Camara/*The
Times*; pic 32 © Mark St George/Rex USA; pic 33 © Geoff Robinson/Rex USA; pic 34 © *Daily
Mail*; pic 35 © Rex USA; pic 36 © Richard Young/Rex USA; pic 37 © *Daily Mail*.

'Come The Wild, Wild Weather' (p1) by Noël Coward. Copyright © The Estate of Noël Coward.
'Warning' (p235) by Jenny Joseph from *Selected Poems* by Jenny Joseph (Bloodaxe Books).

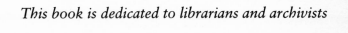
This book is dedicated to librarians and archivists

CONTENTS

Prologue: In Fragrante

IN NOVEMBER 2003, just five months after her husband's release from prison, Mary Archer sang a poignant song on Radio 3. It was written by Noël Coward and called 'Come The Wild, Wild Weather':

> Come the wild, wild, weather,
> Come the wind, come the rain.
> Come the little white flakes of snow,
> Come the joy, come the pain,
> We shall still be together
> When our life story ends,
> For wherever we chance to go
> We shall always be friends.

It was chosen very deliberately as a public declaration that she was standing by Jeffrey. The song comes from a musical called *Waiting in the Wings*, which is less appropriate. Mary has not been waiting on the sidelines to watch Jeffrey's performance; she has had a starring role on the stage of his life. In doing so, she has acquired fame and public status herself. She has had a pivotal

1

role in two of the most famous court cases of modern times: the libel trial of 1987 and the related perjury trial in 2001. In 1987 Mary's evidence was widely seen as crucial to her husband's victory. She made a highly favourable impression on the judge, who gave weight to what she said and how she said it, which influenced his summing up. In fact, Mary had no *direct* evidence of Jeffrey's innocence but she was willing to back up his story and go into battle for him. Her loyalty, intelligence and demeanour brought her sympathetic publicity, made her a household name and gave her a public platform. The libel damages handed the couple a huge sum of money, which according to Mary started their 'giving habit'. They went from strength to strength, and she supported Jeffrey's efforts to re-enter public life. Mary herself acquired a large portfolio of prominent and some public positions.

Jeffrey's court victory in 1987 acted as a brake on journalistic investigation of him; and later his influence was increased when he was given a seat in the Lords. But he could not resist chancing his luck, and when he stood for Mayor of London, with Mary's backing, his dishonest past finally caught up with him. It resulted in the perjury trial of 2001, when Mary's substantial evidence on her husband's behalf – he himself remained silent – had a rather different effect. Again she was the loyal wife supporting her husband, but the perjury trial demolished significant parts of the 1987 evidence and, after Jeffrey's conviction, Mary's own evidence was called into question by the judge, although no action was taken against her. The trial revealed that Mary had known all along about Jeffrey's infidelity, and yet she had been prepared to support him and to 'fly the flag' for him during the first trial in whatever way she could. Had the jury known the truth, he would have been extremely unlikely to have won.

After her husband's imprisonment Mary did not lie low; she strode once more into the public arena to declare that she would fight to clear his name, vowing to defeat his enemies. 'I'm quite combative,' she once said. 'It's not in our natures to hide away.'[1]

She has always been there in the forefront to defend and support him; to rescue him from scandal and disaster; to make light of his wrongdoings; to give him credibility. Because of her cleverness, litigiousness, position and enormous wealth she has had influence and control – some would say far beyond what is justifiable.

For the first half of her marriage, Mary Archer was seen mainly as the loyal, long-suffering and reserved wife of the flamboyant author; she stood back from events, at least publicly, and was once memorably described by a television critic as like 'a swan in a jacuzzi'. But following the libel trial Mary took centre stage and in doing so showed her own flair for publicity and her love of the limelight – a trait that was evident before she ever met him. For many years Mary has put herself and her family in the spotlight, giving countless interviews. She has cooperated with at least fifty profiles about herself, and with nearly forty radio and television programmes. A self-confessed 'wannabe cabaret artist', she has sung on national television and radio, and performed cabaret at an international solar energy conference.

Both the Archers are adept at managing publicity by placing stories and preventing questions. Jeffrey in particular is infamous for bullying and for threatening journalists with litigation. Over the years, guests at the Archers' have included newspaper editors and at least one BBC director general, John Birt. The present BBC chairman, Michael Grade, bought the television rights to Jeffrey's book *Kane and Abel* in the 1980s. When contacted by this author about whether he attended the Archers' parties, Grade – the man who now presides over thousands of journalists – enquired whether it was an 'authorised' biography and, on finding it was independent of the Archers, refused to help. The couple have powerful assets: money, fame and contacts. People are often in their debt or scared of them; this is partly why Jeffrey has been allowed to get away with so much.

Mary has always had her own career and interests and she, too, has gradually emerged as a public figure: on the boards of companies, government bodies and charities; holding honorary professorships; acting as an ambassador for chemistry and solar energy. Since 1992 she has been on the board of Addenbrooke's NHS Trust, an organisation responsible for large sums of tax-payers' money. She is an interesting and multi-talented person who has achieved an impressive CV in her own right, as well as supporting an equally fascinating husband. Some of those positions would probably not have been forthcoming had she not been the wife of a rich, well-connected and famous man. It is therefore hard to disentangle Dr Archer the boardroom academic from Lady Archer the celebrity wife. The fact that Mary is so well known and so well connected is undoubtedly an advantage for the institutions that enlist her, but in some ways her inextricable link with Jeffrey can be a drawback, as the Anglia Television affair demonstrated. Mary was on the board of Anglia, which was negotiating a takeover when Jeffrey made a large profit buying its shares, leading to an investigation into insider dealing. Although no charges were brought, the incident was an embarrassment for her, tainted her name and, in the eyes of some, compromised her integrity. Her support of his campaign to be Mayor of London, when there were so many 'skeletons' in his cupboard known to the media, also made her look foolish. And her very public defence of a proven liar and cheat makes her appear, to many people, highly suspect herself. Notably, the judge in Jeffrey's perjury trial indicated that parts of her evidence might bear closer scrutiny, and indeed the police did look into it, but did not take action. It was all the more surprising when she was appointed to the post of NHS Trust chairman. Mary said in 1998: 'People who stand for public office have to expect to be scrutinised'[2] but she herself has gone to extraordinary lengths to resist scrutiny.

Mary likes to keep her life as a well-respected scientist separate from her role as Jeffrey's wife. While she has largely succeeded in doing so, particularly among her Cambridge colleagues and academic friends, she has always linked herself with her husband's achievements and ambitions, enjoying the money, the contacts, the glamour, the title of Lady Archer – and even the prospect of becoming Mayoress of London. Perhaps more revealingly, she has enjoyed and encouraged the publicity, not only on subjects related to her own career but on matters as diverse as her religious beliefs, her medical problems, her investments, the contents of her fridge and what she wears in bed (a full-length, white cotton lawn nightdress, summer or winter).[3] Mary Archer may claim she values her privacy, but she has allowed her life to be put on public display with astonishing frequency. 'I've enjoyed the fame, that's true,' she said in 2003.[4]

More recently, Mary has been engaged in a media campaign that has baffled even her friends: to try to redeem her husband's reputation and to get his convictions for perjury and perverting the course of justice overturned, asserting publicly that he is an innocent man. In the months following Jeffrey's imprisonment, she appeared on many news programmes to put her case, and was also interviewed on *Richard and Judy*, *Woman's Hour* and *Midweek*. She even spoke of Jeffrey's future on *My Favourite Hymns*. In May 2003 she was the subject of an 'authorised' television programme about her life which was a fifty-minute hagiography where she was given a platform to advance her argument that Jeffrey is a victim of a miscarriage of justice; she made clear to the programme makers that this was her purpose in taking part.

The surprising thing about the programme, which predictably got a large audience, was that it was commissioned by the head of current affairs at Channel 4, where one might have expected a more robust and challenging approach. Produced by Fiona Sanderson, a former girlfriend of one of Jeffrey's friends, the documentary had all the incisiveness of a *Hello!* magazine article. Sanderson's previous film had been *Toffs Behind Bars*, about the politician Jonathan Aitken, another friend of the Archers. Channel 4, Fiona Sanderson, Mary and her lawyers had several meetings to negotiate a contract in which Mary agreed to be interviewed subject to conditions that included being able to see the programme before it was transmitted – not normal Channel 4 pro-cedure. In addition she suggested and helped to contact interviewees, supplied most of the stills and a considerable amount of film and tape footage, and – not surprisingly – refused to answer challenging questions. Channel 4 denies that she had editorial control, but it was as near to it as any self-respecting current affairs department could ever allow.

In short, Mary Archer is a very smooth operator when it comes to getting her message across. But perhaps the programme revealed rather more about her than she intended, and it certainly gave this book impetus. Jeffrey's life has already been explored in detail elsewhere; the reader will find a brief summary of his younger days in the early chapters of this book, because an understanding of his character is crucial to any analysis of the woman who is his partner and knows him best, his wife. Mary is both a contrast to Jeffrey and a likeness of him, and some aspects of her personality are, as the nursery rhyme goes, quite contrary. While Jeffrey has made a big impact on Mary and the sort of life she has led, it is arguable that she has made very little difference to him. At the end of 2003 she thought perhaps he was learning a little restraint from her – but that we have yet to see. She once said, 'Jeffrey thrives on a crisis. He doesn't like life just going along normally.'[5] By the summer of 2004, a year after his release from prison, and while still on parole, Jeffrey was once more in the news, and denying 'involvement' in funding mercenary activities in the African state of Equatorial Guinea.

Mary Archer has long been defined by reference to her husband. It is impossible to write about her life without constant mention of her marriage to Jeffrey; they are inseparable in the public's eyes. It has endured for nearly forty years, much longer than most marriages today. And although this strange and unconventional partnership provides much amusement and curiosity, it has also deflected attention away from Mary's considerable achievements. Mary Archer is a very impressive woman in her own right; and it's possible she might have had an even more successful career without her high-profile husband. The question most often asked about her is: why does she stay with Jeffrey? Perhaps this book will also help answer a slightly different question: why does Jeffrey stay with Mary?

1

In the Genes

AT THE AGE OF FOUR, during a Christmas pantomime, Mary was invited on stage with other children and asked what she wanted to be when she grew up. In front of her proud parents she replied: 'When I grow up I want to be an expert.'[1]

The remark of an innocent child would have caused amusement at the time, but these days it gives pause for thought, because it goes to the heart of Mary Archer's character – with her ambition, her cleverness and her need to be someone who is respected, someone with gravitas. Mary was to achieve her childhood dream, but it has not been as an expert that she has found fame, but as a bedfellow in an unlikely partnership.

In many ways she resembles one of her intrepid ancestors, Edith Wilson. Edith was the daughter of an optician and had led an uneventful life in Hackney helping her mother until she married an adventurer, a sea captain called William Wilson. In 1884 and on her honeymoon, she embarked on the journey of a lifetime, sailing with her husband to the other side of the globe to the Indonesian island of Java (the scene of the devastating Krakatoa volcano the previous year). Edith was well educated, and kept a journal of her voyage, which is today a family treasure. The journal is a vivid description of her experiences and her feelings, and makes fascinating reading, particularly as it reveals characteristics that her famous descendant also shows: a sense of adventure, stoicism, devotion to her spouse, the ability to write well, and a fondness for cats. And like Edith, Mary was a woman who would follow her husband to exceptional lengths.

Almost exactly sixty years after Edith Wilson landed in Java, her great-granddaughter was born. Mary's life began three days before Christmas 1944, as the Second World War was drawing to an end. That year had seen the D-Day landings when Allied troops stormed ashore in Normandy, and in September the black-out was relaxed. Plans had been approved for a National Health Service, and scientists had discovered that genes are made from DNA. The British government had banned all foreign travel but it eased clothing restrictions; women could now look forward to pleated skirts and men to turn-ups. Lloyd George announced his retirement, Glenn Miller went missing, and a musical hit of the year was *Mairzy Doats*. The Education Act had raised the school leaving age to fifteen and married women were no longer banned from being teachers. There was to be no means-testing in grammar, secondary modern or technical schools.

That, however, was not going to be a particular concern to Mary's parents, Harold and Doreen Weeden, whose children were destined for expensive private education. The Weedens were comfortably off members of the Surrey stockbroker belt, an area favoured by many well-to-do families whose menfolk commuted by train to work in the City and enjoyed a more tranquil way of life in the suburbs at weekends. The Weedens lived in a large detached house called Bank End in an area adjoining the Epsom Downs, just a mile or so from the famous racecourse. They already had one child, six-year-old Janet. Their second daughter was born in a nursing home in Ewell, weighed 7 pounds and 1 ounce and arrived 'on the button'.[2] She was named Mary Doreen.

Harold Weeden was a chartered accountant for a pharmaceutical company in London, and had also been born in Surrey but in the less expensive area of Thornton Heath, near Croydon. His father, Alfred Norman, also worked with figures, being a book-keeper for a provision merchant at the time of Harold's birth. If Harold got his financial know-how from his father, he inherited Welsh ancestry from his mother. Elizabeth Maud was the daughter of Sarah and John Davies, a farmer from Cwmdu in the Black Mountains, not far from Crickhowell. Early in their married life, Elizabeth and Alfred moved with their son to Cheam, an undistinguished suburb of London. The Weedens joined the nearby Sutton Baptist Church, which was at that time a flourishing community with a large congregation. A local historian, Joan Atfield, who was a child in the 1930s, remembers the Weedens playing a notable part in the life of the church. Mary herself has spoken of her grandparents as being 'very strict and particular Baptists' and said her father was brought up in his parents' Chapel tradition. Their religion was principled and political: it opposed the opening of cinemas on Sunday, lobbied Parliament about Licensing Bills, and supported the League of United Nations' Peace Ballot some years before the outbreak of World War Two. But there was also a lighter side: the church provided social and educational opportunities for its members, particularly its young people, with many associations and activities. At Sutton Baptist Church the twenties and thirties was a time when membership greatly increased and work among young people was particularly successful, according to the *Manual*, a yearly report of church matters and accounts. The *Manual* paints a vivid portrait of the fundraising and community spirit of a religious organisation in its prime.

The Weedens appear on the church roll in 1923, when their son was a teenager. Alfred was a deacon and church treasurer, and his wife was treasurer of the Missionary Sewing Meeting. The sewing meeting raised funds for overseas work; for example, in 1927, sending a parcel of clothing to the Reverend and Mrs Wooster who ran a school in the Congo. Harold played his part too, being a helper in the primary department of the Sunday school where his parents taught. He sometimes played the organ and was the honorary secretary of the church cricket club. A year earlier, the church had moved to its present site in Cheam Road and into a new building – built in six months and with a credit balance of £31 at the end of the project. Whether or not this was thanks to the skills of Alfred Weeden as treasurer is not reported. 'Mr Weeden was a lovely man, a very nice man, and he did a lot of work for the church,' says Joan Atfield. 'When Alfred died, Elizabeth gave the church a piano in his memory. She had a very sharp tongue, and she upset a lot of people with her comments, but she did an awful lot too, running mothers' meetings and a sewing group.' Eventually the Weedens moved away and Alfred went on to greater prosperity, becoming a company director. These traits of directness of speech and ability with figures – as well as commitment to religion, music, charitable works and public service – were to reappear further down the Weeden line.

Mary's father was twenty-seven when he married Doreen Cox, a twenty-three-year-old local girl. Doreen's ancestors, like the Weedens, came from the London area, but nearer the heart of the city. Doreen's grandfather had been a mathematical journeyman, a scientific instrument maker, who married the daughter of a hatter from Cumberland. Their son Theodore (known to his family as 'Mick') married a Whitechapel girl, Doris, the younger daughter of the sea captain William Wilson and his wife, Edith. Photographs show that the young Mick was a very good-looking and well-dressed man; Doris was slightly built, with fine features and dark hair. Five months after Doris and Mick married, their daughter Doreen (Mary's mother) was born, and a few years later a son and two more daughters. Mick was then a clerk with a company called the Pacific Cable Board, and worked his way up to be a supervisor. By the time Doreen married into the Weeden family, the Coxes were living at a desirable address in Cheam.

Mary's mother, Doreen Cox, met her future husband at the local tennis club. She was good at sport and had been vice-games-captain of netball at Rosebery County School in Epsom, as well as games-captain of her school house and a prefect. Before she left, the school awarded her 'colours' (a tie or sash) for outstanding sporting achievement. According to a member of the family she was also very bright, and worked in a bank before her marriage: 'She was a dependable sort of person.' She was also a good cook who is remembered for making a wonderful steak and kidney pudding. Harold and Doreen's wedding took place on 10 July 1937 (Mary was to choose almost the same date – 11 July – for her own marriage). The following year, shortly before the Second World War, their first child, Janet, was born. There are no electoral registers for the war years, but by the time Mary was born, in 1944, the family had moved to Epsom, where Janet had started school. While Harold Weeden commuted, Doreen was a traditional mother who stayed at home for her family – 'a wonderful housewife . . . those were the days!'[3] Mary said later, although over the years she has commented little about her mother, whose place at home – and maybe in Mary's mind – was overshadowed by her dominant father. A brother, David, came in 1949, and the young Weedens enjoyed a traditional, well-to-do English middle-class upbringing: conventional, quiet, Church of England and Conservative-voting. The family moved several times within the Epsom and Ewell area, but Mary spent the first part of her childhood in a detached family house which backed on to the Downs and had a large leafy garden where the children could play. By the time she was eight, the Weedens had moved to an even larger house called Longdown Lodge near Epsom College. Electoral registers show the names of two other women living with the family in the early 1950s, perhaps nannies, and, in 1953, a serviceman. Mary says one of the houses had a swimming pool in the garden. In the 1960s, their grandmother Elizabeth also came to live with them, after her husband's death. Alfred had left nearly £5,000 in his will – the equivalent of over £100,000 today – and among his bequests was £500 each to his three grandchildren, Janet, Mary and David.

Perhaps because of his Welsh ancestry, Harold was a keen musician and fond of singing. He liked to spend his lunch hours in City churches such as St Michael's Cornhill and the Temple Church, listening to recitals – sometimes being joined by his wife – and he encouraged his children to be musical. At home every evening after dinner he would relax by playing the piano. Mary learned to play from an early age and sometimes they performed duets: 'I remember the trouble my small hands had with the octave chords, and the duets we devised to solve the problem.'[4] But more often than not, she would sing to his accompaniment. Sometimes the whole family gathered round the piano to sing: music which Mary remembers to this day. 'We had lots of songbooks of folksongs and old English songs and little operatic arias and so forth and we worked through a tremendous repertory together.'[5] Mary said it was awful when she went away to school and wasn't afraid of singing solo, and everybody else in the class thought it was 'terribly forward'. To her it was quite natural and she had no idea it was something to be shy about. When Mary was a guest on *Desert Island Discs* in 1988, her first choice of record was an organ voluntary which reminded her of her father, whose sheet music she had inherited. Mary's father also had a passion for model railways and built an elaborate layout in his attic. His elder daughter, Janet, described him as a firm but very nice man with a slightly short fuse.

Another of Harold Weeden's interests was amateur filmmaking, then a relatively new and certainly expensive hobby but common among affluent middle-class families. In 1952 he was a founder member of the Epsom Cine Society, and volunteered to become its treasurer. The first film the club ever produced was a black and white silent documentary of the coronation year, and members also recorded local news events. Harold does not seem to have taken part in club productions, but used his film for personal records: he took hundreds of feet of colour 16mm of his young family, and of special occasions and trips to the local swimming pool. But he was supportive in various ways, held meetings at his home and made an occasional donation to club funds. People joined it partly to share technical know-how, and also for its social side, which brought together like-minded people; the members went on outings together with their families. Harold had been encouraged to join by his good friend Leslie Froude, who was club chairman. At the club's first AGM, Froude declared that the highlight of the year was their coronation newsreel, 'a public show . . . which was attended by all the nobs . . .'[6] Leslie Froude, well known in Epsom, was also a leading freemason. His membership of what was in those days a highly secretive society was something he shared with his friend Harold Weeden, who joined a branch of Surrey freemasons in 1960. As we shall see, Mary was to encounter freemasonry later in her life, at Lloyd's insurance market.

Another friend from Epsom Cine Society days says, 'Harold was a wonderful chap . . . a very gentlemanly fellow; very straight to the point, very honest too, and his wife was charming. He was very fond, very proud of Mary, who was very, very clever as a child. The whole family are clever.' Mary claims she was her father's favourite because, she says modestly, 'I was bright and perky,'[7] and remembers him teaching her multiplication tables when she was only three. Perhaps she was her mother's favourite too: 'She's great fun to be with . . .' her mother told an interviewer in 1987.

Although the background was conventional, Harold Weeden was, in one way at least, ahead of his time – a bit of a feminist, as Mary put it later. Harold did not go to university but educated himself by reading widely, and he was determined his children would have the opportunities he hadn't had. He thought women could do everything that men could do, and Mary says she didn't discover this was not a widespread male attitude at the time, until it was much too late to change her mind about what she wanted to do – which was to enter what was then, and still is, a male-dominated profession. Mary's father believed that girls should be as well educated as boys, and sent both his daughters to Cheltenham Ladies' College, the epitome of the English girls' public school. Mary's mother said, 'We sent her to Cheltenham Ladies' not for snobbish reasons but so she would learn to love knowledge and take enjoyment from simple things.' But the forceful Harold wanted his children to 'get on' in life. He had very high, uncompromising standards, which he passed on to his diligent daughters. And the influence and encouragement of a strong father was a key factor in Mary's life, as it is with many successful women. For Harold Weeden, only the top was good enough.

2

Perfect Prefect

A PRIMARY TEACHER once wrote on Mary's report about a needlework test: 'Mary must learn not to cry when she comes second.' The story, told by a friend, is probably apocryphal, but has a ring of truth; she does not like to lose. And at school, she seldom did. Mary's mother said, 'She's got a very clear brain. When she was first being tested for nursery school at the age of four I remember the mistress coming out and saying, "Mary is the *most* intelligent little girl."' Mary's older sister, Janet, remembers a high school teacher calling Mary a genius, and that their father told the family she must nevertheless be treated like an ordinary girl.

Mary's first school was St Christopher's in Epsom, which was a private mixed junior school run by the Misses Patterson and Moodie. Years later, Mary remembered two teachers in particular: Mrs Lock, who taught her to do her shoelaces, and Miss Case, who taught her to read. Violet Case remembers Mary as 'a nice quiet girl' who wore her hair in bunches. The children were taught in small classes with emphasis on the three Rs and at the end of each year they had a Show Day to entertain their parents. The school was linked to St Martin's Church in Epsom, which is where Mary and her brother, David, were eventually baptised on the same day, she aged ten and he aged six. Mary's three godparents included her mother's sister Sheila and her father's cousin Eleanor. St Martin's, like the Baptist Church in Sutton, was a busy centre of Christian activity. Its magazines record that the parish even had a 'moral welfare worker' called Miss Soul.

Mary confesses to having tunnel vision and being very bookish and says people were forever telling her to leave her books and do something else. One of the things the family cine film captures is her dressing up. The 16mm colour footage, shown in a recent TV documentary, shows six-year-old Mary posing in the garden, wearing a wide-brimmed, flower-trimmed shepherdess hat and long gown. She is also seen playing on the lawn with her mother, brother and sister and the family tabby, in front of a large, creeper-covered house. It was not only from her father that Mary acquired her taste for appearing before the camera and an audience. Her maternal grandmother, Doris Cox, was fond of writing little pantomimes – based on well-known stories – for the children of the family to perform at her house. Home entertainments were quite common in those days, and judging from family snapshots, the Weedens and Coxes went to considerable trouble to look the part, with well-made costumes. The photos show Mary acting as Cinderella and as a princess, as well as wearing a Turkish outfit with a yashmak. Her fondness for performing was to become more obvious in later years.

One of Mary's earliest memories is of 'jolting along in a Greenline bus in Epsom looking around at all those . . . old, dull people staring into space . . . wondering if they were thinking interesting things' like the interesting thoughts in her own head. 'I think that's the reaction of a clever child.'[1] One of those thoughts involved tying an earthworm into a knot. Her father scolded her for being so cruel and she explained that she wanted to see if the worm could untie itself. 'That was probably my first scientific experiment,' she later said. 'That particular earthworm could not untie itself from that particular knot, but I have to say it's a good job I wasn't a trained biologist or I'd have taken a thousand wretched earthworms and tied them into a thousand knots to make the result statistically significant.'[2]

In 1956 Mary joined her older sister at the famous Cheltenham Ladies' College. She had already, aged eleven, been sent to London on her own to buy her new school uniform, because her mother believed in making children stand on their own two feet. Mary has described her mother as a lovely person, very self-sufficient and shrewd, but with a sense of remoteness and detachment, which Mary recognises in herself. Doreen Weeden had reservations about her girls being away at boarding school. 'My mother was the one who was more concerned with, you know, being happy and not being over-stretched and my father was more ambitious for us all and for himself.'[3] Cheltenham would provide ideal nurturing for the budding scientist, and when she discovered chemistry and physics, Mary's mind was made up. She still remembers her first chemistry class, and has kept her exercise book with her drawing of a bunsen burner.

Mary says that while she didn't welcome being sent away to boarding school, she already knew the place because her sister was there, which made life easier, and although she was homesick at the start of every term she loved it. When she arrived, her sister had already made her mark, and was Head of House. One of Mary's contemporaries says: 'Janet was brilliant, and different from her sister. She was blonde, Mary was dark. Janet was very pretty, clever, very good at games . . . she was one of those girls who had everything. You don't get made head of house unless you've got a lot of spark to you. We were little girls who'd just arrived. Mary was razor thin and she despised games. We both played in the house second cricket eleven and were beaten very early on. She wasn't terribly good friends with any of us; not that she wasn't nice, just that she wasn't a joiner-in. We called her the brainbox.' The brainy newcomer was soon to eclipse her clever older sister. Another old girl says that teachers used to admonish them: 'Why can't you be more like Mary Weeden?'

Cheltenham was, and is, a traditional girls' boarding school with high and uncompromising standards of education and behaviour. Some thought it snobbish but it was not a 'glamorous' school, although it had a sprinkling of debs. It stressed high academic standards and the importance of female achievement; among its women of distinction were the first woman master of surgery and the first woman to take a doctorate in chemistry. The school offered a protected and conformist atmosphere; it was, said Mary, '. . . a fairly disciplinarian, tough place, but I enjoyed that. My sister, who was six years ahead of me, was head of house and I was the least significant of the newcomers. That was a little bit alarming and I do remember having the wrong shoes. But I enjoyed it. I wasn't particularly popular, because I was a swot, I tended to have my nose in a book. Scientists were always frightfully apart.'[4] Seventeen-year-old Janet Weeden was already in the sixth form and the school magazine reports that she had just won a place at the Royal Free Hospital in London, where she might well have studied medicine (as her younger brother later did) but she changed her plans.

Mary joined Cheltenham at a fortuitous time: the science wing was being extended, with the help of a building grant from the Industrial Fund for the Advancement of Scientific Education. The school's principal was the formidable-sounding Miss Joan Tredgold, whose name was later to be immortalised in a Jeffrey Archer novel, *The Prodigal Daughter*. Miss Tredgold, herself an old girl of the college, and with a Cambridge first in mathematics, could have provided much inspiration for the woman Mary became: 'an awe-inspiring and godly woman . . . one felt one should curtsey rather than shake hands' was the memory of her pupils. If a girl's misdemeanour came to the attention of Miss Tredgold, a staff meeting was called and the teachers were made to feel like naughty schoolgirls themselves, according to one mistress. At speech day in summer 1957, when twelve-year-old Mary was in her first year at the school, Miss Tredgold reported that: 'At present the general impression is of corrugated iron and chaos, but we look forward to excellent new laboratories . . . Such an undertaking must inevitably cause some inconvenience and dis-comfort, and one cannot lose nine classrooms for a term without noticing it; but we have managed to compress ourselves ... at some cost ... to the staff, who have borne it with patience and great good temper.'[5] The school hoped to increase the amount of advanced work in science, but nevertheless the college would not become 'a place in which science will thrive at the expense of the arts'. An indication of the school's overall achievement was the fact that it topped the list of schools whose girls got scholarships to Oxford and Cambridge women's colleges. Girls of 'really good ability' were able to take their O levels in just four years instead of five. But it wasn't all work: girls went to 'dances and other festiv-ities'; they attended concerts, the local arts and literary festivals, got involved in charity work, debated with boys, went on expedi-tions, acted, fenced, danced, swam and played hockey. And some once enjoyed a film show given by Mr Weeden.

Mary was a good all-rounder, blessed with a phenomenal memory; she even made the green school uniform look good, despite the spindly legs, which she said her mother agonised over. She was just the cleverest girl in the class, says one of her contem-poraries, now the English professor and broadcaster Lisa Jardine. 'It was quite maddening ... She was the prettiest girl, and she sang like an angel and she played the piano like an angel and she was also certainly in the top two percent, and believe me the top two per cent of Cheltenham is extremely clever. Her uniform never got rumpled like mine did, she always was properly turned out for choir, she never had the wrong books.'[6] One contemporary remembers her sitting quietly in a corner doing beautiful embroi-dery. Mary was nicknamed 'Weed' or 'Weedlet' because of her name and thinness, just as her husband-to-be was known at school as 'Pune'. She confessed later that she yearned to be like the young actress Jean Simmons because she had 'a rough approximation' to her looks and 'she was so snooty with men in *Great Expectations*'. But as far as her classmates were concerned, Mary *did* have make-believe good looks: 'She was bright, shiny, flawless – her complexion was immaculate where the rest of us had spots and puppy fat. Most of us had boyfriends by the time we were in the senior school, but not Mary. She was good with a capital G.' The naughtiest thing Mary seems to have done is make an 'apple pie' bed for one of her classmates during their first term.

Mary first lived with about fifty others in Glenlee house, later moving to a senior house, Fauconberg, and then to a temporary house, Marston. The houses were some distance from the main school building, and girls had all their meals there, even walking the half-mile 'home' at lunchtimes. They were looked after by a house mistress and Glenlee's was a formidable woman called Sadie Garner who was known affectionately as 'the hag'. Like Mary, she was fond of cats and had a kitten called Phineas Fogg. There were games four afternoons a week, including Saturday, and three hours of homework a day at senior school. Mary Sambrook, who was the assistant to another house mistress during Mary's final year, remembers her well: 'She was absolute perfection, good at everything, good at acting, in the choir, a brilliant scholar, and she always looked very smart in her uniform. They used to say there was no more they could teach her; exams were nothing to her, she just walked through them.'

One of the girls in Mary's house, Ann Gegg, says her own family were not as wealthy as most parents, and she remembers the first thing Mary did was to boast that she lived in a house with eight bedrooms. 'She was quite isolated, I thought she was a bit sad really. She was difficult to relate to and I didn't even know she had a brother until I saw it on a television programme in 2003. Her sister Janet was much more sociable but quite strict.' As a senior pupil she had to be. There was very strict discipline and girls were scrutinised not only by teachers but every week by prefects, who sometimes wrote reports on a girl's posture, table conversation, manners and demeanour. There was a lot of inspection, from underclothes to library books, and public humiliation was frequent. Girls who did really bad work had a Ref (Refusal) read out in prayers, and were under great pressure. As one girl of the fifties put it: 'People of the right temperament thrived on it, bu[...] conformists into priggishness and non-conformists into re[...] The effect on the two sisters was striking. Although Jane[...] highly successful pupil, she left school 'with a sudden i[...] according to another girl in the same house. Despite her place at the Royal Free, she later became a secretary. Mary was a committee prefect (a superior version of prefect) and Head of House and left school with high distinction: the school's Sparks Memorial Prize for merit in academic work.

Asked thirty years later why she chose chemistry, she said she liked it because it made sense of the world; and it appealed to her 'systematising mind'. Another female chemist, up at Oxford University when Mary was born, was Margaret Thatcher, who would become a close friend. Thatcher, too, was greatly influenced by a strong father. Cheltenham's science society arranged lectures and trips to places of interest, and in July 1960 a small group of girls was taken to the Royal Radar establishment at Malvern, about 25 miles away. There, they saw experiments in progress and apparatus such as spectroscopes, and an 'enormously powerful' electromagnet. At the end of the visit they were given tea and told about the possibilities of a scientific career in the Civil Service. Mary had other ideas.

The college magazine provides a priceless snapshot of life in a traditional English girls' school in the mid-twentieth century. During Mary's time, the magazine – edited by the Misses Tredgold, Plunkett, Fanthorpe and Prigg – reveals a privileged and commendable world of culture, order and security – if not comfort – and a certain self-deprecating humour, with its many contributions from the girls. 'The effect of this earnest desire for knowledge is only slightly marred by the insistent stress on shopping (it is a first-class disaster when expedition day proves also to be early-closing day) and food,' wrote one child wryly. Mary's own memory of the food will be familiar to many schoolchildren of the fifties: 'I remember wonderful sticky buns you had at break with a third of a pint of milk. I don't think I could have made it through the day without them, though nothing would persuade me to drink cold milk now . . . or eat lumpy custard . . . or lumpy meat.'[7]

The Weeden girls feature now and again in the magazines: in 1960 it notes that Mary passed her Grade 6 piano exam, and the magazine's News of Old Girls revealed that her sister Janet was now a private secretary working for Tri-ang Toys. Mary herself contributed – including a report of a Lent lecture about prayer, which she wrote around the time she was prepared for confirmation by the vicar of Christ Church, Cheltenham, John Cavell, now a bishop. Mary appears to be among some girls photographed in the new science labs for the magazine, with her straight dark hair severely cut and neatly parted. She also sang in the choir and once took a male role in a school play, *Quality Street*. By the age of only sixteen, Mary had passed A levels in maths, physics and chemistry and had won a Nuffield science scholarship to read chemistry at St Anne's College, Oxford, whose principal was a governor at Cheltenham. She said matter-of-factly that it was a great surprise, but not very difficult; eight others in her year were awarded Oxford places. Before going up to university she travelled to Austria where she learned German which would be useful in her scientific career and was part of her degree course. It was in the autumn of 1962, around the time of the Cuban missile crisis, that she arrived in Oxford at the young age of seventeen already determined to become an academic.

A traditional, solid, middle-class background; strong religious values; a secure family life; a very good brain; parents who valued independent thought and learning, and had the means to pay for the best; a father who was ahead of his time in his views on the education of his daughters; this was the launch pad from which the young Mary Weeden entered Oxford University. It was a place where she would find excitement, fulfilment, the chance to develop other sides of her personality – and where she would acquire a very colourful husband.

Her chemistry tutor at Oxford still remembers the day she first met Mary Weeden. 'She was 16 and 11 months from the fourth year sixth at Cheltenham Ladies' College and she interviewed beautifully. She was way ahead of the minimum scholarship standard and did a super chemistry paper. I marked it Alpha plus. She put in bits that I wouldn't have thought of,' says Dr Hazel Rossotti, a Fellow of St Anne's. The college never took more than six women chemists a year at that time, and there were scarcely two dozen in Oxford as a whole, although chemistry wasn't as bereft of women as some of the other sciences. Applicants of sixteen were still rarer. Having been extremely impressed by Mary, Dr Rossotti was somewhat taken aback to be told by her fellow examiners that 'one did not give Alpha pluses' to candidates but she later discovered that her mathematician colleagues had also given Mary an alpha plus. Physics gave her a straight alpha.

She was a joy to teach, intellectually and personally, according to her tutor. 'Her chemistry was extremely lucid. I left her essays till last because I could read them with enjoyment.' That year there were four women reading chemistry at St Anne's and they were divided into pairs for tutorials, which they had to attend wearing gowns. Mary, being a scholar, had a special gown which was longer and with sleeves. At first Mary had tutorials with a partner, Christine Jackson, but her tutor soon decided she was so clever she should be taken on her own. Even in those days, Mary was professional in her approach and not over-modest about her abilities, just matter of fact, 'neither pushy nor violet-like'. Two of Mary's fellow students found her difficult to get to know. Gillian Howarth says, 'She got into Oxford when she was quite young and because of that she was relatively immature and found the social environment difficult . . . so she was always quite reticent about what she said and did and she didn't ever let you feel you knew what was going on inside her mind, really.' Christine Jackson said she went along with Mary to the college Christian Union meetings for Bible study. The Union was evangelical and another attender says Mary felt it was too 'literal' for her, and she eventually stopped going. 'She was knowledgeable and contributed,' says Jackson, 'but she was rather reserved and I never got close to her.' Her tutor agrees:

'She was certainly rather shy at first,' says Dr Rossotti. 'She wasn't enormously social and she did work very hard, with a lot of practical work to do, but one of her priorities was singing.' Mary had successfully auditioned for the prestigious Bach choir, and went to choir practice every Monday evening. This meant she was not keen on having tutorials on Tuesdays because she had not been able to prepare sufficiently the previous evening, so the tutorials were held on other days. Although there was a greater social gap between tutor and pupils than exists today, a friendly relationship eventually developed between 'Mrs R' and her star pupil. 'She used to babysit our children, and we had a Siamese cat. She's extremely fond of cats and I think she put up with the children in order to have feline company!'

The student who Mary did get on well with was the fourth in her group, Ann King, who was more than a year older than her. Their friendship was somewhat surprising to everybody else as the two women were very different in background and personality. Ann was the daughter of an electrician from Sussex and had done extremely well to gain a place at Oxford. She was clever, although nothing like as clever as Mary, outgoing and friendly. 'She was a very vivacious, generous person and liked to be out there going to parties and she really enjoyed all the social life of Oxford,' says Gillian Howarth. 'She was a contrast to Mary – about as far as you could get!' Mary had been a self-styled 'contented conformist' at school, and perhaps the fun-loving Ann opened Mary's eyes to a wider world and different attitudes; the freedom of university gave Mary somewhere she could experiment, discover people from different backgrounds, and have fun. And despite her initial reserve, Mary was to emerge from her Cheltenham cocoon as quite a social butterfly.

St Anne's, about half a mile from the centre of Oxford, was friendly and outward-looking. Among its alumnae are the author Iris Murdoch, the poet U. A. Fanthorpe and the hospice founder Cicely Saunders, but the year Mary went up it was suffering from what its principal suggested was 'lack of ambition' among its women. Exam results were disappointing, with only one first and 'far too many thirds'. However, the following year, the college was ambitious enough to send a team to compete in the television programme *University Challenge*. It was an era when long-held traditions were under threat and there was talk of women being allowed to enter men's colleges. St Anne's relaxed its own rules to the extent of abolishing sixpenny passes for entry into the building after 11.15 p.m., and extended its hours for men until 10 p.m. on weekdays and 10.30 at weekends. It was the time when the contraceptive pill was new, but abortion still illegal and women talked 'an inordinate amount' about sex. However, its dress code was firm: women must not wear trousers and no miniskirts with subfusc (the black and white 'uniform' worn by students to sit exams). By the time Mary left, improving the ratings with her good exam results, college life was sufficiently relaxed for a crèche for dons' babies to be enlarged due to popular demand. Academically, Mary excelled at Oxford. 'That was a real surprise to me,' she has said, 'particularly with all these cocky young men strutting around . . . because chemistry was rather male in those days.'[8]

Early in her first year, she and the other freshers were mystified by an incomprehensible lecture about austenitic steels. Mary worried about how far behind she must be, until eventually the lecturer noticed he had lost his whole audience. They told him they were first-year chemists, and he began again. He had mistaken them for the graduate metallurgy class. Mary said she was ambitious to do well and found work a pleasure because it interested her and because she was good at it. She was so good that she narrowly missed the university's Gibbs prize for chemistry, gaining a *proxime accessit*. The chemistry course at Oxford was a four-year course, and most students had done 'prelims' before they came up. There were no examinations for three years until their Part I written papers which led to an unclassified BA, and the students then went on to take Part II which was the research year on which a thesis was submitted. The class of degree was awarded at the end of the fourth year, and Mary was one of two women to get a first in chemistry. It is sometimes said she got a double first, but there was no such thing in chemistry at Oxford.

For the first three years of her course Mary lived in a college house, and although she thought it 'charming', it had its drawbacks. She remembers that in her first winter there, 'the snow lay on the ground for an eternity and these little houses had stuck-on boxes that were bathrooms. They were so cold, I don't think I washed for a whole term.'[9] The weather was so bad that a concession was made to allow women to wear trousers, but only within college. The accommodation was in a succession of roomy old houses, which were pleasantly informal in contrast to the other women's colleges, with their long corridors and institutional atmosphere. Particularly for those who had come to Oxford from single-sex schools, St Anne's was a haven to which they could retreat for a late night session of cocoa and conversation. 'It was perfect for me to have the secure base of an all-women's college but to venture out to the alien but oh-so-attractive world of parties,' says one of Mary's contemporaries. In Mary's fourth year, the research year, she had digs in a terraced house between the Cowley and Iffley roads, an area of east Oxford where many students lived, including a cocky young man called Jeffrey Archer. He was by then also in Oxford, sharing a flat only a few hundred yards away with two student athletes, Adrian Metcalfe and Michael Hogan. Mary herself shared digs with her friend Ann King and the two house-mates once had their tutor and her husband to supper. Dr Rossotti says she did sometimes wonder whether Mary paid the rent for both of them, as Ann had no money.

The digs were somewhat dingy bedsits, but the landlady, Miss Kempson, was nice, kind and thoughtful. She looked after her girls very well, and had only one request of them: that they keep her company watching TV programmes now and then. One of Mary's successors at the house, the journalist and media executive Liz Forgan, says Miss Kempson often spoke wistfully of her former tenant: 'I never met Mary, but the impression I got from the landlady was that she was saintly, clever, pretty and nice, and always watched television with her.' Mary also liked looking after the landlady's elderly black cat. Unfortunately for her, the cat was called Nigger and, even in the non-politically correct sixties, it was embarrassing for Mary to have to be out in the street calling loudly for Nigger to come inside.

Mary had looks that were head-turning, especially in the predominantly male university. She was strikingly pretty, with shiny dark hair and lovely skin, and a slim figure; she was always immaculate, as now. 'Mary was always neat and tidy and seemly,' said one of her contemporaries. 'She had beautifully cut hair; there was never any student scruff.' Some thought her prim, but the men were more effusive: 'She was delectable, the most beautiful face, and very poised and very cool, and just jaw-droppingly beautiful,' says Adrian Metcalfe. 'All the scientists put almost a posse around her to stop anybody who wasn't a scientist talking to her because they felt she was one of theirs and how dare all these arts graduates try and chat her up.'[10] The television science presenter Adam Hart-Davis, who also read chemistry, was in Mary's year: 'I don't think I ever dared ask her out because she was so ethereally beautiful,' he says. 'When we meet now, I'm allowed to give her a big hug and I still fancy her.'

Science degrees generally required longer hours than arts degrees, but there was time to develop new interests and make friends; Mary saw it as a tremendous opportunity and 'an absolute rite of passage'. Apart from the Bach choir, there were parties and boyfriends. The swot was rapidly learning how to be more outgoing. 'Mary was far more extrovert than I was,' says Dinah Harrison, a school friend and St Anne's house-mate. 'She got around far more than I did; she was fairly high profile and she had a lot of male friends.' Mary also took out life membership of the Oxford Union which had just begun to admit women to speak in debates; they were not admitted as full members until 1963. The Union gave Mary a little taste of political debate, which is something she hadn't experienced at home. This was the start of the swinging sixties, a time of exciting developments such as the astronaut John Glenn orbiting the earth. It was a time of cutting-edge fashion: Mary Quant short skirts and Vidal Sassoon haircuts; of the Beatles, LSD and Op Art; of protest and the pill. The sixties were a huge contrast to the austere post-war fifties, and would have mirrored the change between the world of Mary's childhood and that of her late teens. But Mary says she didn't see or hear anything tremendously shocking and didn't fall in with the wrong sort of set.

The set she did fall in with, a few days before the start of her second year, was the crowd on *Cherwell*, the Oxford University weekly newspaper which had a left-wing reputation. The paper's editor, Nick Lloyd, spotted the pretty young girl in the Union gardens near the *Cherwell* office and, with a colleague, went over to chat her up. Within a few weeks, Mary's face was on the front page – for the first, but not the last time in her life, and illustrates how naïve – or ambitious – she was then. The photograph showed her cuddling a kitten, above the headline 'Poor Little Pussy'. Next to another picture inside, the paper explained that Mary Weeden was looking for a home for ten-week-old Priscilla. 'You see, this kitten was going to be anaesthetised, so I took it in,' she was quoted, 'tears glistening in her eyes'. Mary became a bit of a camp-follower and was soon part of the paper's social scene, popping into *Cherwell*'s shabby offices at the back of the Oxford Union. Nick Lloyd says she 'went around' with him and a few others and then became the girlfriend of the paper's sports editor, Jonathan Martin. 'He was in love with her,' says one of the group. 'We used to tease him about her.' In 1964 she went on a visit to France with the *Cherwell* journalists to produce a Paris Special edition of the paper. Another front-page picture shows her on the Champs-Elysées with five men, leaping into the air in a parody of a Beatles pose. She was described as 'a mate'. The trip was something of a lark – one colleague remembers her sleeping on the luggage rack on the boat train. Being in the company of aspiring journalists rather than scientists was something Mary found stimulating, even if the conversation was less than high-brow. 'Colleague Mary Weeden and I were discussing the fashion side of Paris,' noted one *Cherwell* reporter. 'We were amazed at the unanimity of the little Paris birds' choice in clothes. Almost every little bird worth a second stare was wearing a neat, rather classical little coat, with squarish shoulders, slightly flared at the bottom, often double-breasted with military buttons . . . The secret is poise and walk. It's a rather serene little walk, with head held high, and little breasts pushed out . . . Paris birds seem to score over London birds by attention to the extremities. Fabulous shoes and well-cut, uncontrived hair take the Paris birds out in front . . . The only fault Mary and I could find was that they tend to have skinnny, rather tubular legs.'[11] Mary was to learn this early fashion lesson well: neat clothes, good hair, poise – Mary was already rivalling Parisiennes at their own game.

Her boyfriend, the sports editor, Jonathan Martin, also took her with him when he went to interview some politicians in London and she took notes, but she seems not to have written anything for *Cherwell*, nor worked on the business side. Martin remembers a thank-you note from George Brown, in which the deputy Labour leader asked him to pass on his regards to 'that pretty girl you brought to see me'. Later, Martin made an hour-long programme for the BBC's European English-language service which featured young people discussing the future of Britain; Mary appeared, representing Oxbridge. Having beaten her future husband to the front pages of the university newspaper, Mary had also been on the airwaves first.

Many women undergraduates would have been embarrassed to appear as a student-newspaper pin-up, and be described as a 'St Anne's glamour girl' in gossip columns but Mary seemed to enjoy it. 'She was great fun to be with,' says Patrick Marnham, a *Cherwell* editor. 'She had old-fashioned virtues like loyalty, dependability and honesty – that's how she seemed to me, anyway. She was quite shy, but laughed easily.' Despite her apparent shyness she had a strong need for adventure, and Jeffrey's Oxford flatmate Michael Hogan says: 'She might have been shy in a group, but one-on-one she wasn't a bit shy. You don't want to confuse her being shy with being reserved.' But having fun wasn't allowed to interfere with academic work. Mary spent eight hours a day in the chemistry labs in her first three years, and much longer in her final year.

'Mary was a very serious girl, extremely serious,' says Adrian Metcalfe. 'She was obviously going to get a first, and she was ... ambitious in her own quiet way.' Her intellectual life was, as it had been at school, a consolation and the thing which really mattered, as she explained many years later: 'Because you are much more interested in what you are learning; that world is more real to you than any others.'[12] She was obviously aware that she had a lot to learn about young men, from whom she had been shielded in a single-sex boarding school. 'When you come to a place like Oxford, there they all are suddenly, wall-to-wall. I found that a bit of a distraction, but I was pretty determined I wasn't going to be distracted from my work.'[13] Nick Lloyd agrees: 'I think it was a slight voyage of sexual discovery for her, or boy discovery, rather.' One of her admirers was Garth Pratt, who later became president of the Oxford Union and a parliamentary candidate. He remembers Mary in the Union bar, and says she 'decorated the place from time to time; I don't think she was ever active in the sense of putting her opinions on the line'. But Mary found Pratt's speeches at the Union very funny, and she used to invite him to her room. 'She was splendid to kiss,' he says, 'no doubt about that! And willing to learn. I made up to her very consistently, and achieved very little.'

Although disconcerted by the presence of so much testosterone, Mary was in an enviable position, from a woman's perspective. Men far outnumbered women in any case, by about five to one, but Mary's good looks made her especially desirable and she had her pick. 'It was fun being a minority ... you went out with different people; I suppose you shopped around a bit. So it was good, but the girls at the university always suffered cruelly from the competition at the secretarial colleges and from the nurses, who somehow always seemed to be much prettier.'[14] She was clearly interested in men who were going places, rather cultivating those people she thought likely to succeed. Nick Lloyd and Jonathan

Martin both went on to successful careers in journalism – Lloyd (now knighted) as editor of the *News of the World* and *Daily Express* and Martin as head of BBC TV Sport. (Although years later, Mary said of Nick Lloyd: 'we were totally unsuited in all respects'.) Another boyfriend, Nick Montagu, was involved in the Oxford Union, eventually became head of the Inland Revenue, and was also knighted. Tony Bottrill, who worked on *Cherwell*, became a senior World Bank official. 'Mary was a friend who kept a cat and kindly did my laundry occasionally,' he says. Martin Linton, now an MP, says, 'The thought was in everybody's mind that she was a bit ambitious in her relationships. She was someone who liked people on the way up. Nothing wrong with that, but there was a pattern there; she liked to attach herself to a rising star.'

All these soon-to-be-highfliers on *Cherwell* were also academically bright and reading for degrees. The man who would win Mary's hand was neither.

3

I Want to Hold Your Hand

WHILE MARY WAS IN HER second year at Oxford, she went to a party in Nick Lloyd's flat. There was a Beatles record playing and Mary was busy chatting to the *Cherwell* newspaper crowd with her boyfriend Jonathan Martin, when a nice-looking, short, muscular, bouncy young man burst in. She immediately liked what she saw. 'My first impressions are really enduring impressions: energy, fizz, enthusiasm, impatience . . . My contemporaries . . . were like me, bookish and swottish . . . he'd ostensibly come [to Oxford] to do a diploma in education but really he'd come to run.'[1] Just as Mary had enjoyed making friends with Ann King, a woman who was completely different and extrovert, she was drawn to an unusual and exciting man. And appropriately, as it turned out, it was through a newspaper that Mary met the partner with whose name and fortunes she would be entwined for the rest of her life.

Mary had already been at Oxford for a year before Jeffrey arrived. He had come in October 1963 as a mature student to do a one-year teaching diploma at the Department of Education, but within days he had thrown himself into various activities including sport and fundraising, and had turned up at the *Cherwell* offices to introduce himself to Nick Lloyd and the journalists. 'He cut a very unusual and dashing figure in my eyes,' said Mary. 'He was much more interested in running than in anything academic . . . He was terrific fun; he was something different from anything I'd ever met before and I suppose it was the attraction of opposites but I just took to him.'[2] Jeffrey intrigued and 'puzzled' her. She also liked the fact that he was a bit older than her and her contemporaries, although 'I can't say I thought older and wiser,' she admitted. But for Jeffrey, it was love at first sight. He wrote to invite Mary out, which was very formal even for those days, and so she was intrigued and said yes. What she found out only later was that Jeffrey had also written to her then boyfriend to ask his permission to invite Mary, and the permission had been duly granted, which she found 'not wholly flattering'. Jeffrey had different interests and tastes: athletics, politics, the theatre. 'These were relatively new to me and he had a car – that was terribly advanced for those days. And he was just huge fun to be with.'[3] Michael Hogan says Mary saw in Jeffrey a lot of things she would have liked to have had but didn't have, and Mary confirms this: 'I never really wanted a husband who was a sort of lookalike of myself. I've always liked the opposite – I have liked the attraction of the opposite.' Jeffrey's flatmate Adrian Metcalfe, who may have been a little bit in love with Mary himself, said: 'They were the most unlikely pair . . . She was incredibly beautiful . . . astonishingly articulate and . . . composed . . . she was regarded as being the most intelligent girl in Oxford . . . and he said well that's it, that's perfect for my life. That's exactly the woman I want. I don't think Mary had any choice in the matter . . . I think he just bowled her along.'[4] Nick Lloyd agrees: 'He sort of overwhelmed her; he pursued her with fervour.'

The pairing raised eyebrows then, as it does today, and was quickly a topic of amazed gossip in the science labs. 'We were all extremely surprised,' says Eric Bodger, a fellow chemist. 'I think she thought we were all rather boring, but we expected someone more conventionally intelligent than Jeffrey.' Many people admired Jeffrey for the positive qualities which made him stand out from the crowd: his energy, drive, imagination, his sporting ability and his resilience; but, just as today, others found him unbearable, insincere and self-serving, and were suspicious of his motives and integrity. Mary, right from the start, either did not see these negative qualities, or somehow did not mind them. Just as she always has done, in public at least, she was able to minimise and excuse the behaviour which others condemned or ridiculed. 'Perhaps in him she found somebody so extraordinary and so complementary that it's worked,' explains Adrian Metcalfe. Mary credits Jeffrey for ending her one-dimensional existence and opening her eyes to life beyond science. Her St Anne's contemporary Gillian Howarth agrees: 'She sort of blossomed . . . And found for the first time she had something interesting in life besides work.'

For their first date, Jeffrey took Mary to a 'rather chilly' Athletics Club dance where she was introduced to all the people who were important in his life at the time. For their next one, he picked her up in his Morris Minor and took her to see the James Bond film *Dr No*, which Mary, with her sheltered life, had never even heard of. Jeffrey remembers she wore a smart pale pink suit. She was also treated to a lunch of egg and chips at Oxford's least stylish restaurant, complete with plastic tables, where Jeffrey fixed her with his eyes and said, 'I am a poor undergraduate and this is all I can afford.' Jeffrey confessed: 'I knew fairly early on that Mary was the woman for me, and that I wanted to marry her. But I wasn't by any means sure that she would want someone like me because she's so intelligent.'[5]

'There were so many men who adored Mary, that I didn't rate his chances very highly,' recalls one friend. But he grew on her and the relationship developed very quickly after that first date; Jeffrey had made up his mind she was the one for him, and he pursued his 'trophy' with all his charm. Perhaps the chase wasn't too difficult. Mary was impressed by Jeffrey's 'star quality' and the fame he was achieving at Oxford and elsewhere, and was excited and seduced by the prospects he offered.

He was sexually attractive, good-looking in a boyish, clean-cut way; he was older and more experienced, and had previously been engaged – although Mary may not have known this. When they first went out, an obstacle to their romance was Jeffrey's 'fearsome old-style landlady who would knock on the door: "Have you got a girl in there, Mr Archer?" Of course I would cower behind a chair not daring to breathe until she'd gone away.'[6] Luckily, her own 'delightful' landlady fell for Jeffrey's charms. Mary says: 'She liked Jeffrey a lot and used to wink at him and say, "I may be a spinster but I won't die guessing," and that was a great relief.'

During the vacation, Jeffrey took Mary to Weston-super-Mare, where they stayed with his old schoolfriend Geoff Bailey and his wife, and got summer jobs. Mary was a 'very successful ice-cream salesgirl' according to Babs Bailey; Jeffrey painted deckchairs. Back in Oxford, Jeffrey spent a great deal of time on athletics and running, and Mary sometimes turned out to watch him train, passing much of the time at the trackside reading, just looking up from her book in time to see him finish. Their friend Michael Hogan remembers on one occasion Mary challenged Jeffrey, saying if he could run the 220 yards in 21 seconds, she could run it in 30. A week or so later she arrived at the track in her gym shoes and ran it in 33 seconds, though it made her feel sick afterwards. Another of Jeffrey's fellow athletes remembers her confiding that Jeffrey had asked her to marry him. '"What do you think?" she asked me. "He says he's going to get an Olympic silver medal, become a millionaire and possibly become Prime Minister."' A fellow woman chemist thinks she was quite ambitious: 'Jeffrey was a sort of shining star, I suppose, at Oxford, so it was like he was one of the prizes out there to get. It satisfied a desire for what seemed like quality at the time.'

It was eighteen months after they met, and during Mary's final year, that Jeffrey says he proposed, on a romantic trip to Stratford-upon-Avon where they had gone to see *Much Ado About Nothing*. (In fact it was probably *Love's Labour's Lost* – or even *The Comedy of Errors* – as the RSC did not do *Much Ado* in 1965–66.) She said yes straight away according to Jeffrey. 'I had the ring in my pocket: it was a sapphire with tiny diamonds around the outside. It cost £23 and I'd had to save up for it.'[7] Mary says she doesn't recall the proposal; she says they knew they were going to get married before that. Before he popped the question Jeffrey took Mary's father out to lunch at the Regent Palace Hotel in London to ask his permission. It was not granted.

Harold Weeden had grave doubts about the brash young man who had swept his daughter off her feet. He had told his family that Jeffrey was someone who must be watched carefully. An Epsom friend remembers noticing his disquiet. 'My opinion about Mr Archer has never changed since the day I met him. I was standing with Mary's father and we both looked at each other and I thought "Harold looks disturbed" . . . I was rather surprised that Mary was putting her trust in that direction.' Mary's brother David said: 'Jeffrey was a natural risk taker. My father was about as far from being a risk taker as you could be, so I guess the two were likely not to have an immediate bonding.'[8] Harold Weeden also believed that his daughter had a brilliant academic career ahead of her, and he and his wife were very worried about her getting married so young. Mary, with the wisdom of youth, thought she was tremendously grown up. 'I remember my father saying yes he's a very nice boy but you're only 21 and I said, "Oh but that's very grown up, Daddy," and I meant it . . . I think they found him a bit alarming . . . but they liked him . . .'[9]

What Jeffrey's mother, Lola, thought of Mary is not recorded, although she did like her name. Many years earlier, in her 'Over the Teacups' column of 1949, Lola had written: 'I have recently been delving into the origin and meaning of Christian names. One of the loveliest of them, Mary . . . is given as meaning bitter or rebellious . . . but the main characteristics of a Mary I know personally, are kindness and tolerance. Surely no two greater gifts could be bestowed on any babe?' She was to be proved right about the tolerance, and quite possibly the bitterness.

Whatever the views of her parents, Mary had made her decision, and said her family were very supportive after that. She thought it would be an exciting and adventurous life, and she knew she had her own profession as a kind of backstop. Shortly after the end of her finals – in which she was predictably one of the few to get a first class degree – Mary Doreen Weeden became Mrs Jeffrey Archer. Adam Hart-Davis, a fellow chemist who also got a first, still remembers hearing the news. 'I was standing in South Parks Road by the Pharmacology building and she came along on her bicycle and I said, "Oh it's Mary Weeden, isn't it?" and she skidded to a halt, using her feet instead of brakes, and said, "No, it's Mary Archer now." I felt, oh shit, I'd missed the bus!' He would never understand why she married Jeffrey; a feeling eventually shared by millions.

The brilliant chemist with one of the best minds of her generation had chosen a man who was one of the least qualified Englishmen ever to belong to Oxford University in modern times. The remarkable way Jeffrey Archer had achieved this feat was due in large part to a potent combination of characteristics he had inherited from his parents, Lola and William. Lola was fiercely ambitious, pushy, energetic and entrepreneurial, with an impulsive and reckless streak. William was a conman, liar and impostor who had used his charm and ingenuity to defraud dozens of victims and had ended up in jails in at least three countries. By the time Jeffrey was born in London in 1940, William Archer was already sixty-four and leading a somewhat mysterious life. 'He was a wit and a sportsman, and, oh, a lover of women,' Lola said many years later, with feeling.

William and Lola were very different from Harold and Doreen, and at first glance Jeffrey's upbringing – and his unconventional parents – was a long way from the comfortable surroundings in which Mary grew up. But there were some important similarities: the value placed on education and achievement, the importance of money, an interest in the arts, the desire to 'be somebody' and the belief in making the most of one's talents, especially by hard work. Both families were staunch Tories and middle class. Jeffrey's mother, like the Weedens, also placed great emphasis on good manners and Christian values – indeed, she wanted her son to become a clergyman.

Jeffrey was the product of an interesting family history. William was already fifty-nine when the nineteen-year-old Lola fell in love with him, in the early 1930s. Her father had a fancy-goods business which was on the verge of bankruptcy; his father was a cheesemonger. Both William and Lola already had children they had lost contact with: William had three daughters, which Lola was unaware of, and Lola had been forced to give up *her* illegitimate daughter, Wendy, for adoption, partly because of her parents' financial predicament. To add to this extraordinary state of affairs, before their marriage Lola and William also had a son together, in 1934, whom they called Jeffrey. But their relationship was unstable and Lola, much against her wishes, was again forced to part with her child. To begin with, the 'first Jeffrey' was adopted by his own father, but the arrangement did not last and he was later adopted by another family. So when William and Lola eventually did marry, in 1939, and she was able to keep her third child – a second son – it is understandable that she should have idolised him.

When Jeffrey Howard Archer, the second Jeffrey, was two years old, his parents moved to the village of Mark, in Somerset, and later to Weston-super-Mare on the coast. The couple had very little money, and Lola could not be a stay-at-home mother like Doreen Weeden. They set up a publishing business together, producing a guide to local events, but life was a struggle for the young wife. The family lived in rented accommodation and moved frequently. By this time William Archer was almost retired, in poor health, and often away, although when he was at home, he introduced his young son to sport, and gave Jeffrey a life-long love of cricket. He also entertained him with stories – possibly those of his own incredible exploits, or his invented past as a 'war hero'.

Lola eventually got a job on a local newspaper, becoming its first woman journalist, and writing a column called 'Over The Teacups', which frequently featured the escapades of her young son. Being hard up had given Jeffrey a keen eye for business opportunities and these, too, were publicised in his mother's column, just as they would be many years later in the national press. Like Mary, Lola enjoyed being in the public eye. She tried hard to break into national journalism, broadcasting and even acting. She eventually became a local Tory councillor, as her husband William had been, twenty-five years before he met her.

Despite the difference in their economic circumstances, what Lola shared with the Weedens were Conservative politics, a Christian faith and a strong belief in education. (She continued her own education until late in life, even being offered a university place at the age of seventy to study theology.) She had been to a private school herself and she wanted the same for her son, and Jeffrey fulfilled her hopes by winning a scholarship to Wellington School, near Taunton, where he went as a boarder in 1952. A couple of years later, William died and Lola remarried – the second of her three husbands. She and her new husband then fostered a young girl, Elizabeth Fullerton, who was the daughter of a black professional father and a white mother who had placed her in an orphanage in Weston. Elizabeth was later to work for Mary as a nanny. Unlike his future wife, Jeffrey was not particularly happy at boarding school and did not do well academically, but he became a very good athlete, fanatically doing body-building exercises and excelling at gymnastics. His English master also inspired a love of theatre, and Jeffrey acted in school plays. He was fifteen when he got the news that his father had died, and he later spoke of this sad event as triggering a sense of self-motivation. The enormous energy, the driving ambition and an obsession with physical fitness were all harnessed to achieve eventual success in life. The first of these successes was in athletics, distinguishing himself in national events with the school team, and coincidentally meeting the runner Adrian Metcalfe, who was to become a lifelong friend.

Jeffrey left school in 1958 at the age of eighteen with a few O levels and, like many school-leavers, no idea of what to do. His mother had remarried, and his stepfather tried to help Jeffrey get work. He tried several careers: the army, the Metropolitan police, hotel work – and he once said he went to California to study. He eventually drifted back into education, as a teacher in a small private boarding school. He was taken on to teach PE and was a great success, and this job led to an even better one – PE master at the prestigious Dover College on the south coast. There he flourished, somehow acquiring a 'graduate' gown, a costly vintage car, a fiancée (briefly) called Diana, and a helpful 'father figure' in the form of the headmaster, Tim Cobb. Cobb, impressed with Jeffrey's athletic prowess, enthusiasm and teaching talent, saw the undeveloped potential in his young member of staff. He suggested Jeffrey try to develop his skills by doing a teaching diploma at Oxford University. Like Dover College, Oxford University was led to believe Jeffrey already had a degree. Cobb pulled some strings with an Oxford friend, and special arrangements were made to give Jeffrey a place at the university's Department of Education to do a one-year teaching course, normally something reserved for graduates, or those of 'graduate equivalence'. Somehow Jeffrey managed to stay in Oxford for three years in all, during which time he not only met Mary but became president of the Athletics Club and a leading light in university sports; he was picked to run for Britain; he covered himself in glory for the success of the Oxfam charity's million-pound appeal involving the Beatles and the prime minister, Harold Macmillan; he busied himself with other fundraising in which he visited the American president, Lyndon Johnson; and he made a name for himself as a bumptious self-publicist. By the time of his wedding day, he not only had a Diploma in Education and sporting blues, but a Coutts bank account, two houses and two cars. It was in his vintage Morris that he and Mary drove off from their fairy-tale wedding to begin their roller-coaster married life together.

Though lacking qualifications, Jeffrey had undoubted talents and discovered just how far you can get with application, so it is worth looking at some of those achievements in more detail as they reveal quite a lot about Mary, too. The most obvious question

Mary might have asked is how Jeffrey financed himself for an extra two years at Oxford when he was ostensibly doing a vague research project which even his tutor said was meant to be for just one year. Jeffrey came from a fairly poor background; he had not been earning much as a teacher, and he had been lent money by his then-fiancée Diana, who had an inheritance. In Dover, he had been constantly on the lookout for 'sponsorship' for business ventures, and from his digs he had set up a postal bodybuilding advice service, to which customers sent cheques. His landlady's daughter remembers there were many complaints from customers, and at one stage grievances got so serious that a colleague advised Jeffrey to consult a solicitor. Nevertheless, Jeffrey was able to afford to buy a Hillman Minx and a 1926 Bullnose Morris which he used on special occasions, which together must have cost more than his annual teacher's income of around £750.

Jeffrey probably had a local authority grant to do his DipEd but it is unlikely this would have continued for informal research afterwards. In the university vacations, he did some games teaching at Betteshanger prep school, and a bit of private tutorial work in Oxford, but, despite his modest income, Jeffrey was clearly much better off financially than most students by the time he met Mary. During his courtship he acquired at least two houses, which he then rented out through an Oxford lettings agency, using the income to pay mortgages he appears to have had. One property was in Oxford itself – a four-bedroomed terraced house just south of the river; and in March 1965, a year before his marriage, he bought another house in Weston-super-Mare for £5,000. One of Jeffrey's friends recalls asking him with amazement how he could afford to do this. Jeffrey explained that he had taken commission from all his fundraising for Oxfam (which amounted to about half a million pounds) and that such arrangements were quite normal. But former Oxfam officials familiar with Jeffrey's work flatly deny there was any such arrangement. The charity was opposed in principle to paying commission on fundraising. In fact, Oxfam held an informal internal investigation at the time, following complaints from students, and one official says they found the money had been banked in 'a honeycomb of bank accounts'.[10] But Oxfam did not have the evidence to accuse him of embezzlement.

The Oxfam campaign made Jeffrey's name: he was probably the most famous student in Oxford at the time. His involvement with Oxfam, and the exciting new methods he used to bring in the money, would be a seminal period in his life – paving the way for other highly successful commission-based fundraising and, at the same time, raising Jeffrey's own profile as a dynamic go-getter. His links with charities continue to this day, and he is constantly emphasising how much money he raises, mostly now through his skill as an auctioneer. Numerous charities have also benefited over the years from his fraudulently obtained 1987 libel winnings, as we shall see later. But in 1963, he was something of a pioneer in changing the way charities operated; he ensured Oxfam became nationally visible, and some people claim his techniques changed the whole nature of charity fundraising.

With the 1963 campaign, Oxfam had set an ambitious target of one million pounds, and was doing reasonably well towards meeting it. Jeffrey was in contact with Oxfam regarding other fundraising he was organising at the time, and he latched on to the big campaign. His attitude was 'I'm going to do this for you! Give me three thousand collecting tins!' according to one Oxfam employee. He ran everything like a military operation, ensuring press coverage and aiming as high as he could for celebrity backing. 'Will the Beatles get me [sic] on the front page?' he enquired of a *Daily Mail* journalist. The Beatles had just emerged as a musical phenomenon, the hottest property in showbiz, and Jeffrey claims credit for managing to rope them in, although his account has been disputed. Nevertheless, despite their reluctance to be involved, the Beatles were railroaded into the campaign by Jeffrey's tactics. In a now-famous photograph, Jeffrey (wearing a tweed jacket, short hair and beaming smile) and Nick Lloyd posed with the fab four, complete with an Oxfam poster and collecting tins. Such proximity to the Beatles was enough to guarantee the envy and admiration of thousands of young women, not just Mary. However, the Beatles' manager, Brian Epstein, was spitting mad about the stunt. To pacify him, Jeffrey promised to arrange a meeting with the just-retired prime minister, Harold Macmillan, the chancellor of Oxford University. In fact, this meeting never took place, but Jeffrey made the headlines – and suitably impressed Mary – by posing with Macmillan himself, holding a half-a-million pound cheque for Oxfam. The Beatles did visit Oxford, too, and were entertained to dinner at Brasenose College by the principal – with Jeffrey in attendance. The *Daily Mail* ran a profile of Jeffrey, quoting friends as describing him as a ball of fire and a pain in the neck. Another article said he had an off-putting, imperious manner. But to Mary, Jeffrey was a hero; and after twenty-two years of marriage she would still be nostalgic about the Beatles, claiming on *Desert Island Discs* that the 1963 hit single 'I Want To Hold Your Hand' was one of her favourite records.

One legacy of the fundraising was that 2,000 collecting tins were never returned to Oxfam. Jeffrey kept scant record of which students had taken them, or of what happened to them. He appealed in vain for students to return them, and then immediately embarked on his original fundraising scheme which had been to raise £25,000 for an Indian hospital, followed by yet another campaign in 1964, the Oxfam Gift Drive, in which people were asked to donate valuable items rather than money. Numerous famous people gave, and then Jeffrey hit on the daring idea of enlisting the help of the newly elected president of the United States, Lyndon Johnson. Astonishingly, the White House agreed to let him come and get the president's autograph on a record album of Churchill's speeches. Jeffrey flew to Washington, was picked up by an official limousine, and whisked to the White House for a few minutes with the most powerful man in the world. Understandably, the picture of this event is still a prized possession in Mary's photo album today.

Like Mary, Jeffrey was also interested in the famous Oxford Union debating society, and in 1965 found time to run a membership drive there, although his future wife had already joined. He served on the Union's ruling standing committee for a term but most of his Union contemporaries found him difficult to take seriously. Many were planning political careers and several did become MPs and cabinet ministers but what nobody yet could have guessed was that Jeffrey would be the first from that Oxford generation to reach Westminster.

One might have imagined that Jeffrey's time would have been fully occupied with academic work and fundraising projects, but what he seemed to spend most time doing was running, both for Oxford and his country, and working as club secretary for the Athletics Club (OUAC). He won three athletics blues and a further half blue for gymnastics but there was much internal dispute about whether he was a *bona fide* member of the university and whether he should therefore have been allowed to run. Not only were there questions about his university status, but also about his personal suitability to be the club's president, which was an office he sought and won. Jeffrey managed, however, to win over his critics, and was credited as doing an excellent job for the club, improving morale and results, and setting a good training example. With practically no academic commitments, he was out on the track every afternoon, and did weight training too. When she met Jeffrey he was 'extremely clean living', reported Mary.[11] A few months before his wedding, he had hopes of being picked to run for Great Britain in the Empire (now Commonwealth) Games, but was not selected. His disappointment was later alleviated by being chosen for the team to run against Sweden in Stockholm.

Jeffrey began to be seen as a local celebrity, and was asked to present prizes at a city school. He had good relationships with local journalists, and by the time he left Oxford there was a sizeable newspaper cuttings file about him. It is hardly surprising that the naïve and impressionable young woman from the comfortable suburbs of Epsom and the protective walls of Cheltenham Ladies'

College should have found Jeffrey a most unusual and persuasive person; like many dynamic people, he is good at putting on the charm when he needs to. Evidently Mary was able to overlook the bumptious and brash side of Jeffrey's character; perhaps she enjoyed it as a contrast to the sort of people with whom she had always mixed at home and at school, and it must have given her quite a thrill to take her fiancé to a speech day at Cheltenham to introduce him to her former teachers and classmates. She would also have thoroughly enjoyed basking in his limelight and meeting interesting people from outside her own narrow circle. 'He gave her a touch of stardust,' thinks Nick Lloyd. 'Underneath there's a wild woman trying to come out,' another friend suggests. Looking back on their student days, Mary herself once said: 'I'd led such a sheltered life I had no idea that people went up to university to run and watch James Bond movies! We've been an odd couple ever since.'[12]

Mary believed that Jeffrey was responsible for running the Oxfam million-pound campaign, notwithstanding that there were many others, including full-time employees, who had been slogging away at it for months, quite successfully, without Jeffrey. These people, and the hundreds of students who took part, neither claimed nor received the credit due to them. Maybe Mary did not know about the questions being raised about Jeffrey's methods, his character, his credentials. Or perhaps she did know, but chose to trust her own instincts. Maybe she knew nothing of the houses he owned, but she probably knew about the Coutts bank account which would in itself have raised eyebrows in most student circles. No doubt if she did ask a few questions, Jeffrey had some convincing answers, if not necessarily complete ones. Or maybe it was simply that she loved Jeffrey, found that the relationship met her needs and enabled her to relax, and so was happy to accept him as he was. 'Mary adored him,' said an Oxfam officer. Mary wanted to be married and thought the chance of such an exciting partnership would not come again easily. She knew she was attractive, but perhaps until she met Jeffrey she didn't think she was attracting quite the right men for her. Now, as she put it, 'that part was settled'. She was free to concentrate on other things.

Saturday, 11 July 1966 was a hot, sunny day; the England football team was playing in the opening game of the World Cup, but nevertheless about thirty Oxford blues turned out to cheer Jeffrey on. All the planning had been done by Mary's parents, and Jeffrey said all he really did was turn up on time. Even his best man, the Olympic runner Adrian Metcalfe, had to provide his gold cufflinks. The mellow stone of the Oxford colleges provided a dreamlike backdrop for the happy scene, and amateur film footage of the Archers' wedding, perhaps taken by one of Harold Weeden's friends from the Epsom Cine Society, has now appeared many times on national television. It shows Mary arriving in a Rolls-Royce at the university church of St Mary the Virgin, looking picture-perfect in a white organza dress and long veil held in place by a flowered band; Jeffrey wore morning dress. The church (which in the distant past had sometimes been used as a courtroom) was filled with white roses and blue delphiniums, and the blue was echoed in the dresses worn by the two bridesmaids, her older sister, Janet (who had married the previous year), and Jeffrey's foster sister, Elizabeth Fullerton. Mary was given away by her father; Jeffrey's moral tutor, the Reverend Leslie Styler, performed the ceremony and a choir from Betteshanger prep school in Kent, where Jeffrey had occasionally taught PE, sang a William Boyce anthem: 'Examine me, O Lord, and prove me . . . and I will walk in thy truth.' Minutes later, on his fairy-tale wedding day, Jeffrey signed the marriage register stating that he, like his bride, was a research graduate.

The 120 guests enjoyed champagne and strawberries outside at next-door Brasenose College, where Jeffrey had been enrolled when he became a member of the university's Department of Education. The principal of Brasenose, Sir Noel Hall, gave a speech in which he remarked to much amusement that he was the only principal Jeffrey had ever had. Mary changed into a cream-coloured coat with a Peter Pan collar and a green hat and they drove away in Jeffrey's beloved red Bullnose Morris, but Mary claims he had trouble changing gear, as it was 'one of those double de-clutch jobs' and once they were out of the city, they swapped to 'a serious car'. They spent their first night in the Cotswolds, where Jeffrey had worked in a hotel before his teaching days, and later flew to Ireland. Jeffrey had warned Mary that part of every day was going to be spent in athletics training, but there was time for some togetherness, with visits to a drama festival called 'The Cream of Irish Talent', held in a big tent. Jeffrey says he and his new bride went every evening for five nights, and killed themselves laughing at the many things which went wrong on stage.

At first sight, Mary appeared to have everything she could want at the end of her undergraduate years – an exceptional degree, good job prospects, and a dynamic husband. Lisa Jardine summed up the gossip amongst their old school chums: 'We were surprised when she emerged married to this sort of matinee idol . . . I think we were probably pretty jealous, actually! I mean, *we* hadn't landed anything that didn't have spots, and she was marrying this runner, and he was brilliant, and he ran everything . . . I think we probably envied the hell out of her.'[13] Mary was madly impressed by Jeffrey's vigour and his extraordinary, headline-grabbing achievements, but how much did she really know about his life, his *modus operandi* and his character? And if she knew things which she didn't much like, how and why did she excuse or overlook them? These days Mary knows much more about Jeffrey, but the questions still haunt her, and perplex not only outside observers, but friends and acquaintances. Does she know about everything and simply accept it? Does she excuse Jeffrey's unacceptable behaviour because she feels he has many redeeming features? Is she prepared to overlook and turn a blind eye to what she doesn't like because she indulges him like a doting parent? Or is she simply a very strong wife who values loyalty and her marriage vows very highly? Perhaps the answer is some combination of all these possibilities. Mary was under no illusions about the fact that she was taking on a most unconventional man. 'He did all kinds of – to me – extraordinary things,' said Mary, 'but if you'd told me in those days I was marrying a popular author I would truly have been amazed.'[14]

But being the spouse of a best-selling novelist was more than a decade away. First, she was to become the wife of a Member of Parliament.

4

The Dolly Don

MARY AND JEFFREY STARTED married life with jobs, a home of their own and an overdraft. They had taken a lease on a small flat in Cadogan Gardens, near Belgravia, a very smart part of London. Most of their rather drab flat had been decorated for them as a wedding present from two of Jeffrey's athlete friends, Dennis Roscoe and Frank Brown, who spent three or four days working and sleeping on the floor there while the newlyweds were on honeymoon.

They both had good prospects. Mary was doing her PhD – on heterogeneous catalysis in solutions – at Imperial College, London University, spending her working day in a world of spectrometers, laser beams and radioisotopes. The pressure of exams was now off, but she worked an eight-hour day and sometimes left parties late at night to return to the laboratory. Her husband had just been chosen for the post of director-general of the National Birthday Trust (NBT), a charity which promoted the care of mothers and babies in childbirth and researched into perinatal mortality – deaths of babies. It was a fundraising job, and paid £2,000 a year. Jeffrey had applied for it six months or so before their marriage, and put enormous effort into his application, brimming with ideas.

Most importantly, the job application was the first time Mary had been summoned to give Jeffrey a certain credibility, something which would be a recurring feature of their married life. In a glowing reference, the principal of Brasenose, Sir Noel Hall, wrote to the NBT: 'Perhaps it may be useful to you and your colleagues if I add a word or two about his forthcoming marriage. My wife and I have seen the two of them together on a number of occasions. She is an admirable complement to him. She is perhaps one of the best female chemists that this University has had, and is to take up a responsible research position at the Imperial College of Science in the autumn. She is well turned out, graceful in manner and speech, very stable in personality and an admirable foil for her husband to be.'[1]

Jeffrey started his new job with gusto. He had an amazing number of imaginative ideas for raising money, and pursued them with great persistence. But he was over-confident and inexperienced and met with resistance because the organisation was not known to the public in the way Oxfam had been. Mary was a supportive wife: she might not always have been there to cook supper or warm Jeffrey's slippers, but she sometimes travelled with him to meet contacts, cooperated with press enquiries, and had a role in several schemes Jeffrey devised to raise funds for the trust – and at the same time make money for themselves.

The first of these was an idea he submitted to four food companies including Heinz: 'I have invented a bottle which I thought might be of some interest to you and now that the patent is through I am in a position to consider any suggestions . . . My wife, who is reading for a Doctorate at Imperial College, London, has designed the bottle . . . One of the problems that manufacturers such as you have, is that whatever you are trying to sell, whether it is sauce, cream, jam etc. a small amount gets stuck in the bottom . . . and either has to be shaken out . . . or got out with a long spoon . . . I have, of course, looked into the scientific problems and these are being dealt with by my wife at Imperial College . . .'[2] Mary's answer to this scientific problem was a bottle from which the bottom part could be unscrewed, but the idea was, understandably, rejected by the manufacturers.

Another idea he brought to the trust was more successful, at least for Jeffrey and Mary. He thought the trust should run a babysitting bureau, and put ads in *The Times* seeking 250 babysitters who would get 'excellent' pay. It was a brilliant scheme, but the trust was very cautious, feeling it wasn't the sort of commercial activity fitting for a medical charity. So Jeffrey simply continued with the babysitting bureau as a personal business, offering to pay part of the profits to the trust. His foster sister, Liz Fullerton, who was a nurse, suggested he recruited state registered nurses as the babysitters. Nurses were short of money, had irregular hours and were medically trained. Babysitters Unlimited quickly became a success, and took up a lot of Jeffrey's time. Mary became a co-director, and the business may have been helpful in turning round the couple's financial situation. In April 1967 Jeffrey had written to his bank manager at Coutts, enclosing a cheque for £208 which he said would put him on the credit side for the first time in several months. Thanking the manager for being kind and patient towards him and his wife, Jeffrey wrote that although he expected to be overdrawn again, he hoped it would never be as big an amount as he faced after his marriage.

In a taste of what was to come, the young couple were quite often in the newspapers, mainly as a result of Jeffrey's aptitude and appetite for publicity. Less than a month after their wedding, the London *Evening News* reported the news that 'the charmer with the Midas touch' had been made a governor of Dover College, the school where he'd once taught PE. Describing him as devastatingly young, blond, stocky and blue-eyed, it commented: 'He married three weeks ago (his wife is also a success – a First in chemistry at Oxford) but this is unlikely to slow him down.' The story was covered by most national and some regional newspapers, including the *Birmingham Post* which also quoted Mary: '"I am very proud of him,"' said his bride of three weeks. "The thing about Jeffrey is that he is always doing extraordinary things. I get sort of hardened to it."'

Jeffrey quickly got disillusioned with the National Birthday Trust and more interested in furthering his political aims. He had already begun the search for a parliamentary seat and was on the Conservatives' list of potential candidates. He was actually short-listed for Reading, but withdrew. He explained that: 'I thought my wife would finish her Doctorate within fifteen months and there-fore we would be able to live near the constituency . . . It now seems she will not be able to finish . . . before September 1969 . . . and I feel I would be unable to fulfil my duty.' One of the other seats he tried, Bridgwater in Somerset, was particularly impressed – with Mary. The agent later remembered thinking, 'My goodness! A raven-haired beauty and a double first as well!' But despite this, Jeffrey narrowly missed the final shortlist. But he had more luck with the Greater London Council, and had become a candidate almost at the same time as taking up his job with the National Birthday Trust, a fact that was to irritate the trust members greatly. They were particularly annoyed to read in the press that he was paid so well 'he had acquired the freedom to embark upon a polit-ical career'.

Mary went out canvassing with her husband, on one occasion in the Bullnose Morris, which made a nice publicity picture. But as Jeffrey later admitted, even a donkey would have won as a Tory, and the election in April 1967 was a triumph for the Conservatives. Jeffrey was one of three councillors to win Havering in north-east London, and the following month, he gave in his notice to the charity. It was a barely amicable parting and if he had not resigned he would have been sacked. An internal inquiry found that he was spending much of his time on his own business and had a damag-ing personal style which had offended people, not least the leading medical specialists to whom he had referred as 'medicine men'. Evidently Mary had not been consulted over that. One leading 'medicine man' privately assessed Jeffrey as 'paranoid'; but to his credit he could not have tried much harder.

The new GLC councillor got himself on an arts committee and often went to the theatre, once inviting his old headmaster Tim Cobb to see a play at the Old Vic. Mary drove to the station to collect Cobb, who later described how he thought to himself: 'Here I am, being driven about by a slip of a girl who got the most brilliant First in Chemistry . . . Stop wishing you could take hold of her leg and change gear with it!' With Mary immersed in scientific research and academia, Jeffrey set about finding another job. He wanted to make as much money as he could, partly because he saw it as a necessary concomitant of a political career. Television was his first choice, and he tried hard to break into journalism and sports reporting, applying to the BBC and ITV. Eventually it was through a GLC contact, the runner Chris Chataway, that he took another job as a charity fundraiser, this time for the United Nations Association (UNA). Among his duties was organising a grand dinner at Downing Street, and persuading a list of rich people to give money. Jeffrey was a persuasive talker, and a big success at this job, raising about £300,000, a remarkable achievement. His reward was a year's contract worth £5,000, and he was also making some influential and wealthy contacts. The UNA was also the reason why the Archers eventually found themselves in a penthouse flat overlooking the Thames. The UNA headquarters, where Jeffrey worked, was in offices high up in a building on the Albert Embankment, opposite the Tate Gallery. Jeffrey immediately realised that space in the property, with its superb view over the Thames, would make a wonderful investment. Years later, when he had made enough money, he shrewdly bought a flat in Alembic House (now known as Peninsula Heights) and lives there to this day, although he has since moved into a larger two-floor flat at the top of the building. His flat, with its fantastic panorama, is now said to be worth about £5 million.

Both the UNA and the GLC brought out some less attractive qualities in the young councillor. Always with an eye to the 'Midas touch' he set about earning extra income by filling in fellow councillors' expenses claim forms. These were very complicated and time consuming, and several dozen councillors were glad to hand over the job to a willing colleague. In return for this service, Jeffrey charged 10 per cent. It was not illegal – but it was inappropriate, and some thought demeaning; it would have earned him the equivalent of a few thousand pounds, which was no doubt worth having if you have a flat in Belgravia to run and a wife in academia. The 'perks' Jeffrey obtained from the UNA were of a much more serious nature. He was fiddling his expenses, regularly and systematically. Humphry Berkeley, the charity's chairman, claimed Jeffrey had 'deliberately and consistently cheated [the charity] of money'. (In 1998 Jeffrey owned up to a 'discrepancy' of £80, although some years earlier he had recalled it as £150.) Humphry Berkeley was more specific: 'He embezzled from the UNA over £1,000.'[3] He also alleged that Jeffrey had forged his signature on an official document. These allegations were aired during Jeffrey's campaign to become an MP, and he sued Berkeley for libel to prevent the allegations being repeated. Eventually the matter was settled out of court but its effects were to last for many years. Jeffrey settled with Humphry Berkeley just before the case came to trial in 1973 and paid both sets of costs. As part of the deal – which cost Jeffrey around £35,000 – both sides agreed never to disclose the terms of the settlement, which had been brokered by the journalist and future cabinet minister Jonathan Aitken – later jailed for committing perjury in pursuit of his own libel action. Quite what Mary knew of it all remains a mystery – although a wife might well notice when £35,000 leaves the bank account.

It was a stage when both Jeffrey and Mary were forging careers for themselves, and although there were aspects of her husband's life she found tedious – such as cocktail party chit-chat – Mary continued to support her husband wholeheartedly. She was also learning from him the value of making and using important and wealthy contacts and liked to bend the ears of politicians about her scientific interests. Jeffrey was soon able to set up his own fundraising and public relations company called Arrow Enterprises and he also opened an art gallery. The money for this came from sponsors he had met and cultivated through the UNA, and from fellow Tory politicians, including the future cabinet minister Geoffrey Rippon. The Archer Gallery opened in Mayfair in 1969 with a glittering reception; the guest of honour was the Conservative leader Edward Heath. The gallery concentrated on modern art, and employed a female manager with an eye for the off-beat. The finances of the gallery were also off-beat and it lost about £1,800 a month and closed after a year. However, the rise in property values offset the losses, and at least one of the investors got his money back. It also turned out to be financially advantageous to the Archers, enabling them to buy good paintings and sculpture at relatively cheap prices. Mary shared Jeffrey's interest in art, and although at the time she thought he spent too much money on buying it, she later became more closely connected with the art world in her own professional life, particularly with the Fitzwilliam Museum in Cambridge, and with an organisation which supported up-and-coming artists.

One of Arrow Enterprises' clients was an organisation called the European Movement, which was campaigning for Britain to join the Common Market. (Jeffrey has always been pro-Europe, but Mary nowadays sounds like a Euro-sceptic.) Through the European Movement, Jeffrey was able to earn large fees which proved to be his financial breakthrough. In 1969 he was paid £45,000 which would be worth about half a million pounds today. But, oddly, Jeffrey still hoped to become a sports journalist and persuaded the *Sunday Times* to let him report on athletics. The paper's sports features editor, John Lovesey, thought he was motivated by his desire to prove himself to his clever and well-read spouse. 'He was very anxious to make an impression on his wife as a literary man . . . But he didn't write well enough, and there were a lot of objections from people in the National Union of Journalists.'

The young wife was by now getting used to the constant attention being paid to her husband, and she was quickly learning how to deal with the press – in those days far more deferential than it is now. Indeed, Mary was no slouch at getting publicity herself. She was featured as one of 'The Plus Girls' in an article in the London

Evening Standard, written by none other than her Oxford contemporary Jonathan Aitken. The 'brainy young girls on the London scene' who 'make men nervous' included a statistician, a civil servant, and a lawyer. Aitken was effusive about Mary: 'She is one of the most brilliant young women scientists in Britain . . . but all this hasn't made her a desiccated, machine-like person. She's the lucky possessor of a beautiful face, memorable for its Botticelli-quality skin; [she] sang in 10 Proms this year as a contralto in the BBC Choral Society . . . and is happily married to Tory GLC councillor Jeffrey Archer.' There was very little conflict between her work and her married life, Mary told Jonathan. 'Occasionally I'm annoyed to leave the lab to go to some boring cocktail party but on the whole marriage has enormously broadened my outlook and has taught me a fantastic amount – about everything except chemistry.' Mary's outlook was pragmatic: 'It's intelligence that counts in marriage, not a whole lot of academic labels. At home the only practical use of all the science I've done is that I know a bit about fixing the inside of a TV set if it goes wrong but that's all.'[4] She didn't think she was cleverer than Jeffrey, except in her own field. He'd get first class degrees in the things he's really good at, too, she said loyally.

The next summer, the *Daily Mail* ran a very eye-catching photograph of Mary, looking fetching in a sleeveless summer dress, her hand held up to her glossy hair. She easily looked like a professional model, and indeed Jeffrey once boasted that Mary had been offered a modelling contract when she left university. The *Mail*'s article said in fact she had been offered a research fellowship back in Oxford, at St Hilda's College. 'At 23, it makes her one of the youngest – and dolliest – dons in the country,' the article enthused. 'It could also mean that husband Jeffrey may have to do a lot of travelling. For Mr Archer . . . wants to be an MP . . . And he might well be offered a constituency many miles from Oxford. Mr Archer was feeling noble yesterday about the prospect of representing the people of say, a Cornish constituency, while his wife was a Fellow at Oxford. "Whatever happens," he said, "Mary must be near her work. If anyone has to commute it will be me.'"[5] Mary having her own career was, from the start, a mutually agreed condition of their partnership and Jeffrey was proud to be married to 'England's premier lady scientist' – as one paper put it – and has always acknowledged that his wife's work is very important to her; indeed, her earning power was to be crucial in the next few years. In addition, the association with such a clever woman reflects well on him and confers a kind of respectability, especially since he appears to regret his lack of academic qualifications.

St Hilda's is situated just beyond Oxford's Magdalen Bridge, not far from the house Mary had lived in as a student lodger. It had been founded by a former principal of Cheltenham Ladies' College, and retained links with that school for many years. It also enthusiastically espoused women's suffrage and promoted women's rights, so the photograph of their new dolly don would not have found favour with the fellows at St Hilda's. 'I would have shuddered on her behalf if I'd known,' said one, imagining that Mary herself was highly embarrassed, instead of happy to oblige, as is clear from the photographs.

Just as Mary was about to take up her appointment, there was a sad postscript to her undergraduate friendship with the lively Ann King, who had got a third in her finals, and become an analytical chemist. In August, Mary received bad news. Twenty-four-year-old Ann had been killed in a car crash in Essex. Mary attended her funeral; twenty-five years later Jeffrey said he and Mary still had a couple of the coloured sherry-glasses that Mary's room-mate had given them for a wedding present. 'They were really ghastly . . . but we still use them . . . very much in her memory.'[6]

Mary was the first holder of the Mann-Craven Junior Research Fellowship at St Hilda's, although she would have earned only around £500 a year. According to the college 'Report', she worked in the lab with 'a new technique using rotating disc electrodes'. And Mary thought it was important to make contact with those who had funded her research fellowship, to let them know about the work she was doing. 'She built bridges,' says don Sheila Browne, who later knew Mary when they both moved to Cambridge. For the young couple, the job in Oxford was the beginning of what Mary called their 'long split-level existence'.[7] Although tutorial fellows were obliged to live in at St Hilda's, Mary did not have to, and usually commuted to London. In any case, there was pressure for college rooms and the college 'Report' said the year was dominated by the problems of building and money-raising.

The fellows of St Hilda's remember her, with some affection, as reserved, quiet and pleasant, someone who didn't put a foot wrong and 'enjoyed talking about serious things'. St Hilda's was a determinedly women-only college, and still is at the time of writing, and according to Professor Marilyn Butler, who was teaching there at the same time as Mary, the fellows were 'a very jolly lot'. They had been outraged by Butler's treatment at Brasenose where, when she was the first woman to be shortlisted for a teaching job at a men's college, a lot of the BNC male fellows refused to come and see her being interviewed for the post. The St Hilda's dons didn't think much of Jeffrey either, who went round representing himself as a Brasenose man despite having no degree. 'He blew it up,' said one, 'which was a rather despised thing; that caused a bit of mirth.' Margaret Christie, who was also a chemistry examiner, sums it up: 'She was most attractive, beautifully turned out, socially adept, friendly, as honest as they come, very good at attending college functions and well liked in the Common Room. It all sounds, along with her undoubted academic distinction, too good to be true, but that was how it was! The only mystery was her choice of husband. As an undergraduate, she was sought after by many an eligible young man at Oxford, but chose Jeffrey Archer, an obvious rogue, not even a likeable one as far as most people were concerned. Rumours abounded about his false claims to qualifications and his dubious financial dealings but not, to my knowledge, about any sexual indiscretions at that time.'

Another of Mary's contemporaries remarked that she was not

easily knowable, but one don who did get to know her better was Barbara Levick, who taught ancient history. 'Mary did me a great favour once, when I was trying to buy some Siamese kittens, and she went with me to a cattery that she knew outside Oxford and helped me to choose a really quite outstanding animal, a very delightful cat. She was so sweet and helpful over that, it's left me with a delightful memory of her.'

The year following Mary's appointment was the start of an even higher profile for the Archers. Another of Jeffrey's political dreams came true, and Mary metamorphosed into an MP's wife. She had not banked on being drawn so closely into the world of politics. Much to his surprise, Jeffrey was selected as the Conservative candidate for the very safe seat of Louth in Lincolnshire, where there was to be a by-election in the autumn of 1969. The constituency covered almost 400 square miles, and was a very diverse parliamentary seat, including farmland with many small villages, a coastline, and industrial Immingham, with its oil refineries and chemical plants.

Jeffrey had made a big impact at two selection meetings, perhaps because he wrote to say he would be arriving by helicopter on Cleethorpes beach. At the next meeting, he was in a shortlist of three, and had Mary to give him ballast. The candidates' wives played quite a part in the final choice, as they would be expected to join in the life of the community, opening bring-and-buy sales, holding coffee mornings, going to garden parties and the like; Louth was not a progressive seat but very traditional, and run by men. The final selection meeting was a crucial day for Jeffrey, but it also clashed with an important day in Mary's diary: she had been invited to attend the Women of the Year luncheon in London, presumably because she was one of the country's youngest dons.

She had to leave the lunch early to travel to Louth, which she had never visited before, for the three-hour evening meeting, and it was worth her effort. Like the other candidates' wives, she made a short speech, albeit rather unwillingly, and impressed the selection committee with her composure, attractiveness and ability; her manner reminded them of the popular wife of the previous MP; and she was again seen as a contrast to her flashy young husband. He won by just three votes. Naturally, there was considerable press coverage in the following days, and Mary, wearing an up-to-the-minute suit, was photographed giving her husband a 'well done' kiss, and described as 'an attractive 24-year-old'. Some of the papers began referring to her as Dr Archer, Oxford research fellow. Despite being a career woman, there was no doubt in anybody's mind that Mary would be expected to do some work for her husband in the constituency.

She was featured in the local 'Roma's Diary' column which claimed she spent three nights of the week in Oxford and four in London: 'The Archers both live a very full and busy life, where . . . organisation is the whole secret.' The *Louth Standard* said her main relaxation was the theatre and that she had 'a fine singing voice'. The *Mail* said Mary was fascinated by politics although she hated wasting time with too many 'meaningless cocktail parties'. And she had praise for Jeffrey: 'I have been such a frightful wife and my husband has been so marvellous, always backing me up and taking an interest in my work. Now I intend to do the same by him.'[8] She played down the suggestion that she helped him a lot in the selection, saying she didn't think the candidate's wife made a lot of difference, unless she were 'really awful'.

Mary's picture also featured in campaign leaflets. She was shown discussing 'the problems of rising prices and education' with housewives out shopping, and she had a personal message for the voters: 'British women, sensible people that they are, are universally acknowledged to be predominantly conservative. We value particularly our security and our freedom – the security that Conservative incentives to hard work, saving and home ownership bring – the freedom that a Conservative government gives us to organise our own lives, to educate our children as we think best, or even to take our holidays free from petty restrictions. We realise, perhaps more bitterly than any other section of the community, just how much the Labour government has devalued the pound in our pockets. If my husband is elected on December 4th, I wholeheart-edly look forward to supporting him, his work and the constituency, and to making a home in Lincolnshire.'[9]

Jeffrey, whose press release described him as a TV commentator despite his singular lack of credentials in that area, told the local paper that he and Mary would be looking for somewhere to live in the constituency. Not for the first time, he was being confused with Geoffrey Archer, an ITV reporter who later also wrote novels.

It was at this point that the damaging Humphry Berkeley allegations about the UNA expenses fiddle were raised, and Jeffrey offered to resign as candidate. His offer was rejected, but then the press began to investigate and a *Times* reporter confronted Jeffrey with the allegations. He didn't pretend they weren't true, but he became emotional and begged the reporter not to write the story. Although the constituency officials would understand, he pleaded, his wife would be upset by the publicity. In the end, the story did appear and Jeffrey had no choice but to issue a writ for libel and slander to prevent anyone from raising the issue again during the by-election campaign. It was to be a costly bluff. At first, the Louth officials glossed things over as Jeffrey's 'carelessness due to pressure of work' and maybe this is the explanation swallowed by Mary. In any event, Jeffrey remained as the candidate and in early December Mary braved the wintry weather, wearing a short skirt and woolly hat, to support her husband as MP for Louth.

He was elected on 4 December 1969 at the age of twenty-nine, and for many years afterwards, he and Mary claimed he was the youngest member of the House of Commons, although this is not true – he was in fact the fifth youngest, but it was a good line.[10] Mary, at nearly twenty-five, might have been the youngest wife, but that wasn't clear either, as the *Sun* reported in a mini-profile: 'Mary Archer . . . left the cloistered calm of Oxford on Tuesday and came to London wearing a bright orange coat to see her husband Jeffrey take his seat at the House of Commons . . . though maybe not the youngest wife of an MP . . . [she] most certainly takes the prize as the cleverest. She holds a research fellowship in a most unlikely subject for a very pretty girl – electro-chemistry . . . Mary Archer may be bursting with brains but she is gentle and womanly. Entirely feminine. "I'm really a quiet, peaceful person," she said, "and the academic life suits me very well. I'm different from Jeffrey who is loaded with terrific enthusiasm and energy." Mary confessed to the reporter that 'the feminist thing does rather escape me', although she believed women should have equal pay for equal work. Perhaps thinking of her own mother she added: 'I do think that many women are content to be wives and mothers and create for themselves satisfying, happy lives.'[11] The *Sun*'s female reporter was glowing about Mary's appearance. 'There is nothing of the blue-stocking about her. She dresses well, has pretty legs, and the sort of skin that requires no make-up. She is looking forward to buying lots of clothes suitable for an MP's wife.' Mary gave the *Sun* the benefit of her opinions on a range of topics: it was 'most annoying' that she never got to meet the Beatles, who were great composers, as she had met Jeffrey just after he'd finished 'running a great big campaign for Oxfam'.[12] She thought children had a right to be educated by first-class teachers, the problem being how the country could afford to pay teachers properly. And she had no wish for a political career; indeed, she would rather vote for a man than a woman.

Early in the new year, after a brief Christmas holiday, Mary and Jeffrey attended a somewhat grander ceremony than the introduction of a new MP to the House of Commons. It was Jeffrey's turn to be proud as he watched his wife, attired in a black and gold gown, with a gold-tasselled tricorn cap, made a Doctor of Philosophy at the London University Senate House. In fact, Mary had qualified two years earlier, but the delay was normal according to the press. Mary told one paper that some called her doctor, but she did hope everybody wouldn't do it. 'I prefer to be Mrs Archer,' she claimed, unconvincingly.[13] But devotion to one's spouse went only so far. Mary declined an invitation to join the Louth Pussycat Club, whose members eschewed equal rights and dedicated themselves to 'making their men-folk purr with pride and pleasure . . . refusing to let them do the washing up and generally pampering them'. Mrs Archer was said to be dead against that idea.

Nevertheless, Mary plunged into her duties as an MP's wife – literally. She took part in a sponsored swim to raise money for a new pool in Louth, and her very appearance guaranteed publicity, as the local paper rightly pointed out, under a picture of Mary looking pretty and demure. Sure enough, a couple of days later, the publicity was even more eye-catching. The *Daily Express* pictured her wearing a bikini at the Dolphin Square pool in London where she was practising for the event, and it was immediately spotted by the editor of the *Louth Standard*, Gordon Webb, who says, 'I always wanted pictures in the paper of females wearing as little dress as possible! I rang the *Express* and said I must have that photo. A lot of that promotion was Jeffrey: he was manipulating her, I would say.' Mary was then photographed at Louth, this time in a one-piece suit and a flower-petal swimming cap. Despite her husband somewhat tactlessly telling the paper 'Mary is no long-distance swimmer', she managed a very creditable fifty lengths of the twenty-yard pool in 23 minutes 43 seconds, thereby raising £250. Her speed shows Mary must have been rather fit; she also played squash and cycled a lot.

The swimming publicity served its purpose in reminding the voters of their Conservative candidate, and four days later Jeffrey was returned to Parliament in the general election which had been called by the Labour prime minister, Harold Wilson. Mary had dutifully attended dinners, lunches and teas; she went to a ladies' party in Cleethorpes, to the livestock market in Louth, to meetings at Grimoldby and other far-flung places, many of them in snowy weather. She found it an exciting time, but full of stress and at first she had difficulty trying to do public things like make speeches and open fêtes. To strengthen their ties with the constituency, and give themselves a weekend base, she and Jeffrey had bought a property in the area, which had been found for them by the wife of a local party official. Their new weekend home was Church Farm House in the village of Brigsley, although they did not move in for a couple of months.

Much of Jeffrey's constituency work was being handled by a young Cambridge graduate with ambitions of his own, David Mellor, who was studying to become a barrister, and needed outside work. Jeffrey, who paid him quite generously, was good at spotting talent, and Mellor's successor was Richard Ryder; both men would end up round the cabinet table, unlike their erstwhile employer. One of Jeffrey's colleagues said that despite his ambition, he didn't have the patience to master issues and couldn't avoid appearing frivolous. In any case, Jeffrey's energies were being diverted elsewhere and by this time he was earning seriously good money, through his fundraising business Arrow Enterprises. He organised a spectacular royal charity concert for Lord Mountbatten called 'Night of Nights', starring Frank Sinatra and Grace Kelly, and claimed to be raising up to half a million pounds a year for charities. In return, he controversially took a percentage, and countered any criticism of this by claiming he had people queuing at his door every day wanting him to raise money for them. He was prospering, and the couple had a few status symbols to show for it. They moved from their tiny flat to a mews house in Bayswater, a few minutes from Paddington station, which was handy for Mary's trips to Oxford. Jeffrey had a yellowy-bronze MG sports car, and treated himself to a flashy number plate, ANY 1, but Mary still kept her feet on the ground and often used a tatty bike chained to the railings outside Oxford station. They both enjoyed buying more clothes, Jeffrey publicly declaring his wife had good dress sense, and were able to buy paintings by Dufy and Russell Flint. In August, the couple went off on a three-week holiday to Greece and Italy where Mary enjoyed herself looking round old churches. She also decided they should spend some time in Turkey, which was just emerging as a tourist destination. The *Louth Standard* reported that they would be guests of the Leader of the Opposition in the Turkish government who was a personal friend, and that during their stay they would meet celebrities including the Patriach of Istanbul.

In the first few months of being an MP's wife, Mary had become something of a celebrity herself, and the following October she was interviewed alongside Jeffrey for a joint profile in the London *Evening Standard* by the writer Valerie Jenkins (now Valerie Grove of *The Times*) whom Jeffrey addressed as 'sweetie'. Jenkins did not report what Jeffrey called his wife, but he told the paper it was 'very pleasant to have in one's home an Oxford don ... Mary never discusses things in a trivial way'. Jenkins said that their main interests, chemistry and commerce, did not clash and she noted similarities: they were both early morning people, highly organised and methodical, with a common love of the theatre which they went to once or twice a week. Mary's other recreation was singing, and having left the BBC Choral Society she now belonged to a small choir called the Clerkes of Oxenford, which performed Tudor and Renaissance unaccompanied music – very pleasing and orderly. Mary also told the *Standard* that Jeffrey's mind was quicker than hers, 'sharper than a packet of needles', as she put it. Whether intentionally or not, the article portrayed the young couple as very pleased with themselves.

The previous day, another somewhat pointed profile had appeared in the press. It was entitled 'In a world where the party's never over' and was about the lifestyle of an eighteen-year-old debutante, Andrina Colquhoun. Like Mary, Andy was extremely pretty and often in the papers. In an interesting coincidence, on the same day as the report of Mary's Louth swim, Andy had appeared in another paper modelling a 'Noddy and Big Ears' shirt. Shortly before Mary's bikini photograph, Andy had also been posing in a revealing manner to accompany a news item about her career as a photographer. Like Mary, the young snapper was busy acquiring an extensive wardrobe for her new lifestyle, not to mention a large circle of men friends. 'The nicest thing has been meeting the older men,' said Andy. 'Men in their late 20s or early 30s. I've learned to move quickly at cocktail parties. We call it field manoeuvres, avoiding boring men ... Money and background aren't important.' Not that Andrina had to worry about money – her parents were extremely rich, and she had no idea how much the season, with its 300 parties, had cost them. 'I realise I'm lucky and I don't feel guilty about it. Why should I?'[14] Ten years later, Andrina Colquhoun would be employed by a wealthy older man, none other than Mary's husband. And she would be a significant rival for his affections.

5

Sun and Sons

1971 BEGAN BADLY FOR MARY. While she and Jeffrey were out at the theatre seeing a drama about a blighted love affair, their home in Bayswater was burgled. The thieves took, among other things, her electric hair rollers. However, in the main the early seventies were the years when the Archers became used to success, money and fame, and Mary's career took a turn which would ensure her future as an international expert on solar energy. They both worked hard to establish their careers and Jeffrey's business appeared to flourish. By 1973 he was being described as a tycoon and telling the *Guardian* newspaper he had no need to work at all.

Being an MP's wife meant that Mary spent some weekends in Lincolnshire, at the oak-beamed cottage they had recently bought near Grimsby, and she didn't find her new role very easy at first. She was starting out on her own demanding career, and trying to combine it with being a very young and inexperienced political wife. It was tough, she said, 'I think I only learned it slowly and probably imperfectly.' She joined in the political campaigning which she found exhausting but fun and carried out a few constituency duties, as expected of an MP's wife, but she wasn't in evidence a great deal. Although she had always been interested in politics, and wanted to participate, she found it hard fitting everything in, and she certainly did not want to 'tag along' at every event; it would have left her with no life of her own, and besides, she had already heard his jokes too many times. Although she was very proud of Jeffrey, she felt he spent a lot of time doing things that did not appeal to her. She was too single-minded to want to bother with the many things a politician has to deal with in a constituency, but she liked being a close observer. A constituency official remembers Jeffrey insisting that he would stand down if anything he was doing interfered with Mary's work, 'which didn't go down too well!'

Her new role brought Mary into contact with Anglia Television, the company which would eventually appoint her a director, and which in 1994 got caught up in a huge financial scandal involving both the Archers. In 1972, however, the company was simply making a documentary about the lively young MP in their area, and Mary was there to add a little glamour. She was filmed handing coffee to her husband at their formally attired 7.30 a.m. breakfast, while he outlined his plans for the day so she could fit in accordingly. Jeffrey then kisses her goodbye and sets off at a running pace down the path to his car. 'What *are* you doing?' Mary is heard to call out, puzzled. 'Well, I always go at this speed, as you well know, dear!' comes the reply. 'One never comes up to Lincolnshire to relax,' Jeffrey assures the interviewer, 'you have to rush round.'

The combined worlds of politics and public relations brought Mary into contact with a wide range of people, many of them influential and wealthy, some of them members of the 'Establishment', and most of them a contrast to the world of science in which she immersed herself. Mary rubbed shoulders with royalty, government ministers, leading businessmen and prominent members of the arts. She found London life stimulating, and her own artistic impulses were not neglected. She was still singing with a good choir, and in 1971 she entered and won a BBC short story competition. Travelling on the tube from Paddington to Westminster one day, she found herself alone in the carriage opposite a transvestite. Mary was intrigued and struck up a conversation, which gave her the basis of her story. Her literary achievement was reported in the press, but the BBC has apparently kept no record of the entry. Years later, she employed a transsexual gardener, Richard who became Rachel.

Life seemed like plain sailing and Mary assumed she would be destined to lead her life as an MP's wife, mainly in London. The couple had planned to have children when the time was right, and their thoughts were turning to starting a family. Mary was being encouraged by her father, who by now was ill from lung cancer through smoking, and no doubt hoped to enjoy some Archer grandchildren. 'Come on, Mary,' he said, 'it's time for children now.'[1] Sadly, Harold Weeden did not live long enough to see William and James. He died in October 1971, just as Mary became pregnant with her first son. She said his death was one of the worst moments of her life.

Earlier, Mary had left St Hilda's after three years to take up a teaching post at Somerville College, but she was not on the staff and the job was to provide temporary cover. She began thinking of getting a job in London, and she had her eye on the famous Royal Institution in the heart of London, the oldest independent research institution. Since its foundation in 1799, the RI has been the home of scientific research, discovery and education; fourteen of its resident scientists have been Nobel prize-winners and some of the most influential discoveries, such as the electric generator and the atomic structure of crystals, were made within its walls. Among those who have laboured in its labs are Michael Faraday and Humphry Davy. In the early 1970s, the director of the RI was another Nobel prize-winner, Sir George Porter, later Lord Porter, and Mary much admired him for the work he was doing in photochemistry, although she had done her PhD and post doctoral work in conventional electrochemistry.

Jeffrey had allegedly told her, 'What's wrong with telling the world how good you are? If you want to work with him, ring him up! I'll ring him up!' In any event, Mary told Porter she wanted to work at the Royal Institution and he asked her whether there was some link between his research and her own specialism. Mary went off to look and discovered there was such a subject, which derived from work done by the American military who had been interested in using solar energy – sunlight – to provide rechargeable batteries. Porter was interested, and she joined him at the RI in 1972 with what was then a rather esoteric research topic. The same year she attended an overseas conference about solar energy that fired her enthusiasm for the subject. Years later, she said she was lucky to be in the right place at the right time.

George Porter thought very highly of his new researcher, and developed a good, supportive relationship with her. As his widow, Stella, now says, 'Mary was a private person. She was extremely hard working, conscientious, reliable and dependable and George admired her for all these qualities. She had a love of chemistry and great understanding of her subject and she was a good lecturer.' Porter also took on a Canadian scientist called Professor Jim Bolton, who was on sabbatical from his own university in Ontario and working at the Royal Institution as a visiting scholar. He and Mary formed a friendship that would last many years.

But before she joined the famous RI, there was the matter of baby William. Mary was still doing some teaching at Somerville College in Oxford, and had carefully planned her pregnancy so that she gave birth after the end of the academic year. But William had other ideas and started to arrive in May – nine weeks early, in the middle of a tutorial. 'I tend to think things will go the way I plan them, so I somehow didn't believe my body was doing this to me.'[2] Instead of going straight to the nearest hospital, which was in fact next door to the college, Mary treated the event rather like a scientific curiosity, and, as she admitted later, put the baby's life in danger. 'I was losing the waters round the baby . . . only clever people can be this stupid, really. I went on teaching. And then I decided to go to the library to look up what I should do next. Crazy, crazy. Anyway, it said quite clearly that this was quite a dangerous thing, that labour would ensue, and so I cycled to the station and got on the train to London, which was the next thing I was scheduled to do. So by the time Jeffrey met me off the train, I was well into labour . . . Jeffrey, bless him, was punctual as always . . . he's very useful when you need something done quickly. He bundled me into our car . . . and off we steamed at 100 m.p.h. to Guy's . . . [the gynaecologist] was in evening dress, but all scrubbed up. Obviously he had been hoicked out of some dinner party or other, and five minutes later William was born.'[3]

Mary was told that her 4 pounds and 1 ounce premature son would have only a fifty-fifty chance of survival and he was put in an incubator in intensive care. 'They wheeled me along to see him . . . there he was, a tiny, doll-like creature. I felt an overwhelming sense of guilt rather than love. And responsibility and anxiety because he had breathing difficulties.'[4] The following day, the drama of William's birth made headlines: 'MP beats stork in 70 m.p.h. dash.' The baby was said to be 'only fair' although Mary was fine, and asked her husband to bring her some papers to mark, which had been left in the car during the dash across London. William had to stay in hospital for about six weeks until he gained enough weight. He was allowed home in early July, and was duly photographed by the press with his parents. The proud father told the *Sunday Express* that he was having the clock in his car removed and mounted as an ornament because it had stopped just half an hour before his son was born.

A couple of months later, a car gadget of a different kind was mentioned in the *Evening Standard*. It was a 'magic pin' which, it was claimed, dramatically cut the poisonous fumes from a car's exhaust. It seemed an exciting and potentially money-spinning development at a time when the West was becoming aware of environmental problems caused by air pollution and the depletion of oil reserves. The company putting its faith in this pin, or valve, was an obscure Canadian firm called Aquablast, which was hoping to set up a British subsidiary. The paper reported that British investors had recently been piling into Aquablast, but what the paper – and Mary – didn't know was that one of them was the MP for Louth.

Shortly before William's birth, Mary and Jeffrey had moved from Bayswater and bought a large, five-bedroomed house in The Boltons, an exclusive street in Kensington. Their new home was said at the time to be worth well over £100,000, and it was to be the only home in their lives where they were together every night under one roof. Jeffrey also bought a new car, a blue Daimler. His company, Arrow Enterprises, had by now given up charity fundraising work to concentrate on public relations, and on financing entertainment ventures. He was only interested in activities which would make big money, although an analysis of Arrow's financial position is difficult because the business never filed any accounts at Companies House, as it should have done by law. Jeffrey was also going through a phase of being very interested in stocks and shares, and began dealing in the commodities market. He made several business trips to Nigeria, working closely with an oil tycoon called Ely Calil, whom he had met at Oxford, and who would become a family friend. Many years later, Calil and Jeffrey would be accused of financing mercenaries in the oil-rich state of Equatorial Guinea – charges denied by both men. Jeffrey acted as a consultant in Lagos, where his status as an MP would no doubt have been helpful to firms seeking to persuade the Nigerian government to grant lucrative contracts. He also got to know a young American banker called Michael Altmann, who was living close to The Boltons, and it was through Altmann that Jeffrey heard about Aquablast. He believed Altmann had inside information on the company. In those days, insider trading was not illegal and was widely practised in financial circles, despite being regarded by many as highly unethical. By autumn 1972, Jeffrey had taken out a second mortgage on his house in The Boltons to pay for shares, and had invested about £170,000. The borrowing suggests that he was not quite as wealthy as he led people to believe; nevertheless, he went on to invest £350,000 in Aquablast.

Mary, whose subsequent career was very involved with environmental issues and renewable energy supplies, might well have approved of the Aquablast valve, if not her husband's large investment, but at this stage she knew nothing of it. She was getting on with her own busy but very comfortable life. At the end of the year, she was interviewed by the *Daily Mail* about such things as her 'dress drill', holidays, money matters and her views on the 'sexual climate'. She told the *Mail* she had a daily help five days a week, and a live-in nanny (Liz Fullerton, Jeffrey's foster sister) who between them did most of the chores except cooking, which Mary liked to do herself. Groceries were ordered by phone and delivered daily, and every month the couple gave a dinner party for up to ten people. Jeffrey more often than not brought someone home for supper and they had whatever was going. Mary, photographed wearing a fashionable scoop-necked, full skirted and lace-trimmed peasant-style dress, said clothes were not a very high priority with her. She hated spending time clothes shopping and liked durable, comfortable, smart clothes which she got from good quality dress shops, never chain stores. Regarding holidays, the couple chose destinations alternately, and would be going to Florence (her choice) next year. Jeffrey liked total relaxation while she tramped around churches. She never sunbathed because it was bad for the skin. As for money matters, she incautiously left all that to her husband: 'My husband deals with all our finances. I keep an eye on household expenditure and know what things should cost, but that's all.' Her salary paid for all her personal expenses and she had her own account. 'Jeffrey is a very generous man and was when he didn't have a penny.'[5] This was a strange remark, as Jeffrey had always had assets, if not ready cash, since before their marriage.

Mary told the paper she did not find town society as neighbourly as the country, or the surburbia of her childhood, partly because wives in the town had a life outside their domestic routine. 'There are people we don't feel we could borrow a cup of sugar from, exactly.' She said she liked the idea of playing bridge and flower arranging but, being in the city, couldn't sit back and take the time. However, when baby William was older, Mary said she would love to see him romping around the countryside and climbing trees. As for being tempted by other men in the current 'sexual climate', Mary was dismissive and frank: 'How any working mother can squeeze in any extra-marital affairs I don't know. I'm certainly too tired at the end of the day to go looking for any! . . . if people are too tired to make love at the end of their day, they have always the weekend to look forward to. Most people seem to get out of the city then and let their hair down a bit.' She added: 'You see as much as possible of your husband, and I happen to like mine.'

Unfortunately for Mary, one person certainly finding time to squeeze in a few extra-marital affairs was the husband she liked so much. It was easy for Jeffrey to conceal these from Mary, given that she was preoccupied with a full-time job, away from home travelling a lot, and busy with their toddler son when at home. Some of these liaisons were the result of Jeffrey's friendship with Michael Stacpoole, who he met during the Night of Nights fundraising concert. Stacpoole was a charming PR man who came from a wealthy family, mixed with the upper-class Mayfair social set, and had beautiful girlfriends. Over the next few years Jeffrey and Stacpoole worked closely on a range of projects and often met socially. They went to football and cricket matches together, or out for a drink or meal in the evening, when they'd eye up women and discuss conquests, both actual and potential. Stacpoole later described in detail how he had introduced Jeffrey to prostitutes, saying he saw nothing wrong with it.

It was around this time that a prostitute, who Stacpoole and Jeffrey had not yet met, started commuting to London from Lancashire, having decided she could find more congenial work on the streets of Mayfair for a few days a week. Her name was Monica Coghlan; she was twenty-two, dark-haired, intelligent and attractive, with a good figure. She was the daughter of a labourer who had left his family when she was five, and a mother who supported her children by working in the canteen of the Manchester *Daily Mirror*. Monica left school early, drifted into various unskilled jobs and took up a life of petty crime. She was sexually attacked at the age of seventeen and was tempted into prostitution to pay off her debts. She first worked as a streetwalker in the red-light district of Moss Side, but then took on a new identity as 'Debbie' in the wealthier parts of London's West End, taking her clients back to a seedy hotel room. Among the men she attracted were some well-known faces, and she claimed to like her work, which started to pay reasonably well, at £50 a 'trick'. Eventually she moved to London, living in Islington, but later bought a bungalow in Rochdale, Lancashire, with her common-law husband, and continued to live there after his death, bringing up her son, the child of a subsequent relationship. Her life could hardly have been more of a contrast to Mary Archer's, but the two women were destined to lock eyes across a crowded courtroom thirteen years later.

Meanwhile, back at the Royal Institution, just a stone's throw from Mayfair, Mary's scientific career was flourishing, encouraged by her mentor George Porter. She was a pioneer in her subject and she had luck in her timing. Oil prices were high, there were political difficulties with coal, and Britain was about to be plunged into darkness during the government's drastic three-day week energy policy at the start of 1974. The prevailing view, says Mary, was that we were going to run out of oil and gas pretty quickly, and those imminent fears produced a great sense of urgency. Suddenly there was tremendous interest in renewable energy and solar energy – stimulated partly by a scientific breakthrough in Japan – and all kinds of funding and opportunities became available. In her lab, she worked to create a 'sun battery' using the sunlight falling on special blue-dyed plates to make electricity and then store it. She built experimental solar batteries and put them through meticulous and painstaking trials, but her work was highly speculative and not even producing enough power to make a flicker in a torch bulb. 'It is a case of research, research, and more research,' Mary insisted.[6]

Mary felt 'passionately' that while Britain spent £50 million a year on nuclear research, solar research had been almost forgotten. It was after attending a UNESCO conference in Paris called 'Sun in the Service of Mankind' that Mary had the idea to set up a UK branch of the International Solar Energy Society, which brought together members of the solar energy community in the UK. George Porter suggested its chairman should be Professor John Page and Mary became its secretary. Together with considerable administrative help, they built the membership from 11 to over 250 people in a year. At the branch's inaugural meeting, at the Royal Institution, she reviewed research and development in her new field and said British efforts were far behind those in America and Europe. Big savings could be made by improvements in architecture, industrial processes and the development of new storage methods to harness the sun's energy. Mary explained that many homes in Australia and Japan were already using solar energy to heat their water systems, and the United States had so much sun that all its artificial energy needs could be supplied by using the sun that falls on just 1 per cent of its landmass. Nobody, though, had yet come up with an economic means of converting that sunshine into energy and she was worried that the current enthusiasm for creating new forms of energy was in danger of disappearing once North Sea oil started to flow. In one sense, she was correct – the OPEC crisis made other countries look for alternative sources and increase their reserves; however, the concern about the amount of carbon dioxide in the atmosphere continued to grow, along with the interest in renewable energy sources. The UK Solar Energy Society was quite profitable in the early days because of this interest, and membership of the society was higher than it is nowadays. Professor Page raised money from the Wolfson Foundation, and a team including Mary wrote a report for a Commons Select Committee. In the mid-seventies, John Page and Mary took part in a *Woman's Hour* on solar energy and by 1981, the society was able to host an international meeting called the 'Solar World Forum', which was attended by two thousand people.

It was around this time that Mary embarked on her lifelong relationship with broadcasters, which had begun with her breakfast-time appearance on the Anglia TV profile of Jeffrey. She may have been inspired by George Porter himself, whose BBC broadcasts in the sixties had been very popular. At the start of 1974, Mary contributed to a two-part scientific programme on BBC radio called *This Island Now*. In the first programme, on the case for conserving energy, the idealistic Mary spoke in the same precise and careful way she does today, but her voice then was softer and more appealing. She told the interviewer it was rather dangerous to put all our eggs in the nuclear basket and solar power was really the only long-term alternative. But she admitted it was a 'great leap' from things which were feasible on the test-tube scale to making a system that worked in field conditions in an economic way. She estimated the development time could be under forty years. Mary pointed out that there were very few people in Britain working on solar energy research, even though there was great enthusiasm: 'We have been heartened by the interest that has been expressed in our very infant society,' she said, making a plea for more funding.

It wasn't long before Mary became known as a spokesman for solar energy, which led to several approaches from television. One of those who wanted to try her out remembers the occasion well. David Taylor was a young producer with Yorkshire Television working on a popular science programme called *Don't Ask Me*, which was similar to the BBC's *Tomorrow's World*. YTV was on the lookout for presenters and Taylor went to see Mary at the RI for a chat, appropriately enough in the Conversation Room. 'I thought she was an extraordinarily attractive person, very nice to talk to, but she was too kind of "buttoned up" and not "giving" enough to be successful as a TV presenter . . . I thought she was just a little bit too Dresden china.' Taylor asked her what had prompted her interest in solar energy and she said it was seeing a television programme called *Here Comes The Sun*, which Taylor himself had in fact produced. 'I was flattered and I thought, good heavens, here's a good bonding thing!' He doesn't remember Mary being used, and *Don't Ask Me* chose Miriam Stoppard as its female presenter instead. The show's executive producer, Duncan Dallas, says Mary did record one appearance, but it was cut out, because she came over too much like a university lecturer. The only problem was that Mary could not be removed from a final group shot for the credits, so 'she sort of appeared mysteriously at the end of one edition'.

As a newspaper aptly put it, she was taking steps towards solving her own surplus energy problem. Not only that, she had learned from her husband the benefits of getting publicity for her subject, and having it aired more widely. And she enjoyed the flattering publicity it brought to her personally. George Porter thought so highly of the keen, clever and presentable young pioneer that he sent her over to the United States to a seminar in Boston because he couldn't go himself. It was the start of a period when she would travel all over the world, so much so that William, at the age of three, said his father lived at home but 'Mummy lives on an aeroplane'.[7] Jeffrey and he made a joke of it: 'Here's Mum, the hero; good of you to join us.'

Her faltering beginnings as a speaker at Louth constituency meetings were now beginning to pay off, and lecturing was an important area of her life. Part of her job at the RI involved lectures to schoolchildren, and other non-professionals; Mary said it used to take up to a week to prepare such a lecture, and she found it much harder than lecturing to experts. Through her trips, Mary became friendly with many other like-minded scientists, one of whom she met at a conference in Calgary in 1975, Professor Michael Graetzel. 'I had already heard about her,' he says, 'and I was very impressed. She can explain extremely well and I invited her to visit Berlin where I was working, and later when I moved to Switzerland she came for a week's seminar to give several lectures on photoelectric chemistry. We have been running into each other at conferences ever since.'

The press reported that Mary was even being sought after in Nigeria, where the government had asked her to advise them on a £300 million refrigeration scheme, perhaps as a result of Jeffrey's contacts there such as Ely Calil, who was a visitor to their home. Although Mary was by now flying round the world, making her name in international scientific circles, and in demand for lectures, she still found time to keep in touch with Louth. She took part in yet another election campaign in the constituency in February 1974, which saw Jeffrey's majority increased by 500 votes. On a campaign leaflet, under a photograph of Jeffrey and herself with little William on her knee, Mary endorsed another message for Louth voters: 'We are living in a time of great political uncertainty in which powerful sections of the community have not been ashamed to act with self-interest and to neglect the well-being of others. As a housewife I know that increased prices of food and fuel are a real problem . . .'

The long hours of work and travel were fitted in despite the Archers just having started a family. By now, Mary was pregnant with her second child, but a month before his birth she was still hard at work in her laboratory, explaining what she did to yet another reporter. 'She looks slightly puzzled when asked if hers is not an extraordinarily busy life. "People keep asking me that, but somehow I feel more exhausted if I do not do anything. William was born on the evening of a full day's work, but that was not really very clever. I am much happier at my desk working than I am with my feet up." She is musing over whether to take a little time off before having the next baby. "I think I shall." Luckily, the "tall thin house" which is her Kensington home runs like clockwork, with the aid of Elizabeth, an excellent nanny, who also likes cooking, and a Portuguese daily.'[8] An efficiently run home was now essential. Mary took on still more commitments, teaming up with Jim Bolton, the Canadian professor she had met at the RI. Bolton at one time lodged in the Archers' home at – confusingly – The Boltons. He and Mary started writing a book together, which was to be many years in the making, and which eventually led to an acrimonious parting. At the time, however, the friendship was strong and her fellow scientist Michael Graetzel remembers thinking of them as a kind of trio – Mary, Jeffrey and Jim – as he often saw them together.

On Friday, 17 May 1974, Mary had taken some time away from

her labs, and was at home, busy organising a birthday party for two-year-old William. Suddenly, Jeffrey arrived back with some unexpected and devastating news: they were financially ruined. Jeffrey had been trapped in an elaborate share swindle which had swallowed up nearly £400,000 – all of it money he had borrowed. During the previous six months, Jeffrey had watched in mounting horror as the Aquablast share price dropped steadily, knowing his wife was blithely ignorant of the impending disaster. Not an inkling of his plight ever appeared publicly, perhaps for that reason. Jeffrey carried on giving the impression that his business was thriving and he was well on the way to being a millionaire. He had boasted he gave all his parliamentary salary to charity; now he was looking for some charity at home. 'I felt weak at the knees,' Mary said later. 'But there was nothing else to do except carry on with the party. When you are told something like that, a sense of unreality takes over and you are carried along in a state of shock which preserves you from the worst anxiety.'[9] Six days later, Jeffrey was served with a bankruptcy notice, although he never did go bankrupt.

In June, almost two years to the day, Jeffrey and Mary's second son was born in circumstances similar to those of William's birth. Mary said she had something called 'maternal incompetence' (probably meaning cervical incompetence) and James was five weeks premature, but this time Mary took the precaution of phoning Jeffrey from work to tell him she was not feeling well and he raced to the Royal Institution to collect her and take her to Guy's hospital. James, at 6 pounds, was also put in an incubator but did well. A relieved Jeffrey told the press: 'The next time we are hoping for nine months of normal pregnancy and an 8-pound baby.' James, like his brother, soon graced the newspapers in the arms of his radiantly pretty mother. News of his father's financial debacle also reached the press that summer. Jeffrey was urgently summoned to Louth, where he was advised that, with a second election pending because of the precarious political situation, he had no option but to stand down as an MP. If he were shortly to be made bankrupt, he would have to resign anyway, and cause an awkward by-election. But they were sorry to see him go. 'It was a foolish investment and I was a fool to get involved,' Jeffrey admitted candidly. 'I can't expect people to have trust and respect for a man who has behaved so stupidly. So I am doing the honourable thing.'[10] As well as being the victim of a conman, he had been the victim of his own greed and arrogance; yet in the long term the Aquablast disaster proved to be a god-send. Problems are often opportunities disguised, as Mary observed many years later. It set Jeffrey on the road to riches through book-writing and sent Mary off to new academic, social and domestic pastures in Cambridge. As for baby James, he would one day also become a share-dealer – involved in dishonest share manipulation.

6

For Richer, For Poorer

THE CAUTIOUS ACCOUNTANT'S daughter now faced a new and harrowing experience: years of anxiety over money and debts. She was forced to leave the home she was fond of, and had the responsibility of being the main bread-winner. Her husband, to whom she had happily left all the family's financial arrangements, was hundreds of thousands of pounds in debt. Mary was to look back on it as one of the worst times in her life.

First, following Jeffrey's decision to stand down, the couple had to face the press. 'I am very disappointed,' he said. 'I have adored every minute of the five years I have represented Louth ... and I will be leaving many happy memories behind me. My wife, Mary, is also very disappointed. This has been a personal tragedy for both of us.' Mary was putting on a brave face, but the headlines were stark: 'I will earn for the family, vows wife of MP in cash crisis' and 'Back to square one says whizz-kid MP'. Mary was said to be cool, calm and confident: 'We will pick up the pieces – I'm just not given to despair. We'll get through, no question about it.' Pouring tea for a reporter, she even joked that Jeffrey should get a job on the new underground line being built in London, saying it would do marvels for his waistline. 'He'll get another job, I know he will ... to me, he is a splendid husband and a very devoted father . . . one thing I can say: life with Jeffrey has never been dull. With him you never have time to get in a rut . . . You just have to grow to expect the unexpected.'[1] She said she earned a good salary and would keep the family if she had to, 'but it will never come to that'. Her job had been a great help and being at work took her mind off her problems. Mary was relieved Jeffrey would not be standing for re-election, as it would take some of the spotlight off them. Understandably, she was unhappy about his mistakes being made so publicly, but she had not liked his absences as an MP in the evenings and at weekends. 'It is no fun having two children and no husband to share them with.'[2] Oddly, Mary also said they had been living with the crisis for almost a year, despite her having learned about it only three months earlier. Perhaps she had sensed some deep concern in Jeffrey during the months before; or maybe she wanted to protect him rather like a mother might do, to share his plight and make light of it – a stance she would frequently adopt in the future.

In truth, she was deeply distressed, as she admitted years later, and had taken it very hard. It preyed on her mind, her face came out in what she called 'the most hideous kind of spottiness' because of the stress, and she said the aftershock went on for years. 'It was like having a bomb exploding under one. It was pretty stunning, because I just couldn't see how we would ever be free of it. I thought this would be something we'd be living with, paying off, for the rest of our lives. And although I don't mind trying to fight my way out of a tight corner, with one child on the way and one very small one, we felt somehow rather tied by that . . . I had trouble sleeping for a long time.'[3] In interviews, Mary said she sought help from her doctor to see her through although she wasn't offered anything for depression and says she wouldn't have taken it anyway.

There were immediate effects from the impending bankruptcy. The constituency cottage in Brigsley was put up for sale, and Jeffrey sold his Daimler, although he hung on to his cherished ANY 1 number plate. His valuable works of art were surrendered to the bank as security for money he owed, as nanny Liz Fullerton recalled: 'The bank came to take some of the pictures, the paintings, off the wall, and the doorbell rang, and there was somebody standing there and it was just a shock . . . but the amazing thing about it was Mary was incredibly calm through all that . . . she and I just re-arranged the house.'[4] Perhaps more distressing for Mary was having to change her plans about having a third child, the one Jeffrey hoped would be a girl called Lucy. And Mary very much minded the loss of face. She did what she could to help stave off bankruptcy, enlisting the help of a friend from university days, Michael Hogan, who went on her behalf to see the solicitor of one of Jeffrey's main creditors, although he came away disappointed. He personally lent the couple £10,000.

In fact, Jeffrey never did go bankrupt, something of which he is enormously proud, perhaps because he had heard his mother speaking of the effect of his grandparents' money troubles. Although at the time he said he had only £18 to his name, and claimed to be considering taking a job as a dishwasher at the Dorchester, he had many valuable assets to offset his debts – not least of them a good lawyer. Victor Mishcon, now Lord Mishcon, whose firm still acts for Jeffrey and Mary, was able to negotiate a settlement with one creditor which avoided bankruptcy. And a vital distinction to be made is that although Jeffrey was in debt, he was not poverty-stricken. He was able to keep his office in Whitehall and, for a couple of years, his home in South Kensington. He still dressed in Savile Row suits; friends and relations lent him £30,000, a considerable sum in those days; he had works of art to use as security, and some valuable personal contacts. Mary had her university don's salary and additional income from foreign lecture tours. Equally helpfully, Jeffrey was a Name at Lloyd's, the insurance market, and received large sums of money from his membership there just when he needed it. Lloyd's, which was a decade or so away from catastrophe, was later to play an important role in Mary's life too.

Jeffrey's debts were certainly serious but his lifestyle was not greatly affected and the couple were never in real poverty, of the kind which Jeffrey's mother experienced in her early days. Apart from anything else, as Mary acknowledged, they had their youth, their wits, and their earning capacity: they were well-equipped to withstand the crisis. Revealingly, one of the worst things for Mary was that she feared they would be unable to afford private schools for their children. William attended a state primary in Cambridge when she moved there to take up a university fellowship, but Mary wanted her boys to go down the public school route, which was normally via prep schools. 'What did hurt me deeply was that it looked as if we would not be able to give our children a good education. I care passionately about few things, but good education is every child's right.'[5] The experience left her with a feeling of insecurity which would not go away, but she found comfort by retreating into her work in the academic world, where prestige is not measured in money or fame.

One positive effect was that Mary began to take a keener interest in financial matters. She said she had never been ambitious about money until they lost theirs and had felt that wives did not deserve large whacks of their husband's wealth or vice versa. She had known nothing of the Aquablast dealings, but had her advice been sought, she would have advised him not to put so many eggs in one basket. For a while after Aquablast, she used to ring Jeffrey up and ask him what deal he had done that week, making it clear that he should ask for her advice rather more often, and the experience left her 'very frugal, cautious with money'.

The advice which Jeffrey did seek concerned not finance but spelling and grammar. He had decided the best solution to his difficulties was to write his way out of debt, as usual aiming high and hoping to produce a best-seller that could be turned into a film. Amazingly, this dream became a reality, but nobody would have believed it at the time, least of all Mary. She was very surprised when Jeffrey announced he was writing a book because she never knew he could write a letter. Friends, too, were incredulous. But Jeffrey knew he could tell stories and he had a good story to tell –

that of his own financial misfortune – and he called it *Not a Penny More, Not a Penny Less*. In the autumn, he asked his old Brasenose mentor Sir Noel Hall if he could stay with him and Lady Hall at their country home outside Oxford during the week to get a little peace and quiet away from his two children, and there he wrote the story of swindled men getting revenge on the fraudsters who tricked them. He returned to his wife and sons in London at weekends, and it is a sign of Mary's patience, goodwill and open-mindedness that she was willing to give up many hours correcting and editing the rough draft, amending her husband's poor grammar and turning it into a readable script. Most wives would have urged their husbands to get a job, or help with the children, not indulged them in a flight of fancy. Perhaps the scientist in Mary wanted to try out this experiment in an objective way; perhaps the adventurer in her wanted to give it a shot. In any event, 'I thought it would make at least some money.' Nevertheless, the cost of the gamble was mounting debt at a time of high interest rates.

She thought the book was a terrific read, but was not impressed by his sex scenes, which made her laugh. Jeffrey said he had tried to copy Harold Robbins, and have 'girls hanging from lampposts with their knickers torn off . . . it didn't ring true because I hadn't experienced it myself'. Instead, he wrote about a 'fragrant, silk-clad wife' which was much more likely to be approved by Mary; perhaps she even composed the phrase herself, and certainly the adjective became associated with her for evermore. A manuscript was produced and Jeffrey set about finding takers. Among those he approached was a television producer called Ted Francis, but it was another contact who was to provide his breakthrough, leading him to the literary agent Debbie Owen. Jeffrey was determined to be taken on by Owen, and wooed her with champagne, despite his penury. 'I mean, one absolutely hit gold,' he said, 'because the secret is to get a good agent.' She agreed to take the 'glorified film script' home and showed it to her husband, the (then Labour) politician David Owen, who enjoyed it. As a result, it was read by

In the science wing at Cheltenham Ladies' College in 1959. The girl fourth from right could be Mary.

Making the front page in her second year at Oxford University. Mary has always been very fond of cats – and of publicity.

Cherwell

THE OXFORD UNIVERSITY NEWSPAPER 4d.

SATURDAY, NOVEMBER 9, 1963

BALLIOL LOSE QUIZ GAME

BALLIOL COLLEGE has been defeated in the final of Granada TV's top quiz show, "University Challenge." At last week's recording session in Manchester, Leicester University won two of the three decisive games to become the first overall champions of this tent of top brains, which is compered by Bamber Gascoigne, theatre critic of 'The Observer.'

CLOSE SCORING

The scoring in these final games was close. Leicester took the lead by 370 to 270, but Balliol fought back in the second session to win by 30 points—210 to 200. Leicester showed the greater intellectual stamina, however, winning the last dramatic clash by 300 points to 290.

David Wickham, captain of the Balliol team, gave a reason for their failure. "Leicester were more dedicated than us; we might have won if we had taken the thing more seriously." Obviously effortless superiority is not enough.

The other members of the Balliol quartet were Insmas, Ed Mortimer, Olly James and Timothy Ades. Leicester win a first edition of Dr. Johnson's Dictionary. The members of the Balliol team were each given a leather-bound copy of the Shorter Oxford Dictionary. This is in addition to the £80 which the team has won for the Balliol JCR with each appearance. The money is to go towards the rebuilding of the JCR premises to be carried out next year. The programme itself is to continue, first contestant in the new series will be St. Anne's of Oxford and St. Andrew's University.

Poor Little Pussy!

This kitten nearly died. Now it lives!

●Mary Weeden (St. Anne's) smiles Priscilla—the cat with eight more lives left! (Photo. by Stephen Fry).

Full details in Oxford Accent on page 4

OUDS break with tradition and choose Twelfth Night

18,00

CHA

The dolly don. In 1968, at the age of 23, Mary had just been offered a junior research fellowship at St Hilda's, Oxford.

The newly-graduated Mary marries her self-styled 'research graduate' husband Jeffrey in Oxford in July 1966.

Top left: Mary was plunged into the world of politics in 1969 when Jeffrey became the Conservative MP for Louth in Lincolnshire. She made a favourable impression on the selection committee and helped him campaign.

Top right: And she plunged into the Louth swimming pool in 1970 to raise money for charity.

'It's time for children, now' Mary's father told her in 1971. She had William in 1972 and James in 1974 while working at the Royal Institution. She was pregnant with James when she heard that Jeffrey had lost about £400,000 through an incautious investment.

Mary meets the press on her doorstep at Grantchester, on the morning the Coghlan story broke. 'My husband told me he never met this girl and I believe him' she said. She claimed Jeffrey's resignation was 'a monstrous miscarriage of justice'.

Monica Coghlan is offered an envelope of £50 notes by Jeffrey's friend Michael Stacpoole at Victoria Station in 1986. Both estimated the gift was nearly an inch thick, or roughly £5,000. Jeffrey denied he had ever met Monica.

The Archers arrange a photo opportunity by serving coffee to journalists waiting outside the Old Vicarage after the *News of the World* broke its Monica Coghlan story. Despite their problems, they staged this scene three times for the benefit of photographers who had missed it the first time.

Mary and her boys on their way to church just hours after the story broke. She carried them through the trauma of the libel case; at the subsequent perjury trial, they supported her.

'Jubilant is not the right word' claimed Mary after her husband's victory in court in 1987. He was awarded more than half a million pounds in damages. 'The verdict speaks for itself' he said.

The Archers face the press at the end of the libel trial of 1987. What Mary wore became the subject of a news item during the three weeks of the case.

Top left: Monica Coghlan, the prostitute at the centre of one of the most famous libel cases ever. Jeffrey paid her money to go abroad, but denied having sex with her, as she claimed.

Top right: The actress Sally Farmiloe, also a deb, was one of Jeffrey's mistresses. An active Conservative, she claimed to 'hold the largest balls in London'.

Bottom left: Andrina Colquhoun in 1970. A debutante who worked as a photographer, she became Jeffrey's mistress and then his PA. Their affair lasted 8 years.

Right left: Angela Peppiatt was Jeffrey's PA while he was the deputy chairman of the Tory party in 1985. She was the main prosecution witness in his perjury trial of 2001.

Top: Mary became glamorous and sought-after following her support for Jeffrey in court. She appeared frequently in the media and even sang, as Dr Archer, in a television cabaret in 1991.

Middle: Mary has always kept fit by playing tennis and squash, and posed for a Sunday newspaper style profile in 1988, when she was in her forties.

Bottom: Mary joined the board of Anglia TV in 1987 shortly after the trial. She was a woman with whom the men of the establishment could do business, remarked one commentator. In 1994, Jeffrey was investigated for alleged insider dealing in Anglia shares, although no prosecution resulted.

an American editor friend of theirs and finally a US publisher made an offer. The book, as it then became, sold extremely well in America, especially for a first novel, and even more surprisingly the film rights were bought by Warner Brothers. *Not a Penny More, Not a Penny Less* was eventually also published in Britain, by Jonathan Cape in 1976, and sold reasonably well. Jeffrey's comeback had begun.

During this time, Mary continued with her scientific career. She carried on working at the Royal Institution for a while, and was given a Dewar fellowship by the Davy Faraday Laboratory committee, which paid a small amount but was mainly honorary. She was also promoted in the world of solar energy, becoming one of the board of directors of the International Solar Energy Society. But Mary needed some long-term stability in her life and started searching for a permanent academic job which would meet her requirements as a scientist, pay some of the bills and fit in with her young family. Academic jobs are highly competitive but Mary was well-qualified. As luck would have it, the Cambridge women's college Newnham had a vacancy for a chemist, and the principal, Jean Floud, had written to, among others, George Porter to ask if he could suggest anybody. She got glowing references for Mary; Porter was 'dead keen' she says. 'There were other candidates but she walked into the job. She was very impressive academically and personally.' After heartfelt discussions with her husband, Mary moved with her boys to Cambridge in the autumn of 1976, to enter a new phase in her life.

Mary's chemistry fellowship at Newnham was what is known as a Non University Teaching Officer (NUTO) post, in that it was funded by the college and not by the university. There were very few women in Cambridge actually paid for by the university (UTOs) – less than 5 per cent overall, and even fewer in science – and Newnham had a number of distinguished fellows who were unable to get university posts. University posts were considered highly prestigious and were correspondingly competitive, and women had to conform to what was then very much a man's world. Nevertheless, Newnham had arranged that their chemistry fellow should have access to the labs in the university chemistry department as a research associate, and she gave lectures there. Although Mary was on the second rung of the Cambridge academic ladder, which in itself required a high degree of dedication to work, there were many others in similar positions.

The Newnham post was jointly funded and Mary's teaching was shared with the male-only Trinity College across the river. She became one of its first female teachers as a lector in inorganic chemistry, although Trinity already had its first female don, Marian Jeanneret. Because Trinity was a very wealthy college, and Newnham very hard up, it paid most of Mary's salary although Newnham got most of her teaching. Trinity was also able to provide her with accommodation big enough for her family and close to both colleges – 'on very nice terms' she revealed, though Jeffrey once told an interviewer it was free. Her appointments were noted by the faithful *Evening Standard*. '"I'll still continue with my research," Dr Archer, thirty, said this morning from her laboratory at the Royal Institution in Albemarle Street. "But it will mean that Jeffrey will be joining the commuters as we're moving to Cambridge."' Going to Cambridge with two small children, and back into a university environment, felt then like a step into the unknown and Mary was 'terribly uprooted'. Although, as she put it, Jeffrey had become 'portable', she was leaving a home she loved.

Her nanny, Liz Fullerton, nobly went with her for a couple of years to tide her over and after she left, Kathleen Beer took over. Mrs Beer was in her late forties and became a surrogate mother to the two young boys; with Jeffrey in London during the week and Mary often abroad on lecture tours even in the vacations, Kathleen Beer ran their lives. 'I had great fun bringing them up, even though sometimes they were very devils; but boys are boys.' Mary remembers the time when, aged about eight and six, the boys 'cooked up this amazing wheeze' one Sunday when she was out. They dialled 999, announcing their parents had been kidnapped. Jeffrey and Mary got back home to find the police waiting for them. Mary, who made them write letters of apology to the Chief Constable, thinks they did it because they've always had to cope with Jeffrey being well known.[6]

Mary said she was besotted by her sons but she would have been desperately unhappy and frustrated had she stayed at home; her academic life was extremely important to her. In her field, Mary simply had to be single-minded and work very long hours and it helped that she was an unemotional and unsentimental person who viewed the role of stay-at-home mother as intellectually limiting. She worked right up until her children's births, and went back as soon as possible afterwards. While she was breast-feeding Jamie, he spent a couple of weeks tucked under a bench at her lab so she wouldn't have to stop. She got a lot of fun out of work, and, at first, out of travelling, even though it was often during school holidays. And she never regretted her decision. 'One might suppose it matters most to be there when they are babies, but it doesn't; I think it matters more when they get older.'[7] When James was twenty he said he had never heard his mother raise her voice or get annoyed and remembered only one occasion when she said she was cross about something. Evidently, Mary was able to rise above, or ignore, the many vexations of child-rearing.

The accommodation which Trinity College let to the Archers was in Grange Road, just ten minutes' walk from the centre of Cambridge; a nice enough house which they were very grateful for, she said, but 'it wasn't quite what we'd had'. The family occupied Number 58a which was a ground-floor flat with a terrace; upstairs the Archers' neighbours were first a couple called Chung and then an art historian, Dr Lolita Nehru. Another neighbour, Alida Short, remembers the family and says Mary was always very polite, although Jeffrey was rude to her. She says her daughter used to babysit for the Archers, and if they were back home a quarter of an hour earlier than expected, they would deduct money from the teenager's pay. 'I know they were hard up, but they were just a bit mean, so I stopped my daughter doing it,' says Mrs Short.

Trinity College, where Prince Charles had studied, still had a very formal atmosphere and it was not until two years after Mary joined that it began accepting women as undergraduates. The College Record shows that Trinity not only boasted a Foot Beagles Society, it had a Masonic Lodge, which met several times a year in London. The college, famed for its Great Court, was the biggest and richest in Cambridge, and proud of its scientific distinction which the Master, Lord 'Rab' Butler, claimed 'easily outbids any other college of our type in the world'. Mary often dined at Trinity's high table, with its good food and wines, sometimes bringing guests such as her colleague Jim Bolton (which caused gossip) and Debbie Owen, Jeffrey's agent (which caused a flurry when it was realised she was the foreign secretary's wife). According to Jean Floud, 'Mary was a honeypot; the Trinity dons flocked round her, although she was cool and takes herself seriously.' 'We all liked her,' says Lord Garry Runciman. 'She was a very good teacher. But she certainly gave out no suggestion that she wasn't loyally married, and she used to produce Jeffrey at the college occasionally.' Several members of staff still recall her arriving for work in a Mini.

In contrast, Newnham was an un-hierarchical society, well aware of the stresses and strains of juggling professional life with family demands. Women wore their learning lightly, and used first names. Mary fitted into the life at Newnham, and took part in college activities despite the demands of her research and her young boys. 'She was an extremely effective fellow,' says Jean Floud. 'She taught extremely well and took a great interest in the college. Even when they began to live in great style, she played her part and was very helpful, once lending the London flat for a meeting.' Mary's first-year students remember her as strict and rather distant. 'She was as interested in correcting your grammar as in correcting your chemistry,' says Alison Brown. 'Neat, quiet and well organised,' says Olivia Webley. 'It was a surprise when she was so much in the media afterwards.' With those who became more interested in chemistry, Mary warmed up, and was regarded as something of a role model for young women in science, albeit one whose looks were hard to emulate. 'She was well dressed and well maintained, not your typical scientist,' says Sara Gledhill. Ingrid Pickering, now a science professor, says, 'We thought it was a terrible shame she was like a second-class member of the university chemistry department, and thought she might be being discriminated against because she was a woman, but we had no direct evidence of that.' Gledhill and Pickering were among five women in their year who remember being invited to Grantchester for lunch. 'Everyone was highly strung just before finals,' says Pickering. 'It was just this huge treat for us, a really nice thing of her to do. Jeffrey picked us up in his Jag and we had lunch served in the garden. I loved that day; it was super, a nice opportunity for us to relax.'

Although she could be solemn and serious, Mary did have a sense of fun. She sometimes wore a jumper which lit up in places (using a battery) and she suggested a fundraising slogan which could be printed on Newnham T-shirts: 'We are appealing'. Her contemporaries toned this down to 'Newnham is appealing' and put it on their letter-franking machine rather than their clothes. Whether Mary ever wore her T-shirt is unclear, but she is remembered for her poise and elegance, and also for taking part in fundraising; she also contributed financially to the college. There were some who thought Mary was out to impress, particularly when she became rich, and perhaps because they took exception to a 1980 article featuring her in the *Cambridge Evening News* entitled: 'Six Women – a study in maturity', which was about 'attractive people in the 35 plus age group'. Mary said she had always been interested in fashion and 'in relation to my colleagues, I spend on the high side . . . I always shop in London for my clothes. I like Jaeger. I'm naturally thin so I don't need a diet . . . Sometimes I have an exercise routine – patches of jogging and yoga. I like swimming and tennis . . . but mostly I rely on dashing around town on a bicycle.'[8] And she played squash with a Newnham maths lecturer called Stephen Siklos.

Newnham fellows noticed that Mary was very independent of

Jeffrey, although he did come along occasionally to drinks parties. It was also noted by one fellow who had small children that Jeffrey insisted on winning all the games at his young sons' party. William and James occasionally came into college – they were very well-behaved – and Mary took her nanny Kathleen Beer to dinner there on one occasion. Mary also had a very sharp tongue; '. . . you could get quite a barb from Mary,' said one fellow. 'Cold as ice,' said another. 'She would not have been sympathetic if her students had personal problems.' One fellow says it was very hard to get a smile out of her, although she was always perfectly civil. But the college heads liked her, just as schoolteachers and tutors had, finding her courteous, helpful, and conscientious. 'If she agreed to do something, you knew it would be done, done well, and with absolutely no fuss,' according to Sheila Browne, a former principal. Browne's predecessor, Jean Floud, agrees. 'She was very helpful to me when I had the disgusting job of raising money,' she says.

Mary also supported a move to make Newnham a mixed-sex college: a hard-fought battle eventually won – but only just – by those who wanted to preserve its distinctiveness. The argument against single-sex was not confined to the intake of undergraduates but also related to the pool of teaching talent, and staff costs. The college statutes did not allow male fellows, and this limited Newnham's options, especially if it wanted to attract those with positions already paid by the university. Mary felt this was a disadvantage, particularly in scientific subjects that were male-dominated, and where the number of women with university posts was small. To make matters worse, there was competition from the men's colleges which were in the process of going mixed. Another Newnham scientist says, 'Many of the science fellows, including Mary and me, felt that the standard of science teaching in Newnham, which had been high, was in danger of falling. Mary felt it was inequitable that men appointed to college teaching posts could not be fellows. A group of scientists started a campaign to change the college statutes to allow the fellowship, but not the undergraduate population, to become mixed . . . This made those scientists, including Mary, unpopular with fellows who opposed the idea and who believed it would send out the wrong signals to aspiring women academics.' Mary did her share of lobbying: 'She went round campaigning assiduously,' says one of her opponents. 'She even came to see me at home and pressed her case very cogently and politely, in a very restrained, unemotional way.' Although most science dons were in favour of change, they were a minority of the fellows; nevertheless, the resolution only just failed to get the necessary two-thirds majority, so the lobbying nearly succeeded.

Meanwhile, at the university physical chemistry department, Mary set up an experimental research group, her special interest being the question of how the sun's light energy might be harnessed in new and useful ways. Away from Cambridge, Mary still had a public platform to press the cause for solar energy research, and in January 1976 had spoken to a parliamentary select committee on science and technology about the prospects for using photochemistry to supply new energy sources. Her Solar Energy Society made a strong case for more funds to be made available in Britain, which was spending a few tens of thousands a year on research, while America put in £50 million. The receptiveness in America towards her expertise was demonstrated by the offer of another post, that of 'consultant' to the US Department of Energy's Brookhaven National Laboratory in America, which she had first visited in 1975 to give a lecture, according to a chemist there, Dr Jack Fajer. Mary went over to Brookhaven, on New York's Long Island, just as Jeffrey was giving an interview to *Women's Wear Daily*, an American journal, about the way his wife had been so encouraging about his writing. 'At this very moment, she is at the Brookhaven National Laboratory advising your government on solar energy and stealing all the advice she can get from them as well. She's still the most beautiful woman I know and by a long, long way, the most intelligent.' Someone else who found Mary beautiful and intelligent was a young chemistry researcher at

Brookhaven, Dr Stephen Feldberg. The two had met at a science conference in 1972 and struck up a close friendship.

Mary's extra work boosted the family's earnings, and the *Daily Express* reported she was earning over £5,000 a year as a lecturer. She went all over America, as well as to Australia, Europe and Romania. Later, she also visited Japan, where Jeffrey's books were phenomenally successful, and where at a banquet she was given the most surprising thing she ever ate: fried bumblebees. 'They didn't taste bad,' she said, 'it was just the thought of them!' Mary had by now also begun writing her own book, called *Photoconversion of Solar Energy*, on which she was collaborating with fellow scientist Jim Bolton. She visited him in Canada when she could, staying with him and his wife, Wilma. Jeffrey, too, made a trip to Canada at the end of 1975, where he became embroiled in the curious case of the stolen suits. The incident happened in Toronto, where Jeffrey was giving evidence in a preliminary court hearing about the Aquablast conspiracy, which eventually ended up as a big fraud trial. During this visit, Jeffrey went shopping in a department store, Simpson's, and was stopped by store detectives while walking out of the building carrying three suits. Jeffrey was arrested on suspicion of theft, but he convinced the police it was all a misunderstanding and that he had not realised he was leaving the premises. The local police did not press charges, partly because Jeffrey was an important witness in the fraud trial. Ten years later, the British investigative journalist Paul Foot became interested in the story, only to have it completely denied by Jeffrey himself, who said he had 'never been involved in any such incident'. In 1998, however, Jeffrey was forced to change his story, finally admitting he was stopped carrying suits over his shoulder, and giving the explanation that he had been crossing a footbridge, which he had not realised connected Simpson's with another store. The trouble with this 'explanation' is that the bridge had not yet been built in 1975.

A year after the Toronto suits episode, Jeffrey was again able to buy clothes in Savile Row. He had written a second successful novel, *Shall We Tell the President?*, spending two months in

Barbados working on it as the guest of a Canadian millionaire. The book was another good seller, and its success eased the Archers' financial position. A debt-repayment programme had been devised by this time, the lawyer Victor Mishcon drawing up a deal by which one of Jeffrey's friends bought their house in The Boltons. Following his change in fortunes, Jeffrey was interested in buying more expensive things than suits, however; he was somehow able to afford a large flat in Alembic House, the building where he had once worked for the UNA. The Archers were able to pick up, 'really amazingly cheaply', according to Mary, the fourteen-year remainder of a lease on a tenth-floor flat. From there, he looked across the Thames to the Houses of Parliament, and saw an exciting future. He continued to travel to Nigeria on business, on one occasion getting stuck in Lagos after an attempted coup, and he gave numerous interviews about his change of fortune. One journalist noted that he was 'a highly practised interviewee . . . his well-drilled answers are pat, quotable and clichéd . . . He has learned how to box clever.'

At the end of 1977, Mary reflected on the previous three turbulent years in an interview from Newnham College for the *Daily Express*. She said the loss of their money was very tough to take. 'The public humiliation, wondering what our friends were thinking, and not having the money to meet our obligations, this gave me a lot of stress I had to learn to live with. With help from my doctor, I got through this depression and am not sorry to have had that experience. Now my salary insulates me financially and my work insulates me mentally . . .'[9] The reporter suggested that perhaps Mary was the 'ideal' wife for Jeffrey? Mary shuddered, and her colleagues pealed with laughter. Later, 'in the cloistered calm of her quiet Cambridge rooms', the contrast seemed even greater. While the slim, pretty don with a 'polished bob of mahogany hair' sat in her book-lined Cambridge study, waiting for her next batch of students to arrive, her 'firecracker' husband was unpacking at their new London flat where he lived during the week, ready to do more business deals.

In the *Express* interview, Mary defended her dual role as career woman and mother, although some of her views were out of step with the current feminist movement. 'Being a housewife is part of the female role. If a woman works she has to be able to do both jobs. This way the family hangs together. I'm afraid much in the feminist movement escapes me. To be a good mother is one of the ground rules of marriage for me. I have grown up believing this.' Nevertheless, as the article pointed out, Mary had the help of a nanny. A few years later, she also employed a daily, a housekeeper and a gardener, which presumably made the job of 'housewife' rather easier. She also told the newspaper frankly that she would like to see a bit more of her husband: 'Naturally I miss him. If I did not have a job I loved it would probably lead to boredom and mischief! There is a level over which I miss him terribly, but he is often home more than just weekends . . . We both have separate friends as well as shared ones. I think there is a temptation to be possessive that you have to resist. Though I do believe in being faithful. That's another ground rule of mine.'[10]

Jeffrey may not have rewarded Mary's loyalty with enough of his company, but he did give her a generous and unconventional thank-you gift for her support after Aquablast: one hundred thousand pounds, to make her a member of Lloyd's: 'total financial security' as Jeffrey optimistically described it. In fact, it could have been total financial ruin as many thousands of members were riding for a fall in years to come, and it would transpire that Mary had the task of dealing with them. But for now, it was indeed a good time for members – or 'Names' as they are called – who had been enjoying high returns in recent years, and Jeffrey asked his own underwriter, the highly successful Ian Posgate (nicknamed Goldfinger) to introduce Mary to the market. Jeffrey expected the money to produce an annual income of between £10,000 and £15,000 for Mary, as a way of ensuring that she would not suffer if he ever went broke again and he made sure his gift got publicity in the newspapers. Fulsome in his praise as usual, Jeffrey said Mary had been fabulous: 'I made the decision that there was no way she would ever have to go through it again, even if the worst happened to me. She's a hell of a bloody lady.'[11]

For reasons that have always escaped most people, Mary also thought the best of Jeffrey. She explained it this way: 'What people fail to understand is that he is a deeply, deeply unconventional person.'[12] Jeffrey was probably thinking of his wife when he created the character of the doctor Elizabeth Dexter in his new novel *Shall We Tell the President?*. Like Mary, Elizabeth is left-handed, with beautiful dark hair, fine skin and good legs and says work is her entire life. More unexpectedly, the author writes of Elizabeth: 'For all her intelligence and self-sufficiency, she had a touching fragility . . . a pleasant self-assurance, yet without a trace of the bitchiness that mars so many city professional women.' Perhaps part of the touching fragility was Mary's loneliness. She led an independent life at work which was satisfying and busy, but she wanted her husband to spend more time with her, and with their young sons.

On one level, of course, there was no reason for Mary to be suspicious of Jeffrey. She trusted her husband, and appeared to believe what he said. Hadn't he been brought up, like her, with Christian moral values, at least by his mother? Mary knew she was physically attractive; Jeffrey was constantly telling anyone who would listen that she was the most beautiful, the most intelligent woman he had ever met. He was inordinately proud of her abilities, even saying in his *Who's Who* entry that his education was 'by my wife'. Friends felt that he worshipped the ground she walked on, and noticed how he jumped to attention if she came into the room, and frequently commented on her 'glorious' hair. Mary, publicly at least, called him a splendid husband. They shared a bed; twenty years after their marriage, Mary assured a court that she and Jeffrey enjoyed a 'full' life – a euphemism generally taken to mean they were still having sex together. She would not have described herself as a jealous woman, but nevertheless she was covering up feelings of anxiety and irritation that she had to share her husband's time with so many others. She may have suspected she was also sharing her husband with another woman, or women, though perhaps it was not something she could admit to herself. If she had looked, there were hints in the press; Jeffrey had been 'chasing actresses like a stage-door johnnie' and his name was being linked with the 'coquettish' Andrina Colquhoun.

Honey for Tea

THE SEVENTIES DECADE ENDED rather better than it had begun. Mary's brother David got married to Faye, a nurse, which was a happy family occasion, and in September 1979 Mary became the wife of a best-selling author. *Kane and Abel*, the tale of two men from different backgrounds who are born on the same day, is still perhaps Jeffrey's best book, and elements of his own life are woven into it. It reached number one in Britain, on the way to becoming an international best-seller, and was the book that was to change their lives. Mary had by this time given way as his 'editor' to the redoubtable Richard Cohen, senior fiction editor of the publishers Hodder & Stoughton. Cohen spent many relentless weeks improving the drafts and guiding Jeffrey. It paid off; the American paperback rights for the book were auctioned for over one million dollars, an extraordinary figure for an English writer who was still relatively unknown in the States. *Kane and Abel* reached number one in the *New York Times* best-seller list, and continued to sell: 2.5 million copies over the next ten years. Jeffrey was keenly aware of the importance of marketing, and he began to cultivate sales reps – giving them parties and gifts. He was in great demand for interviews, which he gave at every opportunity, claiming now to be a multimillionaire and revelling in his reversal of fortunes. Not only did he love being a celebrity, he also knew it was all good publicity for his books. But he still dreamt of a career in politics.

It was the advance on *Kane and Abel* that enabled the Archers to put down the deposit on a large family home which finally consoled Mary for the loss of her 'very nice house' in The Boltons. Initially, Mary had wanted something similar: a 'well-bred Georgian town house', but they considered other village properties, and even competed with the inventor Clive Sinclair to buy one of them. It was Jeffrey who fell for the house they eventually did acquire. The Old Vicarage, Grantchester, was famous for its literary connections, having been immortalised in a poem written in 1912 by Rupert Brooke. In a village not far from Cambridge, set in a large garden near the river, the seventeenth-century house was on the market for the first time in sixty-five years. It inspired a somewhat more commonplace verse by Roger Woddis:

> Ah God! To see the vampires stir
> To get their claws on Grantchester! . . .
> And will the Vicarage, when sold,
> Be modernised and called 'Ye Olde'? . . .
> Oh, is the littered driveway full
> Of coachloads down from Liverpool?

Brooke had rented rooms in the house between 1910 and 1912 and wrote his poem about it while in Berlin, feeling homesick for England and the Old Vicarage. He had previously described it as a 'deserted, lonely, dank, ruined, overgrown, gloomy, lovely house: with a garden to match. It is all five hundred years old, and fusty with the ghosts of generations of mouldering clergymen. It is a fit place to write my kind of poetry in . . .' The poem became most famous for its last two lines: 'Stands the Church clock at ten to three? And is there honey still for tea?' but it is a lyrical and passionate poem; a hymn to the England he loved.

Fortunately for the Old Vicarage, its new owners had the money and the inclination to restore it to its former beauty, and keep it as a family home, although in time they did often open the gardens to visitors to raise money for local causes. The house cost the Archers £180,000 and they needed to spend a lot more on renovation, new wiring, general refurbishment, work on the garden and, eventually, providing his-and-hers studies in the two-storey Victorian folly in the garden, the one downstairs for Mary, the other upstairs for Jeffrey. They could not move in immediately, and a designer called Julian Dakowski was hired to help modernise the kitchen. Dakowski, whose brother had known Jeffrey at Dover College, had already worked for him at Arrow House, which he turned into a stark modern office, and at Alembic House where he redesigned the flat which had previously belonged to the James Bond composer John Barry. Jeffrey asked Dakowski to go up to Grantchester and guide Mary. 'The main concern was the kitchen and I took her round design studios and state-of-the-art kitchen shops to get ideas. Mary was receptive but pretty definite in her views.' When the Archers bought the Old Vicarage, it was in split occupation, with two kitchens, because it had been used by previous owners to accommodate lodgers. The Archers had fun putting it back together again as one family home, suitable for their two boys, nanny, three cats and various other livestock. The initial building work took about six months while the family lived on the top floor, needing to be on the spot while the plumbers and builders moved in. The boys, of course, loved it, and Jeffrey and Mary were so proud of their new home they allowed it to be featured in several style magazines, put a drawing of it on their writing paper and even had a limited edition of ceramic replicas of the house made to give to favoured guests.

Mary organised her new life with her usual precision, a trait of which she is justifiably proud. As a reporter for *Woman's Own* records: '"I am organised," she said, offering me some home-made shortcake as she let down James's school trousers. "I'm also not extravagant and I'm a great turner-off of lights. I hate waste. I was brought up that way. Even though Jeffrey is a wealthy man, I try to run a reasonably tight ship."'[1] When William was eight, he was once asked to write an essay describing his mother. He wrote: 'My mother is small. She has black hair and a flat chest and she gets very upset if her plans go wrong.'[2] By now, Mary had been able to revive her plans for her sons' education and they both got places at St John's, a private prep school in Cambridge.

Mary was still at Newnham College, dividing her time between teaching (both undergraduates and postgraduates) and doing research into electrochemistry. She published scientific papers as well as articles about the life and work of Humphry Davy, and about solar energy conversion. As well as sitting on an appeals committee, Mary was a member of the governing body where she volunteered to act as treasurer, even though she had to learn how to do the accounts. She later told her colleagues she had found it really thrilling. Mary had no hesitation in using her connections, particularly if it would help raise funds, and on one occasion Ian Posgate, the Lloyd's underwriter, was invited to dinner to foster links between female undergraduates and the City. Another friend, Colin Emson, gave Newnham money which was used to equip the music room with a harpsichord. But a more pressing problem was the college roofs, which needed a £3 million overhaul. A development trust of grandees from the business world was eventually set up when Sheila Browne arrived as principal; the trustees included the property developer Elliott Bernerd of Chelsfield, who paid for part of the work, and also helped fund a college post. Years later, Bernerd's daughter became the fiancée of James Archer.

The Old Vicarage needed restoration work, too, but before getting down to that Mary had a lengthy absence abroad. 'Jeffrey was in America doing research for his latest book and I was on my way round the world lecturing or listening to lectures in the USA, Japan and Australia. We met up in New York, but I didn't get home for a month.'[3] By this time, the extensive travel was not financially imperative, but something Mary felt was important to her career. Her young boys were now both at school, and her role as a mother had taken a back seat in practical terms. 'Fortunately I have a marvellous nanny-cum-housekeeper, Kathleen Beer. I couldn't live the life I do without her,' Mary told *Woman's Own*, ironically a magazine with a large readership of housewives.[4] Like her husband, Mary enjoys working hard; work was, and still is, vital to her. She found academic life relatively easy to combine with motherhood; she had term-times and suitable teaching hours, and she realised, although it was hard to think of it at a time when she had two demanding little children, that they would grow up one day and she would still need something to do. Recently, Mary said she never regretted the decision to carry on working, although she still feels bad about what her sons missed. She was simply not there for them in the way her mother was there for her. 'Certainly William says of one or two occasions which were important in his life, "you weren't there" – making one feel permanently guilty.'[5] One compensation was that Mary loved her time at Cambridge, even though it didn't seem easy. She got home at about 6.30 in the evening, usually bringing work with her, but would first spend some time with her children until they went to bed. 'She just was a very academic lady and she worked very hard,' says Kathleen Beer, who had her own room, furnished as she wanted, and the run of the house during the week. 'I couldn't have wished for a better job; it was a lovely job and I had a nice social life as well. They were very generous, and thought about me and treated me very well indeed.' At weekends, Jeffrey sometimes took over. 'I suspect the children have been systematically short-changed,' Mary once said, maybe with some regret. 'But I am not convinced that full-time mothers always produce independent, lively people.'[6] Although her own mother had done just that.

Mary was also unable, or maybe unwilling, to pay too much attention to what was going on at Alembic House, their London flat. Jeffrey had made it clear that the new home in Grantchester would not replace the flat in London that he had fallen for and which he said he needed for his busy life in town. The situation underlined the unusual nature of the couple's domestic relation-ship: for much of their married life they had effectively led separate lives during the week. Now Mary's home was in Cambridge and

Jeffrey was mostly in London or abroad writing, but they spent their weekends together. Mary was rarely seen at the flat, and only in the late 1990s did her name appear on the electoral roll for Alembic House. This arrangement gave Jeffrey plenty of freedom, and within a few years of their marriage, he was unfaithful to Mary and had a serious affair with one of his staff. Then, as would emerge years later at his perjury trial, Jeffrey began a long-term relationship in 1979 with the former deb Andrina Colquhoun, who was twenty-six and working as a PA for Terence Conran, the designer.

Andy, as she was known, was blonde, glamorous, wealthy and well connected. She had a strong personality and great zest for life. She had quite often appeared in newspaper gossip columns herself, and one of her friends was Lord Lucan, who vanished in the mid-seventies. Colquhoun quickly fell for Jeffrey, and was frequently seen around town with him, at parties and art galleries. Friends say she taught him how to dress well, took him to top-class restaurants, and introduced him to the high-society scene. The couple saw each other for three years before Jeffrey made her his personal assistant. She arranged his monthly men-only lunches at Alembic House (where the guests included such diverse company as King Constantine of Greece, the actor Michael Caine, football manager Lawrie McMenemy, heart surgeon Magdi Yacoub and comedian Ernie Wise), and she accompanied him when he went on book-promotion tours, or abroad to write, typing up his notes, cooking meals and sharing his bed. She was, like Mary, a very good organiser, and bought furniture for the flat and liked to make sure there were plenty of flowers everywhere. She was not keen on the modern look Julian Dakowski the designer had introduced, and she had his uplighters removed and put cushions on his sleek sofas. Jeffrey and his PA made no secret of the fact they were lovers, not even concealing it from a television documentary film crew. She called Jeffrey 'Moon' and his pet name for her was 'Roonette'. Michael Stacpoole says she even put her initials on a new mattress she bought for the main bedroom at the flat. Several people have said that Andrina was seriously in love with Jeffrey, but he was not so sentimental, saying he would never divorce Mary. Jeffrey's editor Richard Cohen recalls the atmosphere being lighter when he was with her: 'Andrina and Jeffrey were like a happily married couple, joshing and teasing each other all the time, and they had a mutually supportive relationship full of fun and humour. The flat would bear eloquent signs of their attachment – bawdy Valentine cards, for instance, left open for anyone to see.' By contrast, Cohen felt that Mary often behaved with Jeffrey 'more like a primary school headmistress'.

An Oxford friend says Jeffrey was quite brazen about his affair. 'He likes sort of running with the tigers . . . Andy was a very pretty lady, very lively and fun, a good person to be with Jeffrey.' The friend says that Andy, being young and impressionable, did expect him to marry her. In 1982, when she had become Jeffrey's PA, a story appeared in the satirical magazine *Private Eye*, proclaiming the nature of the relationship loud and clear. 'Former Tory MP turned best-selling author Jeffrey Archer, who honed the art of fiction writing while working at the UNA . . . and fiddling his expenses, is involved in a real-life drama, as two women fight for his affections. On my left . . . is the divine Dr Mary Archer . . . on my right is the coquettish Andrina Colquhoun . . . Andy is confident of winning the day.'[7] Many of those who knew them agree that if Mary knew about the relationship, she turned a blind eye. One friend of Colquhoun's said, 'I never could understand how Archer could live with her in the flat all week and Mary not be suspicious. We often discussed it. We said, "How does it happen? What happens when she rings?" Andy said, "She doesn't ring."' Another friend, from Oxford days, says, 'You never know with Mary what she knows or whether she chooses not to know things and doesn't ask questions.' Yet another person who knew both of the Archers well says Jeffrey simply lied to Mary. Once when she turned up and asked why the flat was so full of flowers, Jeffrey said they had come from a secret admirer. When the association with Andrina appeared in the papers, Richard Cohen says he asked Jeffrey how he felt. 'Richard, I love her,' he replied and shrugged it off, saying that after twenty years the marriage had different rules.

Colquhoun later explained that there was no attempt to keep the affair secret; nor, she said, did she notice any strain between Jeffrey and Mary over the relationship. She was sometimes asked by her lover to look after James and William during the university holidays, when Mary was away at conferences and the like. Occasionally Mary would come to London, and then Colquhoun would have to disappear, allegedly replacing the pictures of herself in the flat with those of Mary and locking her own clothes in a cupboard. Colquhoun felt she should be treated on equal terms with Jeffrey's wife, and Michael Stacpoole recalls one Christmas when he went with Jeffrey to a jewellers in Hatton Garden to order two identical gifts, with one important difference: he claims Andy's jewels were slightly bigger than Mary's. At Jeffrey's perjury trial in 2001, Andrina Colquhoun said Jeffrey was still giving her presents in 1987, three years after he had supposedly ended the affair, and had paid for her to go on a flower design course.

The early eighties were busy for Jeffrey, and he continued turning out books which sold extremely well – a collection of short stories and two more novels. His sales were helped by his appearance as the guest on *This is Your Life* in January 1981, shortly after the paperback edition of the best-selling *Kane and Abel* came out. *This is Your Life*, presented by Eamonn Andrews, was one of the most popular programmes in Britain at the time, with about 15 million viewers a week. A member of the production team says although they found Mary rather 'blue stocking' and reserved, she was happy to cooperate if it was going to be good for Jeffrey, and gave them contacts to approach (including Michael Stacpoole's name, although he did not appear). She travelled to London the day before the show with her young sons and their nanny Kathleen Beer, to attend a rehearsal. During the run-through, Mary would have heard Eamonn Andrews say that Jeffrey had been to the University of Berkeley in California on an education course. She must have believed this fiction, or she would surely have corrected the mistake. On the night, a beaming Mary bounded delightedly through the famous doors of the set to greet her husband; she was obviously tickled pink by the whole experience. Among those singing Jeffrey's praises were the actress Lesley-Anne Down, the principal of Brasenose College, Sir Noel Hall, and the Hollywood producer Mel Frank. The footage of Jeffrey's early life included colour film of him competing in a race at White City – taken by Mary's father.

Jeffrey was also a guest on *Desert Island Discs*, in which his record choices included the Beatles, Beethoven's Choral Symphony (to remind him of Mary who he said had sung it with her choir at the Albert Hall under Sir Colin Davis), and a song called 'It's Hard to Be Humble When You're Perfect in Every Way'. Not allowed to take Concorde as his luxury, he chose a plasticine model of Roy Plomley, the show's presenter, and a pin to stick into it. He spoke about the time a bank statement dropped through his letterbox showing he was overdrawn by £427,727. No such bank statement ever existed, and this little bit of dramatic fiction earned a famous comment from Mary: 'Jeffrey's talent for inaccurate precis,' was her gentle rebuke.[8] Roy Plomley suggested to Jeffrey that his first two books had brought him a million pounds, but he refused to confirm or deny it, saying archly, 'That's what the tax man keeps telling me.'

The tax man did not know everything, however. By now, the money was indeed rolling in, all the more so because Jeffrey was involved in a tax fiddle. He employed his friend Michael Stacpoole in an elaborate operation to escape paying tens of thousands of pounds in UK income tax. Jeffrey had an offshore bank account in Jersey, and told Stacpoole it was money from the sale of books in foreign countries, and the sale of film and TV rights. Stacpoole says Jeffrey paid him to fly regularly to Jersey to collect wads of cash, the interest on the account which, he said, held a million pounds. 'The sums I brought back varied from £7,000 to £15,000.' He even had two extra pockets fitted to his overcoat to carry the envelopes of notes. The Jersey run lasted about a year, with Stacpoole collecting at least £150,000. Jeffrey later transferred the account to Switzerland and the money was then brought back by another of his aides for a few years. With a top tax rate of 60 per cent at that time, Jeffrey was saving large sums by not declaring the money transfer to the Inland Revenue.

Had it been exposed at the time, Jeffrey's Jersey jaunts would have wrecked any chance of a political job from Margaret Thatcher, the then prime minister. He was still in love with politics, and angling for a post in the government. He undertook dozens of speaking engagements for Conservative associations, for by-elections, for fundraising events. Mary was asked, too, but never accepted unless she found something intellectually stimulating, or could talk about the 'social implications of science'. Jeffrey denied wanting to return to the Commons, but hoped that he would be 'offered something' by Mrs Thatcher, and fed the speculation that some reward was impending for the enormous amount of work he did for the party. There was talk of him being made Sports Minister, or going to Central Office, or even being made a peer, but in the end he was made Deputy Chairman of the Conservative Party. The price was Andrina Colquhoun, a sacrifice Jeffrey was reluctantly prepared to make. Nigel Dempster, the *Daily Mail* diarist, said a condition of his appointment had been that 'he regularises his personal affairs', as the Conservatives traded on being the party of family values. 'Andy was in absolutely floods and floods of tears,' says a friend. 'She looked upon it as politics . . . she didn't blame him.' Sixteen years later, she herself referred somewhat poignantly to this heartbreaking episode: 'He thought that it would be better if he tidied up his personal life.'[9] In January 1985 Jeffrey took on a new PA, Angela Peppiatt, and a political aide, David Faber, a grandson of Harold Macmillan.

The end of the Andrina affair was not entirely the result of interference from the Tory Party whips. Jeffrey got a lashing of a different kind from his wife: a 'free and frank discussion' was the way Mary put it. In autumn 1985, Mary was giving a supervision in Cambridge when she was suddenly rung up by one of her academic colleagues. The colleague told her to look at a diary piece by William Hickey in the *Daily Express*. Mary contained her curiosity until lunchtime, when she went to the Senior Common Room to have a look at the newspaper. She was annoyed to find a photograph of Andy in a revealing open-necked blouse, and being described as 'handy' for Jeffrey's London parties; she was equally irritated to read that she, Mary, had 'always hated the London social swirl and the giddy life of a millionaire author's wife'.[10] Mary's reaction was steely; she did not pick up the phone and start shouting at her husband. She calmly waited until she could talk to Jeffrey in private before confronting him. She insisted the affair must stop, and extracted a promise that it would. Had Mary or her colleague been readers of the *Daily Mail*, they would have seen an equally provocative item the previous year, written by the gossip columnist Nigel Dempster. It referred to Jeffrey's intriguing lifestyle with his 'nubile companion' who made no secret of her admiration for the novelist. 'Guests to his South Bank penthouse . . . are usually greeted by Andy, who once worked as a photographer.'[11]

The knowledge of Jeffrey's affair was a defining moment for Mary. She greatly admired her ambitious and successful husband and appreciated the exciting life he had given her. Now, he had betrayed her, and her admiration was tempered with humiliation. Despite dismissing his affair as 'a fling', Mary was deeply hurt and angry. She carefully pondered on her situation. She questioned Jeffrey, she thought hard, and she made her decision to stay loyal – as she would do again and again. She had to rescue the situation for her own self-preservation.

Following their free and frank discussion, Mary made an effort to be seen more often with her husband, and she coolly gave several interviews about her views on his appointment as Deputy Party Chairman, saying their separate lives suited them very well; it was a 'good deal' for her, and a privileged life. 'I know sometimes he wishes I was around more but I think on balance he prefers me the way I am. Obviously I go along sometimes and it's very interesting to meet the people who run the country. I also like bending the ears of appropriate ministers on the use of solar energy.'[12] She was still involved with his books, but not until the final draft, when her meticulous brain and aptitude for detail was helpful. Shortly after Jeffrey's appointment, she visited her first Tory conference and attended more of the kind of events he had formerly been to with Colquhoun. This was duly noted in the diary columns: 'It was a rare outing in London for blue-stocking Mary . . . who prefers the peace of the family home . . .'[13] She had only stayed one day because she was not keen to be 'an accessory'. Mary told the *Mail*: 'It's not true we have an open marriage,'[14] and earlier the paper asserted that now Andy had taken up full-time employment again, 'public appearances with Jeffrey are at an end'.

But not private ones. The affair had not ended; it simply carried on for another three years in a more surreptitious way, with Colquhoun occasionally staying overnight – as she admitted at Jeffrey's perjury trial many years later. Amazingly she was still going to Alembic House to do the flower arranging, and Mary was fully aware of this, although she assumed the affair had ended, and was under the impression it had already been on its last legs at the time she confronted Jeffrey about it. But she was being deceived. Gradually it did fizzle out, but not before Jeffrey had given Andy a parting gift of his precious car numberplate ANY 1, which she still possesses. Understandably, Mary was furious. Andy's car, with its easily-recognised number plate, was even seen in Cambridgeshire from time to time, and she was still in friendly contact with Jeffrey thirteen years on.

Mary had appeared to turn a blind eye to Jeffrey's affair until it appeared in the press, or maybe she was unaware. Wives are often the last to know, as she herself said many years later. But she would have been dumbfounded had she known that there was evidence to show that, around this time, Jeffrey had also invited a twenty-one-year-old black prostitute, Dorrett Douglas, back to his flat for sex. Douglas described the experience as incredible. She says Jeffrey was 'a true gentleman', very polite, very appreciative. 'He looked good, he smelt good, he was polite even when we were having sex.' She thought he seemed lonely and was grateful to her. 'He just wanted some company and some pleasure,' she says. Her story is compelling for its detail: she noted Jeffrey's works of art and his silver cigarette boxes shaped like books, which had indeed been given to him by a publisher, although he is a non-smoker.

While Jeffrey was bouncing about in London and Conservative Central Office, rallying the party in the country round Mrs Thatcher and making some highly publicised gaffes about government policy, Mary was feeling more at home in Cambridgeshire. She thought it was a lovely home to live in because of its history and she felt it gave her 'a sense of security somehow' that the house had had so many people in it. Mary is a neat and tidy person and likes her home that way. Reporters who visit the Old Vicarage often comment on how immaculate it is, how it seems to be unlived-in. Perhaps it looks more lived in when cameras are not there, but they are there often.

Numerous articles have been written about the house; many photographs of it have appeared in the press; and TV crews allowed in to film it. Despite Mary's alleged reserve, and much proclaimed desire for privacy, she is certainly not camera-shy when it comes to her home, which one might have thought would be the one place to be protected from intrusive lenses. Not long after its renovation, her Grantchester home featured in several publications, and in 1981, a month after *This is Your Life*, Mary was interviewed in a television programme about their new-found fame and riches. She said she was getting used to it, but it seemed like a dream that might vanish. She didn't mind the inevitable intrusion into her life and, indeed, did not even see it that way: 'It's quite fun in a way, you know, in small doses.[15] But the kind of life Jeffrey led wouldn't suit her, and she was glad she could escape to a job where all that kind of thing didn't matter. And yet before long, she was appearing in another documentary made at their family home. It might have been the first time, but it was not the last time the Archers would stage-manage a scene of domestic harmony. Mary was filmed at the piano while her sons performed – James on the clarinet, and William singing. A dutiful Jeffrey sat listening in an improbably formal pose on the sofa.

Some time later, Jeffrey made the point on Terry Wogan's programme that he felt sorry for the children of people in the public eye. 'People don't realise the strain they go through.' Quite why he and Mary were happy to parade their children for the television cameras at a young age was not questioned, but he praised his wife for the way she had brought them up to be tremendously resilient. Perhaps Mary thought they should get used to the limelight from an early age; William and Jamie both made several TV appearances throughout the eighties, and were also regularly photographed by newspapers. Jeffrey is remembered by parents at his boys' prep school in Cambridge for bringing a film crew to sports day, where he was taking part, very competitively, in a fathers' race. The headmaster was reportedly so furious that the event had been 'hijacked' he cancelled the race. However, a television programme was made which included the Archer boys running, with their father shouting encouragement. Later, after William had left school altogether and moved abroad, he spoke of his feelings about the publicity. 'There have been times I wished my parents weren't famous. I've wondered to myself, if they weren't, what would I be? You wonder about your own worth . . . One thing I like about being in America is that I do feel more anonymous. I went there partly to escape . . .'[16]

The renovation of the Old Vicarage became mainly Mary's project and the house very much reflects her own style and tastes. It is full of fine English oak antiques, portraits in oils and traditional good quality furnishings, with flagstone flooring, a piano and spinet, flowers and always a cat or two around, as in Rupert Brooke's day. Brooke's landlady Florence Neeve had a photogenic stripey cat, which appears in an old photograph, perched on her son's shoulder. 'The cat tradition lives on,' Mary once told Florence's daughter-in-law. 'It's definitely a cat house.' Mary loves cats, and once wrote of them as 'watchful, self-contained, inscrutable' – a description which could just as easily describe herself.[17] Some of Mary's favourite cats have been Abyssinians, known for their friendly nature, and she once bought two Bengal kittens from the eccentric breeder Esmond Gay, whose speciality is providing stars with unusual pets. Bengal cats, which can cost thousands of pounds each, are partly descended from Asian leopard cats, and have unusual and highly prized markings; Mary was introduced to Gay by her cat-loving friends the retired Appeal Court judge Sir Martin Nourse and his wife, Lavinia, who says Bengal cats are 'enormously imperious and demanding and talk a lot. They are extraordinary creatures – they're really like little dogs.' Lavinia Nourse, who used to be a Grantchester neighbour, has also bred Abyssinians for Mary. 'She's devoted to her cats. No one could be more loving to her animals than Mary.' Jeffrey agreed, saying one of her Abyssinians, Archie, was 'Mary's first love; I'm her second.'[18] A journalist noted that Mary's kitchen floor is covered with quarry tiles, and, when these were delivered, she saw that some of the tiles had tiny pawprints on them, no doubt made by a kitten walking over the wet clay. Mary had the tiles arranged so the footprints led from her cat-flap to her kitchen table. The Archer cats are allowed to go where they like – even on the kitchen counter – and have a lot of garden to prowl in.

The Old Vicarage garden was wild and untidy when the house was bought, as the previous owners had wanted to keep it unchanged as a sort of memorial to Brooke, but the Archers decided on an overhaul. As well as the famous chestnut trees, there were beech, silver birch, willow and an old mulberry tree; dead and diseased ones, like the elms which succumbed to elm-bark beetle, were removed and new ones planted. Mary wanted her garden to be cheerful, though not a blaze of colour, and characteristically did her homework, reading gardening books and seeking advice from the top – in this case the former director of the Cambridge Botanic

Garden who lived in the village. He provided the odd piece of advice, and later did his stint at the Archer gates when they opened their garden as part of the Yellow Book charity scheme. Herbaceous borders were filled with delphiniums, day lilies and English country flowers; the lilacs, poppies, pansies and pinks were there, as in Brooke's day; roses threaded through the trees, over-hanging the bench where Brooke had sat, the best place to catch the sun. The Archer boys, however, were keen to point visitors to the Rupert Brooke Memorial Garbage Corner. The Archers' cook benefited from the newly built herb garden by the kitchen door; and the fountain was re-created. Mary later had a large pond dug, called Lake Oscar, named after the favourite cat she 'absolutely adored' who is buried nearby. Jeffrey paid tribute to his wife's efforts: 'I would be very hurt if he [Rupert Brooke] didn't like what my wife has done . . . she has spent considerable time restor-ing it.' Despite organising all the work both inside and out, Mary found time to give a talk in Grantchester village hall about her house, and a neighbour suggested she should turn it into a book, *Rupert Brooke and the Old Vicarage, Grantchester*, which was duly published in 1989. A photograph of Rupert Brooke is on the front cover, one of Mary on the back.

Mary also found a home in Grantchester for her musical talents. Shortly after moving to the village she was approached by the then vicar Noel Brewster and asked if she would consider taking on the job of choirmistress at the parish church of St Andrew and St Mary, just a short walk from her home. The choir had dwindled to 'two inaudible girls', as Mary put it, but the church had an organ-ist and a supply of talent on its doorstep, including the two young Archer boys, whose voices had not yet broken. Noel Brewster, cousin of the musician Kit Hesketh-Harvey of the duo Kit and the Widow, said he 'roped her and the two little boys into the choir. One had a very nice treble voice. They sang Sunday morning serv-ices, and some of the choir came in the evening too.' Mary rehearsed her choir every week before the service, and sang as well as conducting, because they couldn't spare a voice. Ian Talbot, the

Grantchester organist, says the role of choirmistress couldn't have been very rewarding 'because the choir is about four elderly people ... she was very patient, but for big events she always brought friends, professional singers, from London. She's clearly been trained and understands a lot about church music especially psalms and plainsong; she knows all the rules and I learned quite a bit from her. She's always well prepared, never caught off guard, never flustered.' Mary said it gave her a tremendous source of pleasure, and she did the job for at least eight years. Jeffrey came to church with his family every now and again, and once wrote a little nativity play in which his son William had the main part as the son of a Roman governor. The play later became a book, *The First Miracle*.

Mary was so dedicated to church music that she had become a member of the Guild of Church Musicians, an organisation that exists to foster the highest standards of church music both amateur and professional. Mary enthusiastically endorsed these aims, saying it was important that musical standards were kept up at parish level. Grantchester choir members testify to Mary's love and knowledge of music; they still keep her robes hanging in the church in case she wants to join in, and she likes to attend the Christmas carol service, following which she would invite the choir and their partners back to the Old Vicarage for supper. When eventually Mary did give up being choirmistress, a job requiring great commitment, she was asked to write about preparing the carol service. 'Being Mary, she was able to charge a large fee which went straight to the church,' says a member of the congregation. In the rather erudite article, which explains the history of carols, Mary said hearing children sing 'Away in a Manger' still brought tears to her eyes, as it reminded her of learning it at her father's knee. She said as a child her father had a version of 'Hark the Herald' which he sang as 'Hark the Harold Angels Sing', thinking it referred to him. She herself had misunderstood a famous line from 'Silent Night': 'Round yon virgin mother and child', labouring under the more embarrassing misapprehension that a virgin was some kind of fireplace. She was so proud of her singing that she sent her friends Christmas cards with a photograph of herself in a church choir. She also performed with a local choir called the Palestrina Singers, who were based at Magdalene College and who sang the Tudor and Renaissance music she liked so much, but it disbanded because, as she disapprovingly put it, 'half its members were too disorganised to come to practice'. (Her own son had to leave St John's College choir for the same reason.) She then joined the Cantus Singers, run by a neighbour, which usually sings for charitable causes, and recently performed in Mary's garden to raise money for the church tower.

Singing is an outlet for Mary; a relief from her disciplined life. She points to an analogy with the physicist Richard Feynman who played bongo drums to relax. Adrian Hutton, a musician who was asked to help her prepare for singing 'cabaret' style songs, says she is 'thoroughly good fun, very easy, very smiley. She really enjoys music.' Mary relaxes by playing the piano and spinet, and also likes to compose lyrics which she frequently sings herself. When the Grantchester vicar Noel Brewster retired she put on a show for him, writing the words and music. Among the songs was 'The Last Noel', based on the carol, which went:

> The Last Noel we all shall sing,
> Is to thank our Vicar for everything,
> For everything which he has done,
> To make our village a Godly one.

She likes the mental game of composing humorous poems – 'ratiocinative verses', as she calls them. In the eighties she also entered and won a limerick competition run by the *Cambridge Evening News*. She was so surprised to be chosen as the winner, she rang the paper to make sure it had been on merit and not because of who she was. Having been reassured, Mary enjoyed her prize – a trip to a pantomime. She evidently enjoys playing with words, and over the years has adapted the lyrics of numerous well-known songs with her own verses, which she performs at various social events.

During the early eighties, Mary was also acquiring a portfolio of influential positions and widening her network of contacts and interests. She became a member of the Council of the Royal Institution, where she had worked earlier in her career; and was approached to take on a fundraising job for the famous Cambridge University Museum, the Fitzwilliam. Cambridge was, and is, a renowned centre of science, and the museum had been somewhat neglected. The museum's director, Michael Jaffe, had set up a Museum Trust whose aim was to get more money for the museum than it received from the university, so there could be major improvements and new acquisitions. Mary was the Trust's first director, alongside Lord (Gordon) Richardson, the former governor of the Bank of England, who became chairman. A scientist who loved the arts, Mary set about her job with the diligence for which she is noted; she was effective and 'very all about' according to one trustee, and naturally her extensive contacts were very useful.

Another important local connection came when Mary was approached out of the blue by the chairman of Anglia Television, Lord Buxton, who asked her to become a director of the company. Lord Buxton is a friend of Prince Philip, who had worked on wildlife projects for the television station. Anglia was one of a number of regional ITV companies which held franchises to make programmes for their local areas and also made some for a national audience, or the 'network' as it was known. Now they wanted someone to bolster their science coverage, and in getting Mary, they could 'tick a lot of boxes' as one manager put it. She was an academic, a scientist, a local, and a woman. And she was part of the local circle of wheels within wheels. 'It did have the feel that the regional TV company was part of the regional establishment,' says board member Roger Laughton. There were two other women on the board, and one of them, Diane Nutting, a countess by her first marriage, was the wife of a QC.

Mary took the plunge. It was not only a boardroom place which attracted her, but the prospect of being part of programme making, and appearing in programmes herself, as well as learning more about her area, and about all kinds of science. 'She was instrumental in persuading the programme people to bring regional popular science programmes to the screen,' says Anglia's then general manager Mike Hughes. It was another crossroads in Mary's life, and her association with Anglia was to have future consequences quite different from the ones she envisaged.

8

Midlife Crisis

ON THE AFTERNOON OF Saturday, 25 October 1986, Mary was at home in Grantchester when she took a phone call from Michael Dobbs, chief of staff at Conservative Central Office, who was desperately trying to get hold of her husband. What he had to tell Jeffrey would have devastating consequences. The *News of the World* was about to break a story entitled 'Tory Boss Archer Pays Vice Girl'. The paper had a photograph of a prostitute being offered an envelope crammed with cash, and it had a tape-recording of Jeffrey talking to her.

Earlier that year, Mary had faced a crisis of a different kind – what she called 'a mid-life intellectual crisis'. Around the time she was being head-hunted by Lord Buxton for Anglia Television, Mary had been at Cambridge for ten years, the longest she'd been in one job, and she began to ask herself what was she going to do in the next decade. She had enjoyed teaching, research – even sitting on college and university committees – but the next ten years looked as if it might be more of the same. She was by now forty-one, still young, energetic and attractive, and like many women of this age, she felt stuck; it was time for a change. Despite the fact that her husband had very high political hopes, she was not content simply to follow in his wake; she wanted to develop her own talents further, and continue with her separate career.

She was unlikely to get much further as a Cambridge academic. In the highly competitive and male world of Cambridge science, she had little chance of getting a university post; these were given only to the most distinguished, dedicated and single-minded of applicants, and men were preferred. One observer claimed there was some personal animosity between Mary and her head of department, Sir John Meurig Thomas, who was critical of her husband, but he now refuses to comment. In any case, Sir John was leaving Cambridge to go to her old place of employment, the Royal Institution, and she felt this change at the top would not improve her chances. Another scientist says she was annoyed that Trinity College did not take her career as seriously as she would have liked, one senior don expressing kindly surprise that she wasn't content to stay at home like his own wife.

Mary was, and is, acknowledged within her profession as a good scientist, but she has never been a future Nobel prize-winner. As the widow of Lord Porter puts it: 'She is not the sort of chemist who will push back the frontiers of science but there are not many of those.' Several professors who worked with her all agree, although none was prepared to be quoted by name. One says: 'I would say history will judge her more as a promoter of ideas than a forefront working-face scientist.' According to a former Cambridge colleague, she has produced 'some very good original work' particularly on solar energy and photoelectric chemistry, but not in sufficient quantity. 'It's not absolutely the very, very top.' Another says Mary's research never matched up to her teaching: 'As a research scientist, she was not very good in terms of creativity, quality or quantity. She would not have been able to compete with people shortlisted for university positions.' A professor from another university who had observed Mary's career says, 'She was a good lecturer but she wasn't any better than that. She's not the distinguished scientist that some people might suppose. Her research was all right; run of the mill stuff you'd expect from a lecturer.'

Neither was there any question of a professorship for Mary. 'She was not even close; she would not have dreamt of it,' says a fellow chemist. Another observer says, 'To be a professor you've got to have a CV that you can hardly pick up, it has to be so weighty. Mary's would be quite nice but she wouldn't have published enough scientific papers.' It is not unusual for a chemist to produce ten to fifteen papers a year and one colleague said, 'I'd be extremely surprised if she was writing that many, even in the early days.' A professor is expected to carry out original research as well as teach students from all colleges, a demanding position with a lot of obligations which might have been difficult to handle alongside bringing up a family and being the wife of a prominent politician, not to mention the amount of travelling Mary did lecturing all over the world. In addition, the academic world of Cambridge was unsympathetic to women: 'There was a strong anti-female element,' says one leading scientist. 'The non-university teaching officers in the chemistry department were all women. There was a feeling that "why should a woman who's already here use up a university position?"'

The experience clearly rankled. Four years after leaving her Newnham job, Mary wrote an article saying the odds were stacked against women scientists: 'As to the practices of our ancient universities, they surely merit referral to the Equal Opportunities Commission.'[1] And later still, she said she felt patronised because of being a woman. 'There was a great change when men's colleges admitted women and many of the men found that hard to take.'[2]

Mary had more sympathy overseas. Her Canadian colleague and co-author Jim Bolton, himself a professor at the University of Western Ontario, thinks Mary was treated very badly by the male-dominated power structure at Cambridge. 'She had an active research effort, worked very hard and, I felt, deserved to have a "regular" faculty position. I believe that she threatened to resign if she were not offered one, and when it was not forthcoming, she did resign.' An American scientist who met her in the mid-seventies, Dr Arthur Nozik, says Mary is regarded very highly in her field. 'What strikes me most is her scientific insight and the crispness of her questions; she makes excellent comments. She's very impressive and smart [clever].' Dr Nozik, who works for the US government's National Renewable Energy Laboratory, and is co-editing her third volume of solar electricity books, says, 'Mary is a good colleague, very warm, with an elegant demeanour – an intriguing lady.' One of Mary's female colleagues also thought she could have succeeded: 'Given Mary's quality of mind, determination and ruthlessness, if she had wanted academic life, she was better equipped than many to survive.' But she did want other things. She had a young family, a home she loved in Cambridge, and a glitzy life as the wife of a wealthy would-be politician. She said that because of Jeffrey she was more aware than many academics of life outside the 'ivory tower' and she decided on a move into management and business, which she found interesting. She said she had already been involved in college administration and handling quite substantial budgets, which she had found daunting, because she wasn't equipped. Now she wanted to go out into the world and get the experience she lacked. Mary went to see the principal of Newnham with her mind already made up. She would be leaving academia.

Meanwhile, well outside the ivory tower, husband Jeffrey was also not being taken as seriously as he would have liked, despite having flung himself into his unpaid job as deputy party chairman. He claimed that in his first year he had visited 276 constituencies, raised more than £420,000, eaten 119 ham salads (taken with a pinch of salt) and drunk more than 300 bottles of water. He liked to tell people how close he was to the prime minister but as usual he had exaggerated his own importance. Although Margaret Thatcher was fond of him, she was too busy to see him regularly. He was an occasional visitor to Number Ten, and he still harboured hopes of being there as the occupant rather than the messenger from the constituencies. His friend Michael Stacpoole says they discussed strategy many times, and the plan was that if Thatcher lost the 1987 election, Jeffrey would stand for the leadership – a ludicrous idea, especially when he wasn't even an

MP. In the meantime, he received a snub when his leader appointed a second deputy chairman, Peter Morrison, leaving Jeffrey to cheer the 'troops' and raise money; these were valuable skills, but he was seen more as the jester at the court of Margaret (and her successors) not just because he cooperated with articles such as 'The Contents of My Wastepaper Basket' but because he was regarded as too lightweight – and by some senior officials and ministers as too suspect – to be taken seriously.

While his books brought him fans and compliments, his return to the political life served to remind him of all those who wanted to 'knock' him. When the writer Lynn Barber went to interview him, he launched into a tirade about 'all these people whose sole purpose in life is to be unpleasant and to bring you down'. Barber reported that interviewing Jeffrey was quite an experience: 'He tells you what you can say and what you can quote him as saying and what you can say in your own words but not in his. When he makes a joke, he tells you, "That is a *joke*!"' Barber said he almost made her dislike him even before they met, by keeping her standing on his doorstep for twenty minutes on a freezing day in Cambridge. To make up for that, she was asked to stay to lunch, but in the end she somehow ended up going to the pub instead and paying for Jeffrey, his wife, his two children, their Costa Rican lodger, the photographer and his assistant. 'You can get this on expenses, can't you?' Jeffrey had said.

The gossip column rumours persisted. Jeffrey was pictured escorting American film producer Kathleen Kennedy to a literary lunch while his wife was away lecturing in Paris. He was quick to deny any impropriety: 'We have just celebrated our twentieth wedding anniversary,' he told the reporter. 'I gave her an antique walnut table.' In June, just nine months after her 'free and frank discussion' with Jeffrey about his mistress, Mary told *Woman's Own* that she despised gossip columns. The article referred to rumours concerning Jeffrey and Andrina Colquhoun and to claims that Mrs Thatcher insisted he should 'regularise' his personal life. Mary told the magazine: 'That sort of untrue story irritates and annoys me.'[3] Four months later, she would also be denying a much more sensational story, one that claimed her husband had slept with a prostitute. Having explored 'For richer, for poorer', Mary was now to be tested on 'For better, for worse'.

As before the Aquablast drama, life for the Archers seemed to be going well, but the events of the next nine months were to have a major impact on Mary's life and career, transforming her from a fairly obscure academic to a leading public figure. Although it might not have felt like it at the time, the court case proved to be a tremendous opportunity, resulting in enormous and largely favourable publicity for her. At the start of the 1986 party conference season, a drama serialisation of Jeffrey's book *First Among Equals* had just started on ITV. One of the novel's leading characters is a politician who is blackmailed by a prostitute. Coincidentally, in the weeks before he attended the conference, Jeffrey had been unsettled by rumours that the *News of the World* had some sort of 'dirt' on him. He had also received phone calls from a prostitute calling herself Debbie who insisted they had met, and that the press were on to her. She said one of her clients claimed to have seen Jeffrey going to a hotel with her, and she wanted the papers off her back. Jeffrey spoke on the phone at length to Debbie, always denying he knew her, but sympathising with her situation. Although Mary twice answered the phone (and mistook Debbie for a 'secretary from the north') Jeffrey made sure he personally took all her calls, not allowing her to speak to his assistant, David Faber. He did not report these calls to the police nor to his colleagues, and rejected all offers of help from Central Office, who had warned him before the party conference that a story was going round the tabloids about him. Eventually Debbie told him that that the source of the story was called Aziz Kurtha, and Jeffrey immediately got his lawyer to fire off a letter warning Kurtha about defamation. Jeffrey suggested to Debbie that she should go abroad to avoid the attentions of the press, and offered to give her the means to do so: she was to meet a friend of his at Victoria Station in London who would hand over some money.

Jeffrey then arranged for Michael Stacpoole to rendezvous with Debbie, who would be wearing a green leather suit, and be waiting at the end of platform three. Stacpoole wore an overcoat, perhaps the one with the special pockets for carrying money.

What Jeffrey had not suspected was that Debbie was helping the *News of the World* corroborate the story circulating in Fleet Street. She was in fact Monica Coghlan, and all her calls to Jeffrey had been carefully recorded by the newspaper in a sting operation to trap him. Now the paper had undercover photographers waiting at the station to capture the moment Stacpoole gave her the envelope full of £50 notes. Monica did not accept the money, and handed it back, although she had a good look at it and later claimed the wad was about an inch thick. The newspaper conservatively estimated the envelope from Jeffrey contained at least £2,000; Monica's own guess was that it was more like £5,000 – Stacpoole guessed the same. In any event, the *News of the World* now had a sensational story, and went to great lengths to protect it, running a 'decoy' front-page story in its first edition to mislead rival papers.

Jeffrey was warned about the imminent debacle when he was returning from a constituency meeting on the Saturday afternoon. He took a call on his car phone from Michael Dobbs – who had warned him weeks earlier of a story going the rounds. Nobody had seen the Sunday paper's copy at this stage, but it had a photograph of Monica Coghlan being offered the money by Stacpoole, and it had a tape-recording of Jeffrey telling her to 'go abroad as quickly as you can'. Anyone reading the story would have assumed that Jeffrey had had sex with Monica, but the newspaper was careful, on legal advice, not to say this.

When Jeffrey got home, he found Mary arranging flowers. 'I shall always remember the scent and colour of the chrysanthemums I was arranging . . . when Jeffrey told me of the story that would break,' she says. 'It was to have been such a nice weekend, the boys home for half term and Jeffrey, unusually in those days . . . home by Saturday afternoon.'[4] Instead, it was a miserable two days, with weather to match, in which Mary 'struggled to understand' what was going on. The couple tried to keep their sons out of earshot and repaired to the kitchen, where a frantic series of phone calls followed. Mary considered making a log of events, but did not feel sufficiently composed to do so. Jeffrey rang the *News of the World*'s editor, David Montgomery, to ask him if it was a story over which he should resign, but Montgomery told him he could not advise on that. Jeffrey insisted there was no truth in the story and Montgomery promised to phone back after speaking to his reporter. 'Can you ring quickly,' Jeffrey asked, 'because my wife is here in tears, which is not making my life easy.' The paper seized on this information, and next day one of its headlines read: 'Tory whizzkid faces weeping wife'.

Although Jeffrey had known of the rumours, and had been trying to find out what the papers knew, the news came as a shock to Mary. There were several more calls that evening, including one from the highly respected *Observer* journalist Adam Raphael, who was told by Jeffrey that he had met Debbie only once 'very casually six months ago'. By now, both Mary and Jeffrey were in a very depressed state. One of the callers was her anxious mother, who had been watching television news and seen the *News of the World* advertising its sensational story.

Jeffrey had desperately tried everything he could to prevent the paper running the story. He lied to the reporter, denying the story; he pleaded with the editor, admitting a lot of it was indeed true; he tried to contact the paper's owner, Rupert Murdoch. Having finally given his version of events to his wife, a defeated Jeffrey, unable to sleep, left Grantchester at 3 a.m. to drive to London for a meeting next morning with his lawyer. Mary had to wait until the Sunday to see the story in print, when she sent one of her sons over the garden wall to the village shop to buy a copy, telling him to avoid the fifty or so press gathering at the front gate: 'a remarkable sight' she would recall. She sat down alone with her sons and explained it all to them as plainly as she could. Fourteen-year-old William found it hard to take, but Jamie, twelve, was more robust. Mary told them there would be some horrible things said at school but they were not to take any notice. By now, the story had been picked up by other papers, and before long the reporters were knocking at the door. Mary answered, still dressed in her floral housecoat and slippers, having no idea there were television cameras there. Cool and composed, despite her distress, she confirmed she was standing by her husband: 'Certainly. My husband told me, and I believe him, that he had never met this girl.' Obscurely, she added: 'There is no affair, neither technical nor sexual.' ITN's Gaby Rado asked her how Jeffrey knew Monica. 'Never met the lady,' asserted Mary tersely, arms folded, nonchalantly leaning on the doorpost. 'Spoken to her, because she kept ringing him up.' Where did the contact between them start? 'She rings him up.' And why did she ring him up in the first place? persisted Rado. 'I suspect she thought there was money at the end of it, I don't know,' replied Mary. What about suggestions that he might have to resign? 'It would be a monstrous miscarriage of justice,' Mary claimed. 'They do happen, however.' Her words were to prove prophetic, but not in the way she intended.

Mary also spoke of 'the despicable motives' of Monica Coghlan. 'I suppose I ought to say something vituperative, but I feel a kind of weariness and distaste,' she added. 'There's enough trouble in the world already without having to make it up, without having to disturb families like mine on stories like this.' Mary said that although she first heard the allegations a few hours earlier, she knew that a woman had been phoning, but couldn't remember the number of calls. 'I knew they were from a woman but Jeffrey didn't seem to be taking it very seriously. She telephoned to allege they had met, which my husband repeatedly denied.' Asked if she thought it strange that her husband had not mentioned this earlier, she replied: 'Both our lives are busy. These things don't seem important at the time. We have funny people phoning up all the time. I take it more seriously when they threaten to burn the house down . . . My reading of the *News of the World* is that they don't suggest that Jeffrey has met this lady. Of course, she suggests she has, but that's a different thing.' Mary assured the reporters: 'I am very strong . . . the children are coping pretty well . . . I hope I am ready for every eventuality, like a good Girl Guide.' It was a foolish remark, she later reflected, '. . . but I made it.'

Despite this bombshell having just descended on her family, Mary was keen to keep up appearances and carry on with her normal routine and obligations. 'It may seem incongruous to you,' she told the press, 'but I am the choirmistress up the road.' She quickly got dressed and rushed out with her children to church, only to return red-faced, several minutes later. 'In all this business, I forgot to put the clocks back,' she explained. Mary obligingly posed for photographs, with an arm around each of her sons, and answered questions, as she later explained: 'I did what I could to keep our end up, playing, I may say, from a very weak position . . . I don't much like saying "no comment".'[5] She was soberly dressed in a dark woollen coat, a white pussy-cat-bow blouse, and a check scarf: a far cry from the green leather suit worn by Monica Coghlan. Some days later, a columnist commented on this little scene and its effect on the children. 'The sight of 14-year-old William Archer blinking into the camera lenses with pure bewilderment on his face was one of the more poignant pieces of television footage this year. At best it was sad, at worst it looked like a cruel PR exercise.' As the writer shrewdly observed, the right and wrong way to act in these circumstances is a tricky question. Disappear and you look guilty, brazen it out and the family suffers greater stress. Mary explained her philosophy two years later in *Prep School* magazine where she had some advice for children with famous parents: 'Stand your ground, do not retreat; do not let them force you into a defensive position when there is nothing to be defended. You must have the confidence to carry on.'[6] Retreating is one thing the Archers rarely do. Resigning was a different matter.

Later that day, Jeffrey rang Margaret Thatcher and offered his resignation. Publicly, he conceded, 'I have been silly, very foolish. What else can I say?' His lawyer issued a statement in which Jeffrey admitted 'lack of judgement' and said he was considering legal action. Jeffrey returned home to Grantchester, and collected his wife and sons from a friend's house, where they had been having lunch. The family again posed for photographers in their immaculately manicured garden. Jeffrey looked subdued and nervous, and fended off questions. How do you feel? Mary was asked. 'I'm merely rather sad,' she replied, understatedly. But her eyes welled with tears, and Jeffrey led her indoors. 'Get off my flowerbeds!' was his parting shot to the hacks.

However, he soon reappeared; the Archers' PR skills were now to be deployed. Having said they would not be making any further appearances, they decided to serve a tray of tea and coffee to the crowd of journalists still hanging around the Old Vicarage; William also helped. Jeffrey told them he was sorry about the weather and Mary answered more questions; after all, the press had been quite kind to her that morning. Why hadn't her husband called the police about the phone calls? 'I think it would have been probably wise to do so, but then you know we all do foolish things under stress, particularly when we choose to be unadvised,' she said, pointedly turning her head away from Jeffrey. The tea-tray photographs were predictably in most of the papers next day, partly because the Archers re-staged the 'coffee round' twice more for the benefit of cameramen who had missed it the first time.[7] Columnists also began commenting on Mary's demeanour. 'She showed no sign of the betrayal, the fury or grief,' said one; 'no sign behind the porcelain complexion of the emotional turmoil she must be feeling'. Mary was contrasted with her 'flash and grab merchant' husband: 'Coffee mornings with the Party faithful leave her cold ... but [she] enjoys the social side of the Tory party. The entire Cabinet and assorted Tory toffs are invited to her famed Champagne and Shepherds Pie parties in the run-up to Christmas. It will be a revelation ... to see who turns up this year.' A certain Anne Robinson, writing in the *Daily Mirror*, said any woman who was prepared to meet reporters and photographers at dawn on a Sunday morning in a dressing gown and minus her make-up deserved a round of applause; Central Office might consider using Mrs Archer's performance as a sort of training video for wives. Robinson thought it was unlikely anything Jeffrey did could shock his wife. 'Maybe catering for Mr Archer's immense and child-like ego is a relaxing alternative to discussing electro-chemistry with her fellow Cambridge dons,' she wrote. 'Dr Archer versus Monica the threatening tart' would be a 'more even contest'. Events would prove the journalist wrong, and Mary would be much more than a match for Monica, at least in public.

In the following days, Mary tried to return to normal. She evaded the press by slipping out at the end of the garden and took one of her boys to the opera in London. Things might have fizzled out had it not been for a follow-up story by another tabloid, the *Star*, which went much further than the *News of the World*, suggesting that the prostitute had slept with Jeffrey, and compounding the damage to his reputation by saying – although Monica denied it – that most of her clients demanded a 'specialised field of sexual perversion'. Jeffrey and Mary, who had believed they were by now over the worst, were very distressed by this latest story, and Jeffrey pounced. He denied both the stories and issued libel writs against both papers and their editors; it was the start of a process which, over the next fifteen years, would produce two of the most famous trials in legal history. Not only that, it would propel Mary into a world where she became a nationally recognised and admired figure.

The central issue was what exactly happened in Mayfair's Shepherd Market, and in Victoria, late on the evening of Monday, 8 September 1986 and the early hours of Tuesday, 9 September. The allegations came originally from an intriguing and wealthy Asian, Aziz Kurtha, who was a TV presenter, lawyer, businessman, politician and academic. He said he had paid Monica (or Debbie as she called herself professionally) for sex in a hotel room not far from Victoria station. Just as he was about to drive her back to her patch in Mayfair, they saw an expensive car flashing its lights at them. When Monica spoke to the driver, Kurtha says he recognised him as Jeffrey Archer. Monica then went back into the hotel with the man, and Kurtha tried to sell his story; he wanted the money for charities in Pakistan. The *News of the World* had some difficulty persuading Monica to help them, as she was reluctant to 'shop' a client and did not want any trouble. Eventually, she agreed to make one call to Jeffrey to see if he would incriminate himself. She was paid for loss of earnings and expenses, but very little by Fleet Street standards. In the end, she made a total of six calls, trying to get Jeffrey to say he had been with her, which she firmly believed.

Consistently, Jeffrey denied having met her, but nevertheless he kept taking her calls. She described to him the pressure she felt under with journalists pestering her, and Jeffrey finally made his extraordinary offer. The newspaper now had a big story, and despatched a team of journalists to Victoria Station to cover the cash hand-over. The paper could never prove that Jeffrey had had sex with Monica, but they had evidence of utterly bizarre behaviour and appalling judgement by a high-profile politician; a politician, moreover, who was infamous in Fleet Street for his sexual indiscretion and who was also married to a photogenic and respectable wife. Attempts were made to try to settle out of court, but finally a trial date was set: 6 July 1987. The participants did not know at the time that the case would go into the record-books.

In the meantime, Jeffrey returned to Grantchester and resumed work on a play which he had begun some years earlier: a courtroom drama called *Beyond Reasonable Doubt*. (He would do the same thing fifteen years later before his perjury trial, writing another courtroom play called *The Accused* which cocked a snook at the justice system.) It was not long before he also resumed his constituency visits and media interviews as though nothing had happened, and Margaret Thatcher showed her support by inviting the Archers to Chequers for lunch on Boxing Day. The couple got 'rafts of kind and touching letters' from both friends and strangers; and they had an unusual amount of time together, which Mary said was good. In contrast, a depressed Monica Coghlan said the scandal had ruined her life and finances and forced her into hiding, but she felt sorry for Mary and wished the whole thing had never happened. Mary's career, however, was progressing nicely. She spent a lot of time working on her book on solar energy, although she was realistic about its prospects: 'I'm not the stuff from which popular authors are made.' She also began reading the financial pages and sometimes sought advice from her brother-in-law Peter Brealey, who worked as an investments manager for the Church Commissioners. In an interview for the magazine *Family Wealth*, Jeffrey said Mary was wonderful with money. 'She has never been the sort of woman who spends because her husband is wealthy . . . she can have what she likes . . . but she is very careful with money.'[8] He said he never told her the prices of some of his paintings because she would have a fit. 'She's not a buyer by nature. She's incapable of spending money and wakes in the night worrying about curtains she's got to buy.'[9]

Mary's interest in things financial coincided with another appointment, as consultant on scientific matters to Robert Fraser and Partners, a merchant bank. For a basic annual retainer of two or three thousand pounds, she would be asked a few times a year for advice on any deals with a scientific angle, and if she couldn't help, she suggested someone who could. The bank's managing director was Colin Emson, a long-time acquaintance and financial advisor of Jeffrey's, and the bank's offices were situated a few yards away from Mary's old workplace, the Royal Institution. Emson recalls when she was asked to look at a specific project about solar energy and wrote an extremely good analysis. 'She is incredibly thorough and uniquely capable. She came in and met the people who were making presentations to us, and would form a view on whether their proposals were sound.' Emson had already been a very useful contact for the Archers, and Mary no doubt felt grateful to him. Firstly, he had warned Jeffrey against the Aquablast investment; secondly, when the Archers were coping with the fallout from Jeffrey's ignoring this advice, he devised an ingenious financial deal to help Jeffrey pay his debts. He offered to buy the house in The Boltons from Jeffrey, with a view to living there himself, but he suggested that Jeffrey should continue to pay the mortgage, so that he could use the proceeds to pay off some of each of his debts as a sign of good faith to his creditors. Emson used his banking expertise to negotiate the unusual deal, which had the support of the main creditors and the involvement of Jeffrey's lawyer Lord Mishcon, who also worked for the tycoon Robert Maxwell. Emson was taking a risk: if Jeffrey defaulted, the banker stood to lose the property and the money he had paid for it.

The Robert Fraser Bank was chaired by another of Jeffrey's friends, Lord Rippon, who had been involved in his art gallery in 1969. Rippon had been introduced to Robert Fraser by Jeffrey and Emson was so grateful he enquired what he might do by way of thanks. Jeffrey asked him to donate a harpsichord to Mary's college, Newnham. Rippon and Emson had numerous dealings with Robert Maxwell, who invested millions in their bank, according to Maxwell's biographer Tom Bower.

He says in December 1990, the soon-to-be-disgraced Maxwell was a guest at the Archers' Christmas party, powdering his face in the lift in front of one of the Archer boys, and leaving after ten minutes when it was clear he was not going to be the centre of attention and despite (or perhaps because of) the presence of most of the Cabinet. Another banker with links to Maxwell was Sir Michael Richardson, whose firm was Maxwell Communication Corporation's stockbrokers. Sir Michael was some years later named in a diary column as enjoying 'a touching friendship' with Mary. She was quick to deny she had ever met him which is surprising given that he was closely associated with the Tory party and an adviser to the prime minister, Margaret Thatcher.[10] Mary was Robert Fraser's scientific consultant for the next five years, and said it brought its own challenges and rewards. 'Knowledge of fields as diverse as retroviruses, metal fatigue and nuclear waste disposal is called for . . . Depth must be abandoned for breadth,' she wrote. The Robert Fraser group, though no longer a bank, still occasionally consults her.

During the months before the libel trial, Mary had also taken up the offer of joining the board of directors at Anglia Television, commenting that 'one does grow like one's spouse in the end – twenty years ago I would never have dreamt of such a thing as going into the media!' It also surprised Jeffrey, whose contacts with the company went back to his days as an MP in the region. 'He seemed nonplussed by her appointment,' says one manager. 'He said to me, "What's Mary going to do? What do you want her for?"' But Mary had plenty to offer; she worked hard, had good political contacts, and was very well connected locally. 'She wasn't a great business woman,' said one senior director, 'but she was ambitious in that area and didn't turn down opportunities.' Anglia's general manager, Mike Hughes, was given the job of briefing Mary about the television industry and still has an image of her sitting motionless at the board table absorbing the information while he explained. As well as being on the main board, she sat on a committee which was responsible for deciding how to allocate money raised by ITV telethons. Mary became deputy chairman of that committee, and put a lot of effort into it. 'She was a great stalwart in helping with fundraising,' says Hughes, 'and she once turned out at 4 a.m. wearing a telethon T-shirt to send off a cycling team from Cambridge.' The head of press, Vic Birtles, also found her helpful and always willing to do PR for the station, but someone who formed a less favourable impression was a drama script editor, Carol Gould. 'Anglia had a wonderful drama department – it was the Rolls-Royce of television drama, and before the takeover, it was being demolished. I collared Mary and tried to tell her this great department was being destroyed, programmes cancelled, and could the board do something about it? She stared at me as if I were from Mars, and just walked away. There was a very steely, cold expression.'

Before Mary's arrival at Anglia, the chairman, Aubrey Buxton, had circulated her CV to put everyone in the picture. Mike Hughes remembers: 'There were a number of A4 sheets attached to it, listing all her academic publications. The director of programmes said to me, "I hope she doesn't want any of these made into

programmes!"' While Mary's speciality might have been too esoteric for Anglia's science output, she was asked to present a popular
science series. In the summer she recorded the first six episodes of
Frontiers of Discovery, a thirty-minute programme about the latest
scientific and technical research being done in the region. Although
she simply 'fronted' the programme, Mary's university contacts
came in useful, as did her home. Some of the filming was done at
Grantchester where Mary gave the camera crew a picnic lunch
with nice wine in her meadow by the river. Gil Edgeley, the director, says Mary was very professional, hospitable and easy to work
with, but all in all the programme makers felt she was not really a
'natural'. 'But she was well prepared,' says cameraman Chris
Holland. 'Her lecturing experience came to the fore and she did it
more or less in one take, with no autocue.' It was just as well that
Mary was getting used to cameramen, because she would soon be
encountering dozens of them.

Shortly before the libel trial began, Mary was cool enough to
give an interview to Libby Purves of *The Times*, because she
wanted publicity for a play which was soon to be performed in the
Old Vicarage gardens for the Rupert Brooke centenary. Mary told
Purves the Monica affair seemed a lot of nonsense to her, claiming
she was rarely upset. Was she ever annoyed with her husband?
'Goodness, no . . . Whatever he does, I have always preferred sins
of commission to sins of omission.' The article was accompanied
by a photograph of Mary sitting in the garden with one of her
beautiful cats. Three days later, she was sitting alongside her husband at the front of court 13 at the Royal Courts of Justice.

9

Hail Mary

MONICA COGHLAN SAT COOPED UP in the Swallow International Hotel in Kensington and worried about her two-year-old son, Robin. The hotel was a rather better one than the place in Victoria she used for her work, as it was paid for by the *News of the World*. Coghlan was devoted to her child, who was looked after by relatives while she went through her ordeal in court. She was being looked after by minders from the newspaper, as she had been ever since the story broke, in order to ensure her appearance at the trial. Female journalist Jo Fletcher had more or less lived with her in Rochdale for most of the week, sitting around the small bungalow, helping with the housework and playing with the toddler – who was not very healthy – and reading pirate stories to him. 'She adored that son,' says Fletcher. 'She was a very good mother and would have walked over water for him.' Like Mary, Coghlan had known the anguish of a newborn son in intensive care. She, too, had had a difficult time when her first child was born; she had been rushed into a Manchester hospital where Robin was very poorly. She gave up prostitution for a while to care for him, but later resumed so that she could 'secure his future'. When the Jeffrey Archer story broke, she had been terrified for Robin, fearing what the rich and powerful politician could do to them both, and had cooperated with the paper to protect herself. She did not yet know that the case was to ruin her.

On the morning of Friday 10 July, Monica Coghlan looked through the smart clothes she liked to wear in her off-duty life. She chose a grey suit with a white blouse; a simple outfit which showed off her figure and legs. She added her gold necklace and bracelet, put the finishing touches to her make-up and left her hotel room with Jo Fletcher. She was about to become one of the most famous streetwalkers in history.

The case of Jeffrey Howard Archer versus Express Newspapers and their editor Lloyd Turner, had begun four days earlier, and was attracting intense media and public interest; outside the famous Royal Courts of Justice in the Strand there were throngs of television crews and photographers, and the courtroom was packed, so much so that the judge, Sir Bernard Caulfield, invited some reporters to sit near him on his bench. 'It was a cattle market,' commented one of the leading lawyers, Michael Hill.[1] It was a hot week, and some of the jurymen removed their ties; the barristers sweated under their wigs. Mary had never set foot in a courtroom before and for her first ever visit she chose to look rather like a member of the legal profession, perhaps deliberately, in a navy suit and a blouse with a dark bow at her neck. During the proceedings she and Jeffrey occasionally held hands.

Mary said afterwards that the trial was an extremely difficult process, win or lose, and she was 'frightened through much of it ... the drama of the thing, because it's very theatrical, and I remember thinking at some of the worst moments "when I've been through this I won't be frightened of much", and now I still have that feeling; I won't be easily frightened again'.[2] She claimed never to have doubted Jeffrey, merely asking him if it was true and believing him when he said no. 'I was certainly not in terrible despair ... because I knew exactly what had happened and it would be more accurate to say I was angry at the folly that had put the thing up and about, and fabricated a malicious story, and so it was ... anger that sustained me through it ... I was very confident; more confident I think than anyone else around me.'[3] Mary also told her interviewer: 'If you have to defend yourself in court, you've got to speak the truth, the whole truth and nothing but the truth.'[4] When it came to her own evidence, however, the whole truth did not emerge.

The trial began with Jeffrey's eminent QC, Robert Alexander, playing tape-recordings of the calls Monica had made to Jeffrey, who was then brought into the witness-box for more than three days of questioning and cross-examination. At one point, he was asked about the state of his marriage. 'It is our 21st wedding anniversary on Saturday, sir,' he replied, evading the question. 'I say this without any reservation. Mary was the most remarkable woman I knew when I was young and she remains that way now, sir.'[5] Mary appeared to wipe away a tear. Jeffrey told the court that, on the evening it was alleged he had picked up the prostitute in Mayfair, he was at Le Caprice restaurant with friends and had then taken his film agent Terence Baker home to south London sometime after midnight. Jeffrey's defence hinged on having an alibi for the night of Monday 8 September and pages from a diary were produced as evidence, purporting to show an appointment with Baker on Monday. This large A4 diary, whose pages were obscured and bound except for the relevant days, was in fact a forgery and the genuine diary showed that Jeffrey had an appointment with Baker for the following evening, Tuesday the 9th. Jeffrey might well have got away with this daring ruse, but a spanner was thrown in the works of his fabrication when there was suddenly a legal mix-up over dates, resulting from a mistake in an affidavit sworn by Monica Coghlan. It meant that Jeffrey had to find two sets of alibis, one for Monday and one for Tuesday. He could not use what was probably the true Tuesday alibi, Terence Baker, because Baker was now committed to saying he was with Jeffrey on Monday. As a result, Jeffrey asked his friend Ted Francis to say they had been having dinner together on Tuesday. This elaborate plot was finally unravelled at Jeffrey's perjury trial in 2001, but back in 1987 the jury knew nothing of it. Terence Baker later told friends he had lied for Jeffrey and after the trial Jeffrey gave him a film and TV deal.

On the second day of the libel trial, Mary was wearing a red and white dress with a red blazer and a 'Los Angeles Olympics' brooch; interest was already being shown by the media in her clothes. She watched as her husband became angry when he was confronted by the *Star* newspaper's counsel, the distinguished QC Michael Hill, who said he had 'lied and lied and lied' when speaking to the *News of the World* reporter on the night before publication. 'No, sir,' said Jeffrey, 'and that is grotesquely unfair.' 'Balderdash,' countered Michael Hill. Facing continued hostile questioning, Jeffrey lost his temper: 'I am innocent of this charge, and nothing you will say, however clever you are in the wording of out-of-context pieces . . . there is only one thing that matters . . . I have never met this girl, I have never had sexual intercourse with her. And that is the truth!'[6] On the third day (Mary in pale striped jacket) Jeffrey was questioned about alternative alibis he had given, which he had variously described as being at a function with fifty people, at a meeting, and in a restaurant. 'We are playing with words,' said Jeffrey, telling the court that when he had said he was at a meeting, he meant a meeting of forty or fifty people in a restaurant. It was a confrontation of opposites: Jeffrey, the man described by his wife as having a gift for inaccurate precis, changing his story and saying he couldn't remember, and Michael Hill analysing every detail with thoroughness and precision. He accused Jeffrey of trying to wriggle off the hook and telling 'a hundred per cent thumping lie' whilst Jeffrey strenuously insisted he was innocent and was telling the truth. Jeffrey's manner was always ostentatiously well mannered, forever calling the QC 'sir' and at one point the judge told both men not to be so polite to each other.

Jeffrey said he had never met a prostitute, a falsehood innocently repeated by his QC, despite the fact that Jeffrey had been seen in the early eighties by an *Express* diarist in a restaurant with a woman wearing a low-cut blouse, mini-skirt and gold ankle chain. Jeffrey himself described her as 'a lady of the night' when he rang the journalist next day to explain, saying, 'I didn't want you to jump to any wrong conclusions. She was helping me with some research for my new book.'[7] (A prostitute did indeed appear in his book *First Among Equals* and curiously, in 1980, one of his short stories, entitled *One Night Stand*, concerned a character called Debbie.)

Shortly before the court rose on the fourth day, Mary was called to give evidence; she wore a blue and white dress with puff sleeves. In some ways, it was an odd decision to call her, since she could hardly provide any direct evidence about Jeffrey's innocence or his whereabouts on the night in question; yet her testimony turned out to be crucial. Possibly Robert Alexander had been influenced by his recent defence of Geoffrey Collier, the first City man to be prosecuted for insider trading. Collier's wife had cried in the witness-box, and he had escaped with a light sentence. Mary duly began by entrancing the judge. 'How old are you?' asked Alexander. 'Forty-two,' said Mary, faintly. The judge interjected: 'You should say, how *young* are you?' He then told Mary to relax, and later he referred to 'an elegant phrase' she had used.

Mary Archer confirmed that she and Jeffrey lived what Alexander euphemistically described as 'a full life' and she said they had a 'very happy marriage'. Despite having confronted her husband about his affair with Andrina Colquhoun, Mary listened silently while her husband's QC told the jury: 'There is not a suggestion that Jeffrey Archer is a man who has affairs.'[8] Alexander later told the jury they would be the judge of whether Mary was 'a meticulous lady' who was being 'very careful to tell you what she did remember'. The description of Jeffrey as a 'very happily married man' was repeated by the judge later in the trial, but it was clearly not a happy marriage as most people would understand the phrase. Fourteen years on, when Jeffrey would find himself on trial for perjury, Mary was asked whether she had felt 'a sense of unease' giving the answer about her happy marriage, given that she knew about his mistress, but she replied she couldn't recall, despite her claim to have 'a good and clear memory'.[9]

Back in 1987, Mary said the allegations were 'absurd tarradid-dle' adding, 'the thought of my husband consorting with a prostitute is preposterous. Anyone who knows him well knows that far from Jeffrey accosting prostitutes, if one accosted him he would run several miles in the opposite direction very fast; it would terrify him . . . I think he has withstood an outrageous barrage of events and comment with great fortitude.'[10] She then pulled out a white handkerchief and tearfully turned her head away from the court. As she was helped from the witness-box by an usher, Jeffrey rushed to her side. But she soon regained her composure, and went off to Aquascutum to buy three new outfits, each costing around £200. She later said she wore something different every day to 'fly the flag for Jeffrey'. The press started to comment on her clothes so she 'started to play their game', but she was not expecting the trial to last three weeks, and admitted that it rather stretched her wardrobe. So fascinated did the media become with Mary that an item about her clothes was even included in an ITN news bulletin, and one paper wrote of 'a wardrobe war' between the two women.

Just as she had done during the Aquablast period, Mary sought medical help, visiting Jeffrey's doctor in London for what she called 'reinforcement'. She said she went to bed feeling 'fairly whacked but I couldn't sleep. I . . . padded around the flat . . .' At 4 a.m. Jeffrey suggested she should try telling herself she *could* face it and the positive thinking worked. 'I said to myself you've got to stop thinking you can't bear it . . . I took the negative out. I said I can bear it, I can cope, and I did find that extraordinarily helpful.'[11] Mary had to screw up her courage, but it made her tougher: 'I do feel the steel entered my soul and it has stayed there,' she said.[12]

Feeling more positive and better attired, Mary was called for a second day of evidence. 'Gone was the quiet mouse in the print dress,' wrote Noreen Taylor of the *Daily Mirror*. 'In came an assertive, confident woman in a chic black and white number with shoulder pads and pearls.' Gone were the tears; Mary now showed her claws. According to the *Daily Mirror* Mary 'looked down at him [the editor of the *Star*, Lloyd Turner] as if he were a worm she

143

would trample underfoot'. She furiously challenged him over a headline in the paper which said Jeffrey had lied and lied: 'Not even the residual courtesy of a quotation mark. It is perfectly proper, I quite understand, that Mr Hill should put the case for the defence, the *Star*'s case, which is, of course, that my husband has told a pack of lies; an unsustainable defence but he has to put it . . . I understand that very well. But we all heard my husband say with equal conviction: "No I did not, I have told the truth throughout." Mr Turner, your paper cannot keep a consistent line between one week and the next. How about that for your next headline?'[13] Michael Hill complained to the judge about her outburst. 'I have long been silent,' retorted Mary. She showed that she felt more than a match for any highly qualified and articulate lawyer, using phrases such as 'textual exegesis' and asking the judge, 'Can I expatiate?' At one point, Hill told her not to be rude and she replied 'Why not?'; she told him, 'It doesn't seem to me you've got a leg to stand on.' The judge seemed impressed: 'The jury may think that Mrs Archer is looking after herself very well,' he remarked.[14]

Like her husband, Mary was asked about the conversation Jeffrey had had with the reporter Adam Raphael, who says Jeffrey admitted he had briefly met the prostitute. Mary's recall of the conversation did not accord with Raphael's. But Mary was careful to qualify her evidence, saying, 'Although it is my genuine recollection that this was the conversation with Mr Raphael, I can't say that that recollection is not overlaid by the wish that it was so . . . I think I recollect that it was Adam Raphael, but I won't say on oath that it was.'[15] Then she directly contradicted Raphael, claiming she heard Jeffrey assert he had never met Debbie, and never had a sexual liaison with her or any other prostitute. She also spoke of being 'dumbfounded' when she heard Jeffrey say, 'If I did meet her, I don't know about it,' and asked him to explain. Jeffrey, she said, had told her it occurred to him the paper may have contrived some kind of meeting at a public function – when women who were complete strangers did sometimes embrace him. Raphael, who unlike Mary had taken notes of the phone conversation, stuck to his story, pointing out that if Jeffrey had said he'd never met Coghlan, the obvious follow-up question would be: 'Why on earth, if you've never met this woman, did you pay her off?' But that was not a question this highly experienced journalist had asked him at the time. Raphael later also disputed Jeffrey's assertion that he had taken calls that evening from forty to sixty journalists; he says the story was known only to a handful.

Following Mary, Monica Coghlan was sworn in. The contrast between the soignée Mary and the glamorous Monica, both smartly dressed and sexually alluring in their different ways – pearls versus gold chains as one paper put it – was highlighted when Coghlan took the stand. Like Mary, Monica had a variety of outfits – carefully chosen suits in attractive colours with matching shoes and bags. The journalist Jo Fletcher says she was passionately fond of clothes and always made a point of dressing nicely in good quality things. Monica began by answering questions about being picked up by Aziz Kurtha, and how they had gone back to the hotel in Albion Street, Victoria, for sex. At this point Mr Justice Caulfield said he wanted a break to cool the atmosphere, as he was finding it heavy; the bewigged counsel agreed and there was a short adjournment before Coghlan was called back. During her evidence, Mary mostly kept her head down and took notes in a ledger-sized book, though she 'visibly stiffened' when Coghlan described the clothes she had worn that night: black fishnet stockings, black wet-look mini-skirt and white top with a wasp-waist belt.

It must have been a nightmare for Mary to sit and listen as the prostitute described in intimate detail her encounter with the man she said was Jeffrey; how he had approached her in Shepherd Market and asked if she was free; how he had followed her to the Albion Hotel in Victoria and paid £70 to have sex with her in room 6A; how she was on top of him for ten minutes of sex, and how taken aback he was by her nipples; how afterwards she took off the condom, washed him down with tissues and dried him before lighting a cigarette and lying down on the bed with him; how he had told her he sold cars for a living (which was just what a fictional character in one of Jeffrey's novels had told a prostitute). Coghlan was matter of fact about what was, for her, a routine experience; for Mary, it was like being 'stripped naked and sort of held up for examination'.[16]

Like Mary, Coghlan was also very nervous; she spoke quietly in a Lancashire accent and several times during her long hours of evidence broke down and cried. But when she was accused by Alexander of lying she, like Jeffrey and Mary, gave vent to her anger: 'Don't try and patronise me,' she told the QC. 'You're the liar and he's the liar. You're the one that's making vast amounts of money, not me. I'm penniless through all this. He can carry on. What's going to happen to me? . . . Do you know what I've been through, through that liar? Just because he's got power and money. Why are you doing this to me? Why are you doing it to your wife? . . . You might be big with words, OK, I might be a prostitute but I've never harmed anybody . . . I've just survived all my life. He knows that it's him, he knows it!'[17]

Monica Coghlan felt the stress, and so did Mary. To help take their mind off things, the Archers sometimes went to the theatre in the evenings and Mary became calm enough to cope with a public performance at Grantchester on the first weekend of the trial, when she and Jeffrey hosted a play about Rupert Brooke to raise money for some new church choir surplices. The event marked the centenary of Brooke's birth, and had been planned for six months, with help from a large team of villagers. Brooke was portrayed by an actor called Mark Payton, who had also given his one-man show to raise money for Mary's college, Newnham. Mary, despite being in the midst of the trial, appeared surprisingly relaxed and, wearing a bright pink and frilly summer dress, told the audience she had been 'quite busy'. Although the performance was mainly for local people, the trial publicity ensured a large audience, and despite having been told by the judge not to speak to the press, Jeffrey could not resist telling a reporter that his wife must take all the credit for the organisation. A reporter from the *Star* was not allowed in. The inevitable publicity surrounding the event had an important propaganda value for the Archers; appearances were what mattered. Quite a few papers showed photographs of them sitting together calmly watching the play, along with son William, as though they hadn't a care in the world. The appearance of togetherness and unconcern was to prove a successful recipe.

But the real drama was being played out in the Royal Courts of Justice. Noreen Taylor, the *Mirror* reporter, summed up the contest which had electrified the court. 'There's no doubt the judge is absolutely in love with Mary . . . you could not find two more different women: the donnish, clean-cut Mary and Monica in her silk suit and ankle bracelet . . . at the beginning of each morning that Monica was in the box, she just stared down at Mary Archer and both their eyes locked from about six feet away. You could cut the air . . . Mary looked at her with disdain [as if to say] what are you doing up there discussing my husband and these intimate details? Monica meanwhile looked down . . . as though to say, "What do you think you're looking at?"'[18]

Towards the end of the trial, Mary made a dramatic reappearance to be questioned on an aspect of Monica's evidence that would become legendary: Jeffrey's spotty back. Coghlan had claimed her client did not have very good skin, saying it may have been dry or spotty. Mary explained how he did have a distinguishing mark following a holiday in Greece and Turkey – 'a very white part around his midriff where his shorts . . . were'. She was asked by Robert Alexander if there were any spots on his back, and she replied, 'No, sir.' But the speech for which the trial is best remembered is the summing up by Sir Bernard Caulfield, which was one of the most controversial judicial summaries in modern legal history, and for which he was widely criticised.

Mary's looks, intelligence and the measured and precise way in which she gave evidence had made a big impact on Caulfield, a man with 'an emotional facet which was apt to lead him astray', according to the former Lord Chief Justice Geoffrey Lane. Lane made the comment when writing Caulfield's obituary in 1994, in which he also criticised him for 'judicial pronouncements of questionable fairness and taste' and said he was 'dogged' into his retirement by the words 'fragrance' and 'elegance'.[19] Caulfield's summing up in 1987 included a eulogy to Mary: 'Remember Mary Archer in the witness-box. Your vision of her probably will never disappear. Has she elegance? Has she fragrance? Would she have, without the strain of this trial, radiance? What is she like in physical features, in presentation, in appearance? How would she appeal? Has she had a happy married life? Has she been able to enjoy, rather than endure, her husband Jeffrey? Is she right when she says to you – you may think with delicacy – "Jeffrey and I lead a full life"?' He suggested to the jury that, with a wife like Mary, Jeffrey would not need to turn to a prostitute, asking: 'Is he in need of cold, unloving, rubber-insulated sex in a seedy hotel round about quarter to one on a Tuesday morning after an evening at the Caprice? . . . It is possible even for the most happy, successful and respected married man to seek adventure in physical contact with persons who will not tell . . . but reflect, would you, upon the position.'[20] Misleadingly, Caulfield also told the jury that Mary was in London two or three days a week, and he backed up Jeffrey's falsehood that on the night the story broke there had been dozens of journalists ringing the Old Vicarage.

The jury reflected for four and a quarter hours and at first they couldn't agree despite the partiality of the summing up. Mary passed the agonising hours memorising Tennyson's poetry and doing a crossword; she also requested a tutorial from Lord Mishcon on the structure of the English courts while Jeffrey and his QC watched cricket on television. 'How can you fiddle with anagrams while my future is in the balance?' Jeffrey complained, pacing up and down. They thought of what they would say if they won, and 'as a reluctant contingency, something to say if we lost . . . but I was confident,' Mary said.[21] Finally the wait was over; the jury returned to court with a verdict. There was complete silence; Mary sat taking deep breaths, clasping her hands in front of her. Jeffrey closed his eyes. 'Do you find for Jeffrey Archer or the *Star* newspaper?' asked the clerk. 'Mr Jeffrey Archer,' replied the foreman. 'Thank God,' Jeffrey muttered. 'What sum do you award by way of damages?' 'Five hundred thousand pounds.' 'Phew,' whistled Jeffrey. It was a record-breaking sum. Mary patted him on the back, and kissed Lord Mishcon. As they left, Jeffrey shook each of the twelve jury members by the hand, though he did not look them in the eye, and he signed an autograph for one. The delighted couple left the Royal Courts of Justice amid crowds of cameramen and popping flashbulbs. 'The verdict speaks for itself,' Jeffrey said; Mary said she was over the moon, although jubilant was 'not an appropriate word, it really isn't'. The first thing she wanted to do was collect one of her sons (the other being away); they would delay a holiday until Jeffrey's new courtroom drama, *Beyond Reasonable Doubt*, had opened. Jeffrey took the opportunity to tell the press the details of the play's run.

There was no champagne and no great celebration that Friday evening. What Mary did next was to give a pre-arranged interview to the *Mail on Sunday* whose editor, Stewart Steven, was a good friend of Jeffrey's. Not a word of the evidence had appeared in his paper throughout the three weeks of the trial. Steven sent one of his favourite reporters, Susan Douglas, who says she was chosen partly because she had a background in biochemistry. 'I remember sweeping through the gates at Grantchester past the assembled television crews and Fleet Street journalists,' says Douglas. The trial had ended only hours before; Mary tried to look calm, but she was still very tense, and told Douglas that she felt nothing, nothing at all. 'We didn't shout for joy in the car on the way home. I phoned my mother, Jeffrey phoned his . . . and we listened to that song in *The Phantom of the Opera* ["The Music of the Night"]'.[22] There was no sound at all in the house, Douglas reported. 'It was strange: the silence in the house, and all this furious activity outside,' she now says. 'Bizarrely, Jeffrey was upstairs throughout the whole interview, not allowed down, almost like a naughty boy. We were in the kitchen and he wasn't allowed to join us. Mary controlled it totally; she was totally emotionless. I remember that odd spectre of Jeffrey hovering on the landing in his pyjamas.'

Despite the fact that she was expecting a hundred guests for a previously arranged party on the Sunday, Mary gave at least two more interviews that weekend, possibly because it was cathartic for her to speak about the events to seemingly sympathetic women reporters. The *Cambridge Evening News* the following day had a photo of Jeffrey in a chef's hat serving breakfast to his wife, and also interviewed Mary after her party. Going over her thoughts and emotions Mary said she never thought for a second that Jeffrey wouldn't win; she wasn't cross with him for getting them in the mess; she claimed she never had any niggling doubts in the middle of the night – even though she couldn't sleep. She said she was out-raged that 'a generous and foolish action' could be so wrongly interpreted. 'What happened, happened. We don't look back. I did what I did at the trial because I had to,' she said.[23] She was angry with herself for weeping, but had found it hard to listen to 'the wholly fictitious account of the things Jeffrey was supposed to have done ...' Most of the press coverage of Mary was favourable – she was 'devoted', 'calm', 'attractive' and, of course, 'fragrant' – but there were occasional dissenters. Anne Robinson scorned the judge's remarks and thought it was 'a quaint idea that anyone in possession of a fragrant, elegant, radiant wife is auto-matically above a spot of illicit bonking ... perhaps in some cases precisely because their wives are fragrant, elegant and relentlessly radiant, they dash in search of something refreshingly third-rate and seedy'.[24]

Despite her anger and contempt, Mary told reporters she felt charitable towards Monica Coghlan, and pity for her wretched life. Needless to say, this drew a swift retort from Coghlan that her life wouldn't be so wretched if it hadn't been for the court case: 'I don't need her charity and she doesn't need to patronise me. I didn't start all this and I never asked for money,' she told Paul Henderson, a *News of the World* reporter, who would reappear later in the Archer saga.[25] Coghlan said the court case had made her feel cheap, worthless and dirty, something she had never felt through all her years on the street. Mary, however, would thereafter be known as 'fragrant'. 'I was very touched to be thus described' she once commented, and found it hard to know whether to live up to it, or play it down.

It was generally agreed that Mary had won the case for Jeffrey. She had been central to his defence, and willing to support him in the most public of arenas despite knowing he had been deceiving her with his affair, and that neither of them was disclosing the full picture of their marriage to the jury. As the journalist Ian Hislop pointed out, throughout his life 'she has always impressed the right people, stood by him and given him a credibility he would never have had on his own'.[26] Not for the last time, the papers also speculated about why a woman like Mary should go through such an ordeal in the defence of a man who had humiliated her. It could have been a combination of reasons: her Christian belief in the sanctity of the marriage vows, protective and maternal feelings towards the disgraced spouse and the children, a wish to restore his self-esteem, refusal to admit her own misjudgement. A woman who could do this and keep her own dignity, wrote one columnist, was someone who held all the aces.

Certainly Mary had come up trumps financially. The award of libel damages was a new British record, and is still one of the highest ever libel awards. Express Newspapers (owners of the *Star*) had to pay both sides' costs; and three months later the *News of the World* also settled with Jeffrey: £50,000 damages plus £30,000 costs. The award was thought to express the jury's disgust at the entrapment methods used by the papers. Indeed, the strategy of Archer's QC had been to turn the case into a trial of the ethics of tabloid journalism. In his closing speech he asked: 'What we have to consider in this case is whether there are any boundaries, any limits to what can be tolerated of the press?' Was it right the paper should create a web of deception to trap Mr Archer? *The Times* had an answer, following the verdict, which was that the justification must be in the public interest and that the ends should be in proportion to the means. While it was indeed of public interest whether the deputy chairman of the Conservative party told the truth, the public interest was 'below the level that could justify the tactics used' and the attempts to encourage lies. Interestingly, the same argument would raise its head at another Archer court case.

The former MP Woodrow Wyatt, a friend of the Archers and an admirer of Mary, wrote that Judge Caulfield's summing up 'must have been one of the most biased in history. The Judge was an innocent abroad. Nevertheless, though I think the prostitute was telling more of the truth than Archer, it was probably a good thing that Archer won his case. It may curb newspapers writing about the private lives of politicians and others when there is nothing in them to affect the nation's security or policies.'[27] Wyatt's views reflected what was then a more deferential attitude towards politicians by society in general, if not by the media.

Initially Express Newspapers and their QC Michael Hill considered that the judge's summing up gave them good grounds to ask for the case to be re-tried. But they realised it would be almost impossible to persuade Monica Coghlan to appear in court again. She felt very bitter about the way she had been treated in the witness-box, especially in comparison with Mary Archer, and made to look foolish and cheap. Even if she did agree, a retrial might take another eighteen months and she would have to be 'minded' to ensure she didn't vanish, as the case was hopeless without her. Quite possibly, the Tory proprietor of Express Newspapers, Lord Stevens, also felt that any further court action would hurt the Conservative party. It was odd how little emerged at the trial of the potentially damaging material known by journalists about Jeffrey, although eventually, this evidence was published.

What it revealed would have devastated Jeffrey's case. Michael Stacpoole later gave an account of how Jeffrey paid him to go abroad during the trial to prevent him from giving evidence: he knew about the state of the couple's marriage and a lot of detail about Andrina Colquhoun. The *Star* had gathered evidence linking Jeffrey with the prostitute Dorrett Douglas. Two reporters had been asked by Jeffrey to change their stories; one of them was Adam Raphael who later wrote a detailed analysis of the case which threw up many inconsistencies about the evidence that Jeffrey and his allies gave in court. For instance, Raphael counted twenty-seven different accounts by Jeffrey as to when he first knew that stories about him and Monica Coghlan were circulating in Fleet Street.[28] In 2000, Michael Crick included a new chapter entitled 'What the Jury Didn't Hear' in a revised edition of his book *Stranger Than Fiction*, which detailed the evidence the libel case jury was never told.[29] As a result, the jurors at Jeffrey's perjury trial in 2001 were asked if they had read the book, as it would have disqualified them from serving on the case. But what the jurors and the journalists did not yet know was that Mary was well aware of Jeffrey's infidelity, not just his lack of judgement.

By the end of July 1987 Jeffrey Archer, the politician who gave thousands of pounds to a prostitute he said he had never met, was more than half a million pounds richer. The sum was an unexpected bonus for the Archers, but did not come as a surprise to the editor of their local newspaper, Bob Satchwell of the *Cambridge Evening News*. At eight o'clock that morning, he had pasted up his front page with the words 'Archer wins half a million' but the verdict had come too late for his final edition. Instead, Satchwell took along a copy of his front page to the Archers' celebration party that weekend. 'Mary thought I was clairvoyant, but it was a guess based on my experience, and the summing up,' he says.

The truth was that Jeffrey had perverted the course of justice and lied; his wife had supported him in court; and the judge's summing up had been biased. Fourteen years later, the case came back to haunt the Archers. By then, Terence Baker and the judge had died, Aziz Kurtha had emigrated, and Michael Stacpoole had suffered a stroke. The seedy hotel in Albion Street was bought by a property magnate, Firoz Kassam, for a reported half a million pounds.

10

In Her Element

SHORTLY AFTER THE VERDICT, Mary Archer sat down and wrote a list: her first thoughts on what should happen to the half a million pounds her husband had just been awarded. Appropriately, perhaps, the list was written on headed writing paper from the Savoy, one of the most expensive hotels in the world, and one of the couple's regular haunts. Jeffrey and Mary had gone there during the trial where Mary 'would play with lunch' and she had put quite a lot of Savoy notepaper in her briefcase.[1] According to someone who saw the list at the time, the Archers also decided to buy shares, and indeed a couple of weeks after the trial Jeffrey did buy £400,000 worth of GEC shares.[2]

Despite intense press interest, Jeffrey was at first reluctant to say how he would spend the money, saying it would be at least a month before he decided. 'Mary and I are not going to rush into it and say we are going to give it to x, y, or z. We will give it a lot of thought, but I think you can assume I am going to give it away to charity.'[3] He said he was not keeping the money because he was only interested in clearing his name and later admitted: 'I frankly did not need the money. That is the truth.' Perhaps for once he *was* telling the truth, as the couple were by then extremely wealthy, and, despite Aquablast, Jeffrey was still a speculator; just before the trial he gambled £400,000 on a plot of land overlooking Auckland harbour, in the hope New Zealand would win the next America's Cup yachting competition (they didn't but the land appreciated in value anyway); he had spent roughly £1.6 million on Debenhams shares in 1985, and he had previously tried to buy Hatchard's bookshop for £9.5 million. A year or so after the trial he bought the Playhouse Theatre in London, which proved a costly venture.

The libel award was paid in two parts; the first £250,000 went into Jeffrey's account the month after the verdict. The Archers received many begging letters – three thousand according to Jeffrey, who claimed he and Mary read every single one, and found it a 'hell of a task' deciding how to allocate the money. Their friend the former politician and columnist Woodrow Wyatt advised them to keep it. 'On no account should you give your half million to charity. Buy a decent car and a yacht or something like that . . . It's the only tax free thing you get.' Whether or not the Archers took this advice on board, some donations were announced two months after the trial by Mary, who said Jeffrey had put the matter largely in her hands. She issued a statement in September to her local paper, the *Cambridge Evening News*, which said: 'Following the successful outcome of their recent action for libel against the *Star* newspaper, Jeffrey and Mary Archer have made [sic] donations to several charities, institutions and individuals. The major recipients were [sic] the Ely Cathedral Restoration Trust, the *Cambridge Evening News* charities, the Newnham College Development Trust, the Royal Watercolour Society, the Sports Aid Foundation and the Fitzwilliam Museum Trust, Cambridge. Eighteen other charities and institutions received donations, as did nineteen individuals.' (These included her brother and sister.)[4] But, as with many statements by Jeffrey Archer, things were not quite what they seemed. In 2001, Mary admitted 'we never intended to [distribute the damages to charities straight away]'.[5] And some charities seemed unaware of the Archers' largesse. The Sports Aid Foundation could find no record of any money, and although initial reports had said Jeffrey was giving £50,000 to Mary's old school, Cheltenham Ladies'

College, the school later said the sum was £1,000.[6] (Although now it will not confirm this, saying Mary 'would prefer that we do not make any comments'.) It was also said that Kew Gardens would get one of the 'largest slices' but a spokeswoman said that the donation, whilst gratefully received, was small. But close examination of what happened to the money was still some years off. For now, it was time to spend a bit, in celebrating their good fortune.

The Sunday after the verdict, Jeffrey and Mary finally allowed themselves a few glasses of vintage champagne, at a garden party originally planned to mark their 21st wedding anniversary. As a local band called the Froggits played light jazz on the sunny afternoon, guests who mingled in the Old Vicarage gardens included Michael Havers, the new Lord Chancellor, and the new chief secretary to the treasury, John Major, as well as other politicians including Norman Lamont, David Owen and David Mellor; businessmen Sir Clive Sinclair and Sir Michael Edwardes; the actor Anthony Andrews and the writer Clive James. Mary told the insatiable reporters at her gate that the buffet included delicious puddings and, although she personally had not prepared the food, she had 'worked quite hard on aspects of the party'. Jeffrey calculated that they had had an 80 per cent acceptance rate, compared with their more usual 50 per cent. Just who would have turned up had they lost is a matter of interesting speculation. Many people, including members of the establishment and the Conservative party, are willing to overlook Jeffrey's wrongdoing because they see him as a likeable rogue who does generous things, rather than a man who has contaminated public life. Quite a lot, of course, are in his debt. Jeffrey's tireless work for the Conservative party, his kindness to friends and his lavish entertaining created, in the words of his friend Adrian Metcalfe, 'a thick carpet of favours', which he would be able to draw on in later years. This was a lesson not lost on Mary. Jeffrey even enlarged on this philosophy to another friend, the television presenter Martyn Lewis, saying he liked everybody to be in his debt so that he could call on them one day to come to his rescue or come to his help.[7]

Now Jeffrey was in debt, to his wife. Without her he might never have won, as was widely acknowledged, and there was widespread sympathy towards her. It was a landmark in both their lives, enabling Jeffrey to bounce back into helping his party – and eventually getting a peerage – and giving fame to Mary, who was emerging from her mid-life crisis. An old friend from university, John Bryant, says, 'I think she changed virtually overnight in the libel trial. She realised she could move out of her own patch . . . It was a pretty formative moment . . . knowing she could take on lawyers.' Jeffrey himself called her a 'superstar' and said the trial gave her a whole new confidence, and made their relationship stronger than it had ever been. Mary was quick to exploit Jeffrey's gratitude. At a first-night party shortly after the trial, Nick Lloyd noticed that Mary was wearing a 'rather spectacular evening dress' and complimented her on looking more 'Hollywood than Cambridge' to which she replied it was a Dior dress which Jeffrey had bought. 'From now on, he is really going to pay for it,' she told Lloyd.

It was the start of a period that saw Mary become almost as much a celebrity as her husband, and in the aftermath of the court case she was much sought after for interviews and appearances. Organisations wanted her support, or asked her to give talks or award prizes. Mary found this new platform gave her a taste for public performing, and she revelled in the attention. Over the next two years she was featured in *Hello!* magazine (in an article written by the prime minister's daughter, Carol Thatcher), chose her *Desert Island Discs*, was filmed conducting her church choir, was photographed in her bedroom with her cuddly toys, as well as (fully clothed) on her bed with Jeffrey, discussed her favourite piece of furniture (a four-poster bed) on Channel 4's *Hot Property* programme, posed in a track suit and in her favourite grey business suit for an article called 'Our Weekend Togs', and in another called 'My Style' she modelled a strapless black velvet dress which showed off her 'creamy, lightly freckled shoulders'. She wrote several articles including two which publicised Jeffrey's play *Exclusive* and one which publicised a talk she gave for charity about Rupert Brooke. She became a TV critic; judged a pickled-onion competition; she gave the cartoonist Gerald Scarfe a tour of the folly in her garden; she was a guest on the *Wogan* show. Terry Wogan asked her, somewhat unnecessarily, if she wanted to be more in the public eye. She replied that, having been a backroom academic for years, she did indeed want to give it a try. 'At this rate,' wrote John Preston, the profile writer, 'future generations may look back on Jeffrey outplayed at his own game, reduced to a reluctant hermit, his column inches quite shrunk away while Mary sweeps to global domination.'

She became, for a few weeks, a radio reviewer for the *Sunday Telegraph* in which her extensive literary and musical knowledge was evident. Interestingly, one programme she reviewed was a discussion of Clause 28, the government measure to prevent the 'promotion of homosexuality' by local councils. Mary took the anti-government view, writing that the case against the clause – as put by a leading actor who opposed it – was 'unassailable'.[8] She wrote other articles too, helped with several profiles of her life and career, and took every opportunity to promote her scientific interests, even explaining the finer points of solar energy to a bemused audience on the *Kenny Everett Show*. Her sister-in-law Faye was persuaded to cooperate with an article about their relationship, which she possibly lived to regret. Mary described Faye as 'a lovely girl' and full-time mother: 'I don't really have much in common with her . . . We meet people like her in our village and we certainly need more. She would make a very good Good Samaritan . . . I would like her and respect her even if we weren't related but most of my women friends are academics and Faye isn't an academic.' Faye Weeden, who helped run a mother-and-toddler group, remarked that Mary 'couldn't comprehend how I could exist the way I do. It's alien to her way of thinking . . . Mary doesn't have the same sort of relationship with her children.' Faye also revealed that Mary and her brother were not particularly close and might not see each other for a year or more at a time, and that every year Mary gave them a plate depicting the twelve days of

Christmas – which they stored in the attic. In return, Faye once gave Mary a Tupperware mixing bowl. 'I think she wondered what on earth it was.'[9]

The *Desert Island Discs* presenter, Sue Lawley, put to Mary that no corner of her life was now sacrosanct. '. . . one is private inside one's head. Invasion of privacy can't really be complete if you keep your thoughts to yourself,' was Mary's reply. She thought being an independent-minded person also helped her cope, but, although she had independence from Jeffrey professionally, they were very inter-dependent in other ways, which was also important in dealing with what they had been through. At the end of the programme, Mary was naturally asked which book and luxury she would take with her on the desert island. She chose Proust's *Remembrance of Things Past*; and whereas for his 'luxury' Jeffrey had taken pins to stick into the programme's interviewer, Mary chose needles to embroider some hangings for her four-poster bed.

One of the most revealing programmes was a BBC television documentary called *The Archers: Not an Everyday Story of Country Folk*, shown a month after the verdict. Mary and Jeffrey were interviewed at home in Grantchester and they spoke about what they liked about each other and why they stayed married. Jeffrey admired Mary's honesty, she his energy; Mary said she thought she would find it 'a little monochrome, a little grey, to have a more conventional life with a more conventional husband'. You couldn't expect marriage to be roses all the way, she said, but there had been serious rows only twice in their married life and neither was a jealous person. The interviewer, Dilys Morgan, asked how important fidelity was to Mary, and her reply has been quoted many times since. 'It's moderately important. I think loyalty is important. If you mean strict sexual fidelity, it doesn't rank that ter-ribly high on my scale of the importance of things, in a quite objective sense.' Jeffrey sat on the sofa beside his wife looking uncomfortable. 'Yes,' he concurred, 'I think probably the same, though loyalty is everything, I agree.' Despite knowing about the Andrina Colquhoun affair, Mary also told Morgan that the gossip columns had been wrong. 'I think they were wrong in this instance. I was angry for quite a long time.'[10]

Some of the filming for this programme (originally planned as a segment for a series about couples) had been done during the run-up to the trial and the producer, Jeanne La Chard, had been surprised that the Archers had agreed to it at such a sensitive time. They were quite happy to give further interviews for the programme after the trial. La Chard had to put up with Jeffrey haranguing her about what he thought were the iniquities of the BBC, and she found the Old Vicarage incredibly cold. 'You couldn't get an impression of a lifestyle from it, it was a strange place; very, very tidy.' Perhaps for Mary it was sometimes an extension of her labs. Her son James says that he once found her in the kitchen and asked her what she was doing. 'I'm considering the cooling regime when you drop a uniformly warm ball-bearing into a beaker of treacle,' she said. When he asked her what she meant, she 'went into a soliloquy for ten minutes . . . and completely lost me. She often forgets that other people are less educated than herself.'[11]

The publicity Mary received following the trial led the journalist Ian Hislop, now editor of *Private Eye*, to comment: 'Mary Archer used to complain about being harassed by the media; but she has got her revenge. I now feel harassed by Mary Archer. It is getting impossible to open a newspaper or turn on the television without seeing her. She has become an up-market celebrity and is on course to become the new "thinking man's crumpet". My own loyalty to Joan Bakewell remains firm and, of course, Joan Bakewell has the advantage of not being married to Jeffrey Archer . . .' The word *fragrance* acquired an ironic life of its own, as Mary soon discovered. 'It escaped into gossip columns and dinner table conversations, and pursued me round the world . . . to the unsuitable venue of an international conference on electro-chemistry in Hawaii,' she said.

The timing of Mary's new high profile was helpful to her ambition of widening her career horizons. An acquaintance at Lloyd's described her as 'nakedly ambitious: calculating and very socially ambitious'. In addition, both her sons would be away at school; William at Rugby and James at Eton. Although Mary had never given high priority to hands-on motherhood, she was, like many mothers with adolescent children, in a better position to think about what she was now going to do with her life. Before getting to grips with her new non-academic life, however, Mary joined her husband for a holiday to Italy in August; in October, she went with him to Japan.

When they returned, Mary set about applying for a position that would extend her commercial experience – membership of the Council of Lloyd's, where she had been an external name for about nine years since Jeffrey's financial gift to her. No woman had yet been *elected* to the 28-member council, which regulated the market, although for a short time there had been a nominated woman member called Elizabeth Freeman, also a don. Mary stood as a representative of the external names – those members who did not work within Lloyd's – but at first she failed, although she did get more votes than the other unsuccessful candidates. The narrow miss encouraged her, and she stood again the following autumn. There were rumours that she had also applied to become the High Mistress of St Paul's Girls' School in London, one of the most academically successful schools in the country, although Mary denied it. In the meantime, she worked on her solar energy book and learned about television. She had joined the board of the ITV company Anglia at a time of change in the industry, with new work practices and technology such as electronic news gathering (ENG) and the introduction of satellite and cable systems. She commented that it was a new experience, after life in a college appealing for money to repair its roofs, to work with an organisation that made a tidy profit.

Among the changes in the broadcasting industry at this time was the expansion of local commercial radio and Mary was asked to join the board of a Cambridgeshire radio station, Cambridge and Newmarket FM (CNFM, later to become Q103), which was bidding for the city's first commercial licence. Companies needed to have board members with good local contacts and knowledge, and Anthony Durham, a former neighbour and managing director of the *Cambridge Evening News*, originally approached Jeffrey but he was too busy. 'The paper had invested in local stations. I was responsible for collecting a group of people to apply for a licence and I went to see whether they wanted to invest. She was the ideal person to have, we were glad to have her on board. She made it her business to be well informed.' Local businessman David Ball, also on the board, says Mary played a key role in the bidding process. Three-quarters of the investment came from CNFM's parent company, but local investors had to raise the rest. 'With her contacts and my contacts, and various networking, we managed to gather a group of investors . . . and demonstrate we had the resources to put it on air . . . Mary had lots of good media contacts who were helpful to us.' The CNFM station, with its formula of pop and phone-ins, also had the backing of two Cambridge colleges, including Mary's former workplace, Trinity. It won the licence in 1988 against competition from two other groups and was very successful, eventually being bought up in 1994 by GWR, the profitable station that owns Classic FM. CNFM's holding company was called Mid Anglia, whose managing director was Stewart Francis, a former broadcaster and, years later, a member of the panel which interviewed Mary for a top job in the NHS. Francis says Mary did a lot for the radio station's charity, which raised money for local people with disabilities. 'She was particularly helpful in the way she could be with her contacts, and used to bring Jeffrey along to do the raffle at a number of prestigious dinners we had which were attended by John Major, who was patron of the appeal.'

Mary's links with Newnham were not severed, and she was made a bye-fellow – an honorary position – and continued to take an interest in college affairs, not only in scientific areas. An English don, Jean Gooder, remembers Mary's quick and helpful response in 1989 when the English department had to set about raising £100,000 for a post which was at risk. 'Mary asked if there was anything she could do to help, and was as good as her word. She organised an illustrated talk in college about Rupert Brooke, and because she knew Dadie (George) Rylands socially she got him to come along to do the readings, which was a big pull, and shortly afterwards we had raised enough money to be able to advertise the post.' Rylands was a fellow of King's College and a renowned expert on Shakespeare, whose plays he produced. He had been a governor of another Cheltenham school during the time Mary was at the Ladies' College, and she had worked with him in 1980 when they were both involved in an 'Entertainment' to raise money for the Newnham Development Fund. On that occasion, Dame Peggy Ashcroft took part, the Duke of Edinburgh attended, and guests enjoyed a menu of 'ham mousse and Newnham souffle'. Jean Gooder says Mary also used to organise private literary events at home in Grantchester. Fundraising had by this time become a large part of Mary's life, and while she claimed that the libel award had 'started our giving habit', what the Archers often give is the use of their homes (to host fundraising events or to allow charities to hold events in their garden) and the use of their talents, such as Jeffrey's auctioneering skills, and Mary's popular talk about Rupert Brooke and the Old Vicarage.

Mary was now in her third year as director of the Fitzwilliam Museum Trust, which was doing nicely in raising funds, partly thanks to a donation from the libel winnings. Mary was well versed about different sources of money available to the arts, says David Thomson, who became chairman and also knew Mary from his connections at the RI. 'Mary's role was entirely positive. We went to receptions given by the appropriate minister . . . She was very well informed and kept a very good record system at her home. She's an extremely good organiser.' Mary was also helpful in getting money to hire a professional fundraiser working for the trust itself, who liaised closely with the university to make sure the Fitzwilliam got its fair share of bequests. The appointment of a professional was part of a drive to bring the museum more up-to-date in a world where galleries must be customer-friendly. Up to this point, the Fitzwilliam had been inward looking, administered by a group of university dons called the Syndics, who were there on behalf of the university, and who, although distinguished, were 'hopeless' about raising money. 'When I was an undergraduate,' says Sir John Margetson, a trustee, 'the Fitzwilliam had a wonderful collection but it wasn't run for the undergraduates – nothing was done to entice anyone to visit it, despite it being founded for the university. Mary's great thing was to land a lot of Japanese money. She was in fact running the show.' Oliver Dawson, another of the trustees, agrees: 'Mary Archer is someone who's good at getting her own way.' And her husband's worldwide reputation as a best-selling novelist came in handy, too. The trust was eventually able to raise a substantial sum for the Shiba room, a print gallery, from a Japanese businessman to whom Jeffrey had access through his literary contacts in Japan, where his books were popular. The donor's condition was that the gallery be opened by the former prime minister Margaret Thatcher and that he should be introduced to her; naturally, the Archers were able to oblige. In 1990, Anglia TV made a documentary about the museum and the following year, when Mary resigned after seven years as director of the trust, a lunch was held at King's College to honour her achievements.

Back in December 1987, however, Mary had the honour of being commissioned by two Sunday papers to write about her trial experiences. She did so, writing 'for the first and last time' about what it was like to live through, despite saying the events were 'better forgotten'. One article, entitled 'My Time of Anguish', was for the *Sunday Times*, a paper from the same group of Murdoch-owned titles as the *News of the World*, which had paid damages in the aftermath of the libel case. Mary described how the immediate consequences of the trial were all-engulfing, with kind letters pouring in, 'mendicants at the church gate' and autograph hunters at Tesco's check-out. In an outline of what she had done in 1987, she wrote that she had travelled 'in pursuit of science or pleasure (not mutually exclusive categories in my book) to Canada, the United States, Italy, Japan, Hong Kong and Hawaii' and been affected by the great gale which blew down four trees at the Old Vicarage, and by the death of her Abyssinian kitten, Archie, from a virus. Summing up the year, she thought she had emerged from the experience 'savvier rather than sadder, warier rather than wiser'. Poetically, she said she had reached the 'tranquillity of the far shore in safety after the long storm', and 'put it all behind me with much relief'. But she was wrong; it was by no means all behind her. The libel case would eventually be investigated, and Mary was also to become deeply involved in dealing with some of the consequences of 'the great gale'.

Around Christmas that year, Jeffrey and his PA Angie Peppiatt parted company. Jeffrey alleged that she had paid herself and another secretary bonuses which he had not agreed, and also made unauthorised expenses claims. Peppiatt disputed this, saying Jeffrey had promised her the money after the trial, but eventually tendered her resignation, saying the trust between them had broken down. She left Jeffrey's employment knowing a great deal about his personal life and, more importantly, taking with her photocopies and several diaries. Years later, these would be of great interest to the police.

It is sometimes said there are no victims of Jeffrey's wrongdoing, but the evidence suggests otherwise. Monica Coghlan suffered greatly from the injustice, and no doubt so did her son. The health of the *Star*'s editor, Lloyd Turner, also declined following the trial, and his wife wondered if it had hastened his death. Two national newspapers were defrauded. The journalist Adam Raphael was damaged by the untrue accusation that he betrayed his sources – a charge made by Jeffrey's friend Stewart Steven, editor of the *Mail on Sunday*, and which led to a libel action won by Raphael, although the case took eighteen months of his life. For Monica Coghlan, there was no happy ending. In contrast to Mary's career, Monica's life never recovered; she went back to work on the streets, but her fame made things difficult and she was again fined for soliciting, and eventually went bankrupt. As we shall see, bankruptcy was also to be the fate of a second woman who crossed swords with Mary Archer in court years later. But well before that, it was the spectre of bankruptcy for hundreds of Lloyd's Names which quickly turned Mary Archer from fragrant to fearsome. She was soon to become, for many, a figure of hate.

11

Lime Street Blues

ON 15 OCTOBER 1987, a BBC weatherman told the nation: 'A woman rang in and said there was a hurricane on the way. Well, if you're watching, don't worry, there isn't.' Within hours, southern England was being battered by winds of a hundred miles an hour which blew off roofs, brought down phone lines and uprooted trees, including a third of those at Kew Gardens and several at the Old Vicarage, Grantchester. Four days later, Black Monday saw stocks and shares crashing in the City; a month on, thirty-one people were killed in the King's Cross station fire. These domestic disasters were just some of the many catastrophes that blighted the end of the eighties: the Piper Alpha oil rig exploded in the North Sea; Libyan terrorists blew up a Pan Am jet over Lockerbie in Scotland; there was an earthquake in San Francisco and Hurricane Hugo in the Caribbean. It was all very bad news for the insurance industry and just as devastating was the huge and growing number of claims in the United States relating to asbestosis and pollution. Many of these bills landed on the doorsteps of insurance syndicates at Lloyd's of London. They did so just as Mary Archer, fresh from a cruise on the *QE2*, was trying once more for a place on Lloyd's Council. This time she was elected.

She joined the governing body at the worst moment in Lloyd's

300-year-old history. After many years of seemingly guaranteed profits, from which the Archers had both done very nicely, the world's oldest and most famous insurance market was heading for a colossal financial disaster that was to threaten its very existence and plunge thousands of individual investors into serious debt or bankruptcy. The losses totalled billions of pounds and many investors – known as Names – simply could not meet these 'calls' because they had joined Lloyd's with insufficient means and even less understanding of the horrifying implications of unlimited liability; nor were they aware of the incompetence and – as was found in some cases – breach of duty to Names that had infected some parts of the organisation.

Mary had made history in November 1988 when she became the first woman to be elected to the ruling council. Her sixteen proposers had included four MPs – John Wakeham, Nicholas Baker (both government whips), Michael Jopling and John Moore – and the soon-to-be-MP Jacqui Lait, as well as Jeffrey and the Hon. Sir Clive Bossom (of whose father Churchill once remarked: 'Funny name, Bossom, neither one thing nor the other!'). In winning one of the eight places allocated to 'external' Names, she got more votes than any of the seven men. A female rival, Lady Rona Delves Broughton, complained of being overwhelmed by the Archer publicity machine. She was reportedly angry that a short story written by Jeffrey in the *Lloyd's Log* magazine dropped through members' letterboxes at just the right moment, even though candidates were not supposed to promote themselves. The editor of the *Log* was Michael Wynn Jones (husband of the cookery writer Delia Smith who, like Jeffrey, had Debbie Owen as a literary agent) who had acquired the second rights to *Twist in the Tale*, Jeffrey's new collection of short stories. In September, *Lloyd's Log* published an 'exclusive' extract, a story entitled 'The Loophole', which was about two golfers who plan a swindle involving a libel writ. (One of the characters points out that civil case damages are tax free, as Jeffrey would have discovered the previous year.) Not only was the story good publicity for Jeffrey's new book, it didn't harm his wife's chances of election at Lloyd's. Mary was unapologetic. 'Name recognition is undoubtedly a help. The publicity machine is not of *my* making . . . I'm not such a fool as to turn it down.' And she felt she was every bit as qualified as the experienced Lady Rona Delves Broughton: 'I know what I know by being married to a very wealthy man, and by talking to people in the City. My father was a chartered accountant and a lot does rub off.'[1] Not everyone on the Council was convinced Mary was right for the job; some had hoped that having two women candidates would split the vote.

After her victory, Mary said Lloyd's was an institution she very much admired and, as a woman with no real experience of City institutions, she would be bringing a different perspective to her work from most of the men. She also had a significant aim: 'It is my hope that the relationship between Lloyd's and Westminster could be improved.'[2] This was odd, since there were already about sixty Conservative MPs who were Names. Some of them were her friends: Wakeham, Norman Fowler and Michael Howard. Jeffrey, who had been a Name for sixteen years, said his wife's victory was a very important 'first'. 'Mary will not be intimidated by the men on the committee,' he added. Mary, as the daughter of a freemason, may also have felt at home in a man's world where freemasonry was allegedly practised. There were three masonic lodges at Lloyd's: the Lutine, Fidentia and Lloyd's, and according to Martin Short, author of *Inside the Brotherhood* (published in 1989), 'Freemasonry's power over Lloyd's can scarcely be over-estimated.'

Mary started her four-year post in January 1989 amid further publicity, including one article she wrote herself, explaining that she wanted to learn a lot about the insurance market. She had positively enjoyed serving on university finance committees: 'It sounds extraordinary but it's a fact that balance sheets can make fascinating reading . . . I find that business decisions about . . . finance are no less intellectually challenging than those posed in academe . . . I am pretty confident that I'll find the . . . sliding dollar, the Single European Market . . . every bit as interesting as solar cells.'[3] Being a Name was much more exciting and less remote than just having shares in ICI, and she had fun comparing her results with Jeffrey's, while acknowledging his unchallenged status as the money-maker in the family. 'It's something I've never done and never will and it's something I admire tremendously. The country *needs* wealth generators like Jeffrey.'[4] Privately, however, there were misgivings among some Council members. A 'working' Council member was taken aback at first by Mary's presentation. 'She speaks comma exactly comma as if she were reading comma everything terribly precise and very particular.' And the former MP Woodrow Wyatt reveals in his diaries a conversation with Sir Marcus Kimball, an external member. Kimball (now a Lord) said there were worries Mary would be letting Jeffrey know what was going on through 'pillow talk'. Wyatt reassured him that he didn't think there was any fear of that. Kimball, who was a Lincolnshire MP at the same time as Jeffrey, remains unconvinced: 'I think she was put up to it by Jeffrey, and she always had an eye on the publicity.'

As a pointer to what would be her attitude, she wrote that being a Name was a gamble: 'People become Names at Lloyd's to make a second income on their capital, but they must always be aware of the risks. The general idea is that Lloyd's syndicates pay the Name profits. Naturally enough that occasionally means the Name finds himself or herself paying losses too. That happened to me for the first time last summer, a reminder that cycles of feast and famine are inherent in the nature of the business and that membership only makes sense as a long-term venture.' Thus, she was 'on-message' on behalf of the Council: 'Lloyd's falls outside the Financial Services Act 1986, but the Council ... aims to provide Names with protection comparable with that afforded by the Act.' This view would be greeted with hollow laughter by many ruined Names in next few years, and even at this stage, Mary was beginning to wonder whether it was wise to be part of a husband and wife team there, even in different syndicates.

A lot of the external Names (i.e. those not working within

Lloyd's) Mary was representing had been encouraged to join during a big expansion of the market in the seventies and eighties, when there were twenty consecutive years of profit, and when all they needed in order to show sufficient assets was a bank guarantee against their homes. In the mid-seventies, some Names had to show only £37,500 in assets to begin underwriting, although £100,000 was more usual; in 1986 more than half of the members underwriting had declared assets of under £150,000.[5] Membership of Lloyd's was therefore within the reach of people of 'middling' wealth, many of them near retirement, attracted by the cachet of joining an exclusive club and the expectation of an agreeable extra income. Although many Names were very rich and famous, those who were to be worst hit by the crisis were mostly neither.

There had been warnings within the closed circle of the Lloyd's insiders about the impending crisis, including one which spoke of 'unquantifiable losses' in connection with asbestos claims, but many external Names were seriously misled because they were not told of the extent of the risks to which they were being exposed. As Cathy Gunn, the author of *Nightmare on Lime Street*, pointed out: 'The Names are highly dependent on the skill of the individuals running their syndicates . . . Becoming a Name was effectively handing over your entire personal wealth . . . to a bunch of strangers to gamble with against the probabilities of this ship sinking, that oil rig exploding, this city being rocked by an earthquake . . . and ancient oaks ripped out by a hurricane-force wind . . . When things fell apart under the treble assault of asbestosis, pollution and natural disasters in the late 1980s, the impact soon made the Stock Exchange's Black Monday crash . . . seem just a breeze.'[6]

By the end of the year, the storm among Names was so strong that Lloyd's had to take action. There was already a hardship committee in existence, but until then it had dealt with only a handful of cases. It had been chaired by Lord Kimball, who says he was only too happy to be rid of it, and was under the remit of Lloyd's former chief accountant Graeme King, who by then was in charge of Solvency and Accounting Standards – making sure the Names paid up. Although he had never met Mary, King thought she would be just the person to chair the hardship committee, because of her own experience of near-bankruptcy and because a feminine touch was needed to counter the cliquy male atmosphere. 'I felt she was right: she was analytical, thorough, and had research and consultation skills.' In October 1989 Mary accepted the job because she 'felt a commitment' to protect those whose liabilities outweighed their assets, and was particularly keen to ensure they avoided bankruptcy and litigation. The Conservative MP and fellow Council member Sir Nicholas Bonsor says '. . . it was a matter of deep concern to all of us, and especially to Mary' that a lot of people were in a plight through no fault of their own – people, for example, who had been made Lloyd's Names as part of a divorce settlement, or who had been given membership by their employers as a leaving present.

According to Andrew Duguid, the secretary to the Council, it was Mary herself who persuaded the Council that there should be hardship assistance to those who had suffered the most. 'Mary came to be seen as sometimes harsh in her judgement . . . But the truth was she had pretty well single-handedly persuaded everyone there should be some assistance. I can remember how hard she had to work in persuading some of the Council, speaking quite forcefully. She broke fresh ground and eventually views changed.' Bonsor, who was Mary's deputy on the hardship committee, agrees: 'Certainly she was one of the people who tried to get the Council to be as lenient as they could be.' And Nicholas Pawson, also on the committee and Council, says: 'The scheme was softened; the terms were improved once we began to realise the true problems out there. She had to set up a framework that was fair and sustainable, and once terms were established, they had to be rigorously followed. You can't go beyond the rules for individual cases. Mary could see the potential Pandora's box she was opening.'

Mary's committee was backed up by a team of employees mainly working at Lloyd's offices in Chatham, including case officers, lawyers and accountants. By 1993, more than 6,000 Names owed money – a fifth of the entire market – and the Council needed to distinguish between those who couldn't pay and those who refused to pay. Mary was always conscious that, in not collecting debts, Lloyd's was in effect giving away other people's money, including her own, and that her job was 'a very difficult balancing act' between the aggrieved who refused to pay and those who had paid in full, sometimes impoverishing themselves. With some debts running into millions, many faced bankruptcy and the loss of their family home, but felt the alternative of applying to the hardship committee was hardly more appealing. The hardship committee required ruined Names to make over all their assets to Lloyd's in return for being able to retain a 'modest' roof over their heads and an annual net income, for a single person, of about £11,600. They were required to acknowledge their debt and even had to agree to hand over any proceeds they might eventually recover through litigation. (These stringent terms were eventually relaxed in 1992 when it was accepted that it was counter-productive to insist that Names could never be freed from their debts, whereas a bankrupt could obtain a discharge after three years.)

Mary, who chose to be known as Dr Archer, said that she took very great care that the terms offered were better than bankruptcy, and there were around 2,300 applications to her committee (many of them retired people who needed security for their later years) although fewer eventually settled this way. 'It was a very unattractive scheme for innocent Names,' says Christopher Stockwell, a leading member of one of the Names' action groups which had sprung up to fight Lloyd's. 'I think she thought it would be possible to deal with it in the traditional Lloyd's way of sweeping it under the carpet, but I was of the view that Names were innocent victims of gross incompetence and serious negligence, and that Lloyd's should arrange compensation. Her view was that Names had a duty to pay. She wasn't prepared to entertain the possibility they had been duped.' John Mays, chairman of the Merrett Action

Group, says, 'I don't think she acknowledged . . . that our affairs had been mishandled, and we'd been lied to. I think she felt most of the litigation was unjustified; she thought everyone should pay up like her.' But hardship committee and Council members defend their stand. 'We couldn't go round making admissions on behalf of Lloyd's – that would have led to all sorts of trouble!' says Nicholas Bonsor. Nicholas Pawson agrees: 'For Mary or anybody else to make a judgement about whether or not there was corruption wasn't part of our brief.'

There was great resentment from Names that they had to appeal for help from the very body which had, as they saw it, brought about their ruin, and dozens of groups of Names decided they would sue first, pay later. Their case was that Lloyd's had failed to regulate the market and provide adequate information to investors. It was pointed out that 30 per cent of the Names were bearing 70 per cent of the losses. The way Lloyd's saw it, Names were whinging because they didn't like to lose, the losses were the result of worldwide recession and Names had known about the risks when they signed up. They also had to deal with 'filibusterers' – Names who applied to the committee without the slightest intention of reaching a settlement, in the knowledge that they wouldn't be forced to pay their debts as long as they were in negotiation.

Graeme King went round the country holding seminars to explain to Names what hardship applications were all about. 'The Hardship was formed to help those who couldn't help themselves . . . but I would say to the Names: You've got to be an active investor; did you look at the syndicate accounts? Caveat emptor.' However, King himself had been through the paperwork in great detail when he had become chief accountant: 'I had been dealing with asbestos claims in my previous job in Canada. I went through every set of currently available accounts when I was employed by Lloyd's in 1984 and the word asbestos was not mentioned anywhere. I went through the Council minutes – not a single mention of asbestos. So I thought, well it's not a material factor.'

Some Names suspected that they were the victims of insider

dealing and of the pervasive influence of freemasonry, both very difficult to prove. The author Cathy Gunn wrote: 'Secrecy is the perfect breeding ground for abuse and even fraud, and Lloyd's has been secretive enough without adding the double jeopardy of a secret society within the Society. Worried Names understandably feared that the oathes sworn by lodge members to help each other could have sufficiently outweighed their sense of obligation towards the Names whose money provided their living ... Though still pervasive, the influence of the lodges seemed to have declined in the 80s.'[7] Christopher Stockwell claims: 'We found minutes to do with the new building which had plans for a space for masonic activities. It was entrenched at the top ... But unless you've got evidence from a mason who says this is what was going on, you can't do anything. One of the interesting things is why there was never an investigation by the police or Serious Fraud Office. There were a whole series of separate affairs worthy of police investigation – tax frauds in the late seventies and "spiral" reinsurance arrangements – but no investigation.' These views are not shared by all the Names affected, and fraud was never proved. John Mays says he never encountered freemasonry. 'If you were a golfer, that was more useful than anything!'

At the start of 1992 Labour MPs, prompted by Tory backbencher Names who had lost large sums of money, alleged that external Names had been deliberately dumped on loss-making 'spiral' (multiple reinsurance) syndicates. The same year, there was an investigation by Sir David Walker, chairman of the Securities Board (and an independent member of the Council), who censured some of what had gone on, but said there was insufficient proof of insider dealing. Sir David, described by the Lloyd's chairman as 'so pure he makes Snow White look smutty', succeeded in silencing the most serious accusations, although it was no comfort for the militant Names, who thought his report a damning indictment. Some of the press was also scathing: 'The professionals of Lloyd's are not fit to regulate a flea circus, never mind a multi-billion market,' said one paper. The accountant Graeme King disagrees. 'To the best of my knowledge, there was no collusion or plan to spread the losses amongst uninformed and unprotected sheep. There was a series of individual corporate failures and a lack of accountability. Those management practices were standard practice at the time; hindsight is a great teacher.'

In dealing with angry, articulate and desperate people, Mary had a thankless job and, to her credit, even some of the embittered Names admit she did it as well as it could be done. Her cool, analytical, unemotional personality was an essential ingredient in performing her task; she was in the thick of the human drama, where there were many sad stories, and quite a few suicides. It was at first thought she would be sympathetic in view of her own experiences, and indeed she professed to be, saying she knew how 'really unpleasant' it could be to go through hard times. 'I know it's horrible. I know what it's like to have to move and to not be able to put your children in the school you thought you were going to.' Her son James said it bothered him to read pieces that suggested she didn't care about the people who lost money. 'She works extremely hard, often until 2 a.m., trying to work out ways to help them,' he claimed. But for the people who had to deal with her, she exuded no sympathy or warmth whatsoever; moreover, she was now extremely wealthy, and perceived as sticking up for Lloyd's management. Behind the scenes, though, Mary was pushing for what she thought were much more lenient arrangements: 'I remember I had a lot of trouble getting them through Council because it was thought to be very soft.'

Although Mary was in daily contact with angry Names, her role as chairman was to take a strategic overview. She was based in London, and most of the day-to-day work was done at the hardship offices in Chatham, Kent, where she was assisted by a team of staff dubbed 'bloodhounds' and a solicitor known to Names as 'The Rottweiler', whose job was to scrutinise the assets of applicants and draw up their contracts. Members had to fill in a very detailed questionnaire about their earnings, assets, spending, tax position and so forth; the hardship committee had to know

176

everything, and came to be viewed as the Lloyd's equivalent of the workhouse. For many Names who did meet Mary, she presented a carapaced front; they variously described her as the poisoned cactus, icy, unpleasant and heartless. One Name was outraged that Mary addressed a meeting 'wearing a socking great diamond on her bosom'. Another said, 'You could crack eggs on her.' Mary was hurt when she read these descriptions, but commented, 'It is not my job to be a pushover.'

The writer Julian Barnes, in an article about Lloyd's written for *New Yorker* magazine in 1993, commented memorably that, 'there is something about Dr Archer that gets up people's noses like a gigantic dose of snuff . . . She is small, dark, pretty, poised, groomed and very, very precise . . . I mentioned [to her] that there was a good deal of resentment out there among her current constituency. "Resentment, anger, distress," she replied. "All that is very understandable." But she listed the nouns as if identifying base metals rather than volcanic emotions.'[8] Barnes also tackled Mary about a newspaper photograph that had enraged Names. It showed Mary modelling an expensive designer cocktail dress, set off by a head-dress confection of feathers and described by one Name as 'like a circus-pony rider'. Julian Barnes told Mary that the photograph of the frock was being satirically circulated among the burnt Names, 'and she responded, with a mid-November smile, "I don't blame them."' She saw herself as someone who came to the rescue. Describing her role to *Hello!* magazine, Mary said, 'I always feel like the person who comes along in a van to unclamp your car, setting you free eventually.'

Mary's chairmanship style was extremely methodical and collegiate; she would go round the table asking everyone for their say. As the volume of work increased, her staff fervently hoped her deputy Nicholas Bonsor would chair the meetings. His method was to explain the staff's recommendation and then ask if anyone disagreed. 'With Mary it might take an hour and a half to do one case, whereas it would be five minutes with Nick.' At the end of 1995, the hardship committee gave way to the more all-encompassing reconstruction and renewal scheme overseen by the new chairman of Lloyd's, David Rowland, which introduced reform and a rescue package which members voted to accept. The new Lloyd's building was put up for sale to release funds – and with typical *folie de grandeur* one of the early would-be bidders was Jeffrey, although he soon dropped out. The building was sold for more than £200 million; Lloyd's stayed on as tenants.

The Archers themselves lost money during the bad years at Lloyd's but the forty-two syndicates to which they belonged by 1989 were generally among the more profitable, and they were with one of the more successful brokers, Willis Faber. As Mary said in 1996: 'Both Jeffrey and I sustained quite substantial losses, though not in the millions.'[9] One report in 1993 estimated their losses at £100,000; another, in 1995, thought £50,000. The couple paid up, although Mary said of the rescue package: 'There is a sense of the goodies paying for the baddies here . . . In principle, the non-payers should, I believe, be pursued.'[10] In doing relatively well financially at Lloyd's there is no suggestion that Mary was involved in anything improper, but getting herself elected to the Council could have been quite a hard-headed exercise in becoming an insider, someone at the very heart of the market, and as with all markets, the closer you are to the centre, the more you know what is going on. Indeed, one informal analysis done by a ruined Name of the losses revealed that the largest were concentrated on very few syndicates in 1989. His analysis showed the professionals were over-represented on the best syndicates and under-represented on the worst hit. This gave weight to the Names' allegation that Lloyd's was run for the benefit of the insiders, at the expense of external Names, who provided most of the capital.

Some years later, in 1994, the Labour MP Peter Hain used the privilege of the House of Commons to point out how fortunate some Names, including the Archers, had been in deciding to leave certain syndicates 'before the worst happened'.[11] Hain also alleged that none of the Tory MPs who were Lloyd's Names had suffered destitution, bankruptcy or the tremendous losses that other external Names on exactly the same syndicates had suffered. The significance of his claims was that John Major's government had a very small majority and, had the MPs in Lloyd's gone bankrupt, they would have been forced to resign and the government would have fallen. Major angrily told Hain if he had any information to suggest impropriety he should come up with it. Mary denied her scheme was a way of bailing out Tory MPs or that there were any special deals for them. There is no evidence that MPs got 'sweetheart' deals in dealing with their hardship, and Graeme King, the man formerly in charge of solvency at Lloyd's, says the claim is 'rubbish'. King, who is now general secretary of the Society for Promoting Christian Knowledge, looks back on Mary's appointment without regret: 'I do think she did it with the best of intention and she applied her professional skills in a beneficial way.' As for an overview of the whole debacle, he says, 'Lloyd's is a bit like a domestic dispute. It depends on who you talk to after the divorce.'

Although Mary's chairmanship of the hardship committee was controversial, the Council felt she made a valuable contribution overall. 'She added value,' says one, 'and we had to have a woman.' Another, Peter Nutting, says, 'It was a complete bed of nails; she must have had many moments of regretting it bitterly, but I think she did an extremely good job. She was always well prepared for meetings – she's very good when she is prepared; off-the-cuff is not her forte.' Mary had a manner which seemed unsympathetic but she was also constrained by what she could do; she was in the middle, trying to reconcile opposing views. 'You may feel we haven't got it right,' she told Names, 'but I can only tell you that we try.' A lawyer who was close to events says, 'The lot fell on her; she didn't do a bad job. It was very difficult because she had the Names aggressively shooting at her because she was Lloyd's messenger, and some right-wing members of the Council on the other hand who probably wanted to bankrupt the lot of them and couldn't understand why they didn't pay up. She was just matter-of-fact about it: "An earthquake has hit Lloyds and we'll do the best we can to sort it out. This is what we're offering; take it or leave it."'

Several Council members pointed to the fact that Mary was not a 'businesswoman'. 'Lloyd's is a people business, and I'm not sure that's where her talents lie,' one noted. Whether or not she was a businesswoman, Mary was doing her utmost to learn about business life, and she took on a number of other commitments in the late eighties and early nineties, mainly linked to her expertise in science, music and education. If Names at Lloyd's had a long list of disparaging epithets for Mary Archer, those with whom she sat round a boardroom table elsewhere had much praise for her abilities: dedicated, professional, helpful, enthusiastic, generous, superb, committed, well informed, straightforward, meticulous, hard-working, pragmatic – some even found her warm and friendly. Mary clearly relishes the peculiar demands of board and committee meetings; she has good powers of concentration, an eye for detail and an understanding of figures. 'She could turn up a set of accounts and turn to page four, for example, and say, "I don't think that figure is correct," and we'd say, "Oh, didn't notice that." Business people like me were often shown up by Mary's astute abilities,' says David Ball, the Cambridge company director. 'She put us through our paces.' As a chairman, she was focused and good at bringing people back to the point, which was appreciated by secretaries: 'The meeting would have been six hours, not two, if it hadn't been for Mary. She cut through the crap,' said one media PA.

Shortly after she joined Lloyd's, Mary was asked to become chairman of the newly established National Energy Foundation (NEF). Her former mentor George, by now Lord, Porter became its first president, a position Mary herself was later to hold. The foundation's aim is to promote energy efficiency and the uptake of renewable energy sources, which is Mary's line of interest. Another trustee was David Puttnam, the film director, who was also on the Anglia TV board. The NEF is based at Milton Keynes, but sometimes the trustees would hold their board meetings in the Archers'

London flat. About a quarter of the meetings were held in that way, according to the economist Professor John Chesshire, who took over from Mary as chairman. 'It was a very gracious offer. She provided coffee and sandwiches and it saved several hundred pounds' hire of rooms.' Mary was unpaid as chairman, and never claimed expenses, which saved the NEF even more. To practise what she was preaching, she began – somewhat belatedly – to install energy-saving measures in her own home which had scored an embarrassing 3.7 out of 10 on the Home Energy Rating scale when first tested. Mary, who said she was taught as a child to turn off unwanted lights, added extra loft insulation, secondary glazing, and a jacket for the hot water tank – measures which cost nearly £8,000 but which she expected would cut her fuel bill by more than £1,000 a year.[12]

She managed to squeeze in time to launch her short book about Rupert Brooke and the Old Vicarage, which was sold to raise money for Grantchester parish church. Journalists were invited to a garden party and one remembers: 'Jeffrey was nowhere to be seen and she said he was down in Somerset. It was a lovely summer's day and we were enjoying tea and suddenly Jeffrey bounded into the garden wearing a hat and boating blazer. He totally upstaged her. He stood on a chair and told us to gather round and he gave her a parcel wrapped in brown paper – a surprise present. She just put it down and didn't even open it; she was very irritated. It ruined her little day.' A couple of years later, Mary the writer was asked to give a talk at the Cheltenham Literary Festival, when the director was Richard Cohen, Jeffrey's editor. He had also invited Jeffrey and said the two of them 'would ring me regularly to find out about advance booking figures, and Mary was delighted to pip Jeffrey's final tally by about 50 seats'.[13]

Mary also took up two honorary appointments: in April 1989 she took over from Sir Bernard Lovell as president of the Guild of Church Musicians, which she had joined some years earlier. Strangely, the guild is unwilling to discuss Mary's involvement other than to say she is much appreciated. Mary was also made a

Senior Academic Fellow at de Montfort University, the former Leicester Polytechnic, partly because, according to de Montfort's Professor Roger Linford, 'She was a high-profile chemist and doing a lot of work for women in science. There aren't that many senior female figures in science even today.' She became a trustee of the Science Museum in London, yet another board to sit on, and joined the judging panel for the *Daily Telegraph*'s Young Science Writer of the Year award. (The award is co-sponsored by BASF, whose chairman, Barry Stickings, was one of Mary's fellow chemists at Oxford.) The growing mounds of paperwork produced by all her commitments meant that Mary needed more workspace than her little office under the stairs or the one she shared with Jeffrey; and she needed more help.

In 1988, Mary had hired an efficient PA called Jane Williams, who soon became 'her Mission Control'; the two women moved into a large office on the ground floor of the newly renovated Victorian folly in the garden, which was 'opened' at a champagne party for 150 guests by John Major, who referred to it as 'Mary's second folly'. Jeffrey's office was above them, and sometimes he would bang on the floor calling for silence as he concentrated on his writing. The folly was described in an article in *Hello!* magazine, marking Mary's first solo appearance in its pages – a sure sign of celebrity – although she had already featured earlier that year as novelist's wife. Mary's Folly – complete with castellations – consists of a two-storey tower, conservatory, offices, library, kitchenette and cloakroom. It is decorated with pictures, plants and family photographs. And while Jeffrey writes in longhand, Mary is high-tech with computer and laptop.

Jane Williams had come to Mary's attention through writing a speculative letter to Jeffrey asking for a job. Mary responded, saying *she* might be needing a full-time secretary, and eventually Williams was interviewed and taken on. 'She struck me as bright and ambitious,' said Mary. 'Her performance was entirely satisfactory. She was hard-working and keen to learn . . . Over time, I taught her how to use certain software applications, such as how to draw diagrams.' The PA was at the centre of the family, privy to some of their secrets. In her letter of engagement, quoted later by an employment tribunal, Mary had written: 'I hardly need to add that some of my work is confidential . . . In particular, Anglia Television and Robert Fraser papers sometimes contain commercially sensitive information which must not be discussed with or disclosed to a third person, not even a spouse.' Williams's duties included coordinating Mary's professional, academic and personal engagements; she oversaw the household staff, paid bills, made sure appointments and birthdays were not forgotten, and answered fan mail. She was told she could 'share whatever we happen to have in the fridge' for lunch. She did everything from bleeding radiators to liaising with the prime minister's protection officers, and was introduced to Thatcher with the words: 'Margaret, I would like you to meet my loyal and dependable PA.' This satisfactory state of affairs lasted for about ten years, but was to end in calamity.

By the end of the eighties, Mary's portfolio of charity, commercial and public positions was so extensive that she was deemed suitable for inclusion in that bible of the well known, *Who's Who*. Her first entry, in 1990, listed her hobbies as 'village choirmistress, theatre, squash, cats and picking up litter'. (She says she can't go out without emptying the wastepaper baskets.) Her growing prominence had also been marked by television appearances. One of her colleagues on scientific committees, Professor Ian Fells, was a prodigious programme maker and working on a populist science series called *Take Nobody's Word for It* (which discovered the presenter Carol Vorderman). 'I used to interview some frightfully grand person, a Nobel prize-winner or someone like that,' says Professor Fells, 'but the trouble was we could never find any women of the same sort of calibre . . . I knew Mary and I was rather against having her on the programme because she didn't compare with the other distinguished people I'd interviewed, but my producer was insistent we had some women. In the event we did quite a nice piece; I got her to do an experiment to gild some lilies, literally.' The series was made in Bristol, where Mary arrived in her chauffeur-driven car. Ian Fells remembers the women on his research team being very impressed that Mary turned up for rehearsals on the same day that she was holding a big party. 'They were clearly under the impression that when she got back home she would have been buttering little slices of toast, and I said I don't think it's quite like that: all she has to do is walk into the penthouse! She came back the next day and did a very good job.'

In 1994 the BBC also made a documentary about Lloyd's, and two of the badly hit Names, Fernanda Herford and Denis Meyer, were filmed questioning Mary. 'She made us travel to Chatham to do the filming,' says Herford, 'and it was a very hot day and we had to wait because she rang up from her car to say she'd be late. We were all very hot and sweaty by this time, and she arrived as cool as a cucumber. We asked her whether she agreed there had been an injustice, but we got nowhere.' All Mary would say on that point was that she was not an apologist for Lloyd's past: 'We can't undo the past; we can only try to cope with the consequences.' The interview was not included in the programme.

Someone else who felt he got nowhere – some years later – was the former MP Tom Benyon who ran the Society of Names and had met Mary for his Names' magazine. 'I sought to interview her to find out the real Mary. I take some pride in being a friendly cove, and can get on with most people and oddly enough I was at the same ghastly school as Jeffrey. But it was like interviewing the north face of the Eiger,' he says. 'It was amazing. I got absolutely nowhere at all. Perhaps she was a bit uptight because the press were waiting for her, although I tipped her off to go out of the back entrance. She later seemed rather surprised that I had written nothing.' The reason the press were waiting for Mary was that another scandal had just broken – Jeffrey was being investigated for insider dealing. It was alleged that he had bought shares in Anglia Television at a time when the board was negotiating a takeover; and on that board sat Mary. Her reputation in the City was about to be seriously damaged.

12

Mary Quite Contrary

THE COUNCIL OF LLOYD'S and their wives looked on in astonishment as Mary Archer walked on stage and took the
microphone. They were at the end of a lavish dinner – known as
the In and Out – held by the chairman, David Coleridge, to thank
the outgoing Council and to welcome the new. The sixty or so
guests had enjoyed the best food and wines in the sumptuous setting of the eighteenth-century Adam Room. 'There were masses of
flowers, string orchestra, champagne – the entertaining was regal,'
says one Name. Now, as they sat back with their *digestifs* to enjoy
a performance by the musical duo Kit and the Widow, they were
unprepared for the entertainment in store for them. Lady Archer,
baroness wife of the newly ennobled Jeffrey, chairman of the hardship committee, newly elected board member of Addenbrooke's
NHS Trust, was about to sing the cabaret. Wearing a slinky, low-
cut dress, Mary launched into a rendition of 'Who Wants To Be A
Millionaire?' with words carefully adapted to suit the organisation – 'Who wants to be a member of Lloyd's – I don't!' The new
chairman, David Rowland, who had already set about making
changes to Lloyd's and who later put a stop to such royal entertaining, was horrified: 'The song was crushing to him,' said one
guest. 'Half the room was amused and half appalled. It showed a

lack of taste.' A member of Council said: 'Here was the outgoing Chairman giving a very grand party as if nothing was happening outside. The evening started on a grotesque note and got worse!' Another says the cabaret turn was 'not very appropriate. But if you live with somebody whose life is governed by publicity, some of it must rub off. Maybe she was trying to appear more human.' What the devastated Names would have thought, can only be guessed.

Mary's performance had been inspired by the response to her 1991 New Year's Eve public debut when she had appeared with Kit and the Widow on Channel 4 television singing Tom Lehrer's witty 'The Elements'. Announcing herself as Dr Archer, and wearing a tight, strapless red evening dress, matching *manchettes*, sheer black tights and very high heels, she proceeded to reel off, to piano accompaniment, the list of ninety-two elements in her precise choirmistress's voice. She was later photographed for a publicity shot draped across the piano. It was an audacious performance for an amateur musician, and could only have been done by a person of supreme self-confidence, not to say vanity. Her friend, Kit Hesketh-Harvey, said she chose the song herself, carefully rehearsed it and thoroughly enjoyed doing it. 'It's such a delightful side of her character. She's less ice-maiden-like than her public image suggests.' The performance was all the more incongruous because of the contrast with Mary's more sober roles. She had just taken up an honorary position of visiting professor at Imperial College, London; she was a member of a DTI committee, the Renewable Energy Group, which advised the government about energy issues; she had recently been asked to join the board of her local NHS hospital, Addenbrooke's; and was also a council member on the governing body of her old school, Cheltenham Ladies' College, whose motto, incidentally, is 'May she grow in heavenly light' . Limelight, perhaps, in Mary's case.

Mary's cabaret act had also been featured at the couple's silver wedding party, held in a marquee on the lawn of the Old Vicarage, when she had joined the musicians to sing the Lehrer song and 'There's No Place Like Home' in front of several hundred close friends including Margaret Thatcher and John Major. This star turn, which would become a regular feature of Archer entertaining, was 'sung with a choirboy purity that left no soul unmoved' commented journalist and party guest Valerie Grove; Mary had found the elements song 'inordinately difficult to learn' because the periodic table of elements was 'listed out of its predetermined order'. A musician and chorister, Adrian Hutton, helped her rehearse for several parties: 'At first, she was quite hesitant, but in the end she was jolly good. Her adaptations are witty, sometimes with oblique references to politics and the guests.' The Archers' silver wedding party had been a grand occasion, attended by many leading lights in the Conservative party, House of Lords, and show business. Mary wore a glamorous pink gown and pearls which showed off those 'creamy shoulders' and William and James, now nineteen and seventeen, wore white dinner jackets. Jeffrey gave Mary a portrait of herself with her favourite cat Oscar, which he had commissioned from Bryan Organ – an artist who had also painted Lord Porter and, more famously, the Princess of Wales. In turn, Mary admiringly gave Jeffrey a grotesque (gargoyle) of himself which was installed on the wall of the folly. One of Mary's most loyal friends, the Tory MP Peter Bottomley, was so taken with her singing that he suggested she should make an LP, which she duly did later that year.

Among the silver wedding party guests were two Kurdish business associates, Broosk Saib and Nadhim Zahawi. The two men had been prominent in campaigning for Kurdish refugees, whose plight had been much covered on television earlier in the year. In the aftermath of the Gulf War between Iraq and Kuwait, more than 800,000 Kurds were trapped on Iraq's mountainous northern border with Turkey, having fled from the regime of Saddam Hussein. In the spring of 1991, James had prompted his father to get involved in a major fundraising effort for the Kurds by arranging a concert similar to the 1985 Live Aid organised by Bob Geldof, which had raised millions for Ethiopia. Jeffrey had set about this task with his trademark gusto; his efforts, according to his biographer, 'would encapsulate many of Archer's best and worst qualities. On the one hand he brought to the Kurdish appeal his compassion, energy and unquenchable self-belief; yet at the same time his efforts suffered from his customary lack of attention to detail, bad judgement, and exaggeration of his own achievements.'[1] The project was named Simple Truth, and turned out to be highly controversial – and far from simple or truthful. One of the first people to complain was Lorraine Goodrich, a Devon housewife who had been running a relief organisation called British Aid for the Kurds and who claims she had already begun organising a concert with Peter Gabriel and Sting when Jeffrey came along and simply hi-jacked it. 'He took the idea from me,' she says. 'He's taken all the credit for what a lot of other people were already doing.'

As Lorraine Goodrich had done, Jeffrey teamed up with the Red Cross but he had the crucial advantage of backing from John Major's government. A public relations team including Tim (now Lord) Bell, Margaret Thatcher's advertising guru, was hired; big names like Rod Stewart and Chris Tarrant were signed up to perform; and Jeffrey himself worked tirelessly, calling on his numerous well-placed business and political contacts, even travelling to see the UN secretary-general, and later embarking on a trip to Kurdistan. The Simple Truth concert itself was a big success, with five hours' live coverage on BBC2; Jeffrey greeted the Princess of Wales and then sat with his wife and John and Norma Major for the show. Among the VIPs was Paddy Ashdown, leader of the Lib Dems, who thought that Mary was much prettier than she appears on television, but was less impressed by Jeffrey: '. . . he was there too, poncing about and generally being obnoxious'.[2] A few weeks later, at a press conference, Jeffrey held up a placard announcing the total he claimed – but was never able to substantiate – the event had raised: a staggering £57,042,000, the second highest sum ever announced by a British appeal. Within weeks, the claim was being investigated by the *Observer* and the London *Evening Standard*. Kurds were beginning to question whether such a sum was ever raised, and, with many Kurds still starving and suffering, how it had been spent. The Kurdish Disaster Fund even vented their frustration in a full-page ad in the *Guardian*, saying Kurdish children were still dying for lack of enough help. It became obvious that nowhere near £57 million had reached the Kurds, although £7 million, administered by Simple Truth and the British Red Cross, was accounted for and had been sent immediately in direct aid: lorries, tents, blankets, medicine and food. The £57 million claim – a gross exaggeration – would later have even more damaging effects on Jeffrey's reputation, which was not helped by his subsequent involvement in a company called Systems Engineering and Technology Co (SETCO) established to link Kurdish leaders with an American oil company to explore the possibilities of exploiting the oil and gas reserves beneath Kurdish soil in the interests of their economic independence. SETCO was set up by a close friend of the Archers, Henry Togna. Nevertheless, the Kurdish leaders were grateful that Jeffrey had at least drawn the world's attention to their plight; and Jeffrey put the £57 million claim in his *Who's Who* entry for the next seven years.

The early nineties was a period of political comeback for Jeffrey, and one of increasing glamour for Mary. The Archers were on close personal terms with the past and present prime minister and many Cabinet ministers. When Margaret Thatcher's leadership came to a messy end in the autumn of 1990, Jeffrey was well placed to support John Major, whom he had first met in 1979 when Major succeeded the MP David Renton in Huntingdon. When Major became prime minister there was speculation, naturally fuelled by Jeffrey, that he would be given a ministerial position, but there is no evidence that Major seriously considered this. Despite the friendship between the two men, Major told one colleague that he 'supped with a long spoon'. Nevertheless, in June 1992, Major gave Jeffrey a life peerage, after two previous rejections by the Political Honours Scrutiny Committee. This time, it was easier to justify because of his fundraising work for the Kurds, as well as for the party. Lord Renton, as he had become, was one of Jeffrey's proposers; the other was Lord Denham. The first time the new Lord and Lady attended the State Opening of Parliament by the Queen, Mary wore a long black taffeta outfit, only to be taken aside afterwards and told that black should only be worn when the 'court' was in mourning. She describes it as her most embarrassing moment.

As with Thatcher, Jeffrey was a source of unofficial advice and cheerful flattery, a valuable commodity for premiers whose lives are often isolated. He was popular with political correspondents who liked his name-dropping and gossip, which was rarely malicious. He went to the right parties: the Archers were among the select group of twelve who were invited to Margaret Thatcher's 65th birthday celebrations at Downing Street, and in 1991 they spent New Year's Day at Chequers with the Majors. Jeffrey was called to Kensington Palace to hear that Diana, now separated from the Prince of Wales, was going to announce her 'retirement' at a charity event where he was auctioneer. 'The Prime Minister put me in charge – at her request – on the day of her leaving public life,' he declared. She did scale down her public life, but maintained contact with Jeffrey through her work as vice-president of the British Red Cross. Jeffrey also had his own television programme, *Behind the Headlines*, a weekly afternoon talk show on BBC2 which he co-presented with the Labour MPs Tony Banks and Paul Boateng. His life was one of writing, book promoting, media appearances, charity functions, constituency visits and the House of Lords, not to mention party-giving in his new flat. The flat, still in the same block, was three levels higher and over two floors – a genuine penthouse apartment with specially built large-scale furniture and gilded decoration, and no expense spared, according to *House and Garden* magazine. One of those involved in its design, Jane Davies, said it was 'very glamorous and on a theatrical scale', but another view – from a business acquaintance – is that 'there's a sniff of fake royalty about the whole environment'. Mary was very much part of the design team and took Davies to the American Embassy to show her an interior which Jeffrey admired. To set off his collection of paintings, which included several Vuillards 'with their look-alike Lady Archer women', the walls were coated with a special 'polished plaster made from marble dust mixed with pigments'. There was even a marble staircase – perhaps with a Mary cabaret performance in mind.

At the end of 1992, Mary brought out an LP of herself singing carols with the Salisbury Cathedral Girl Choristers and the Cambridgeshire Boys' Choir to raise funds for them and the Iris Fund for the blind (as it then was) – one of whose patrons was Lord Anthony Colwyn. Colwyn, who had a dance band that some-times played at the Archers' parties, says Peter and Virginia Bottomley suggested to him that the record would be a good idea. Although he was not convinced, Colwyn put Mary in touch with various musicians. The musical arranger, Colin Frechter, was amazed that Mary was physically able to record all eighteen titles in a day or so. 'The voice doesn't usually last that long. Goodness knows how she did it, but that's Mary Archer. She's a very focused lady, very helpful, very businesslike.' For the launch, Mary's house-keeper had made mince pies, but few members of the press turned up, although Mary was able to promote it – including an 8.30 a.m. Christmas Eve appearance on *TV-am*. Mary told a friend she hoped her name would give the record novelty value and opti-mistically thought it might make at least £20,000. But, for whatever reason, it was not so profitable and Mary was disap-pointed. She was a very supportive Boys' Choir patron and did not want to let them down and, a year or so later, Jeffrey raised £1,000 for the choir. Colwyn was never told the record made any money for his charity: 'Mary's got a sweet little voice, and it would have been lovely had it worked. But as far as I know it wasn't success-ful.' In July 1993 the Iris Fund received £750 from Mary, but the girls' choir did rather better. In January 1994, Jeffrey gave them £5,000 and in June they received a further £3,000 from Mary, which they think may have been proceeds from the record. Mary then joined the Girl Choristers' appeal committee and played a large part in organising a successful fundraising dinner at Number

Ten Downing Street, hosted by Norma Major. Mary kept a meticulous eye on every detail. The evening had specially designed programmes and a colour scheme of green and blue (to echo the choir cassocks) which were also the colours of Mary's dress. She gave her fellow organisers gifts of scarves made from the same material, and arranged for the choir to have supper at the London flat before specially arranged transport took them to Downing Street. Among the guests were the wealthy Indian businessman G. P. Hinduja, who made a donation, and Ely Calil, the long-standing family friend of the Archers.

The Christmas carols marked the end of another busy year, and she was about to take up yet another honorary academic appointment as Visitor at the University of Hertfordshire. The appointment was originally for five years, but Mary's work was so 'sterling' that she was kept on for longer. Senior academics at Hertfordshire are inexplicably reluctant to discuss her contribution. By now, Mary's job with the Robert Fraser bank had ended as the company had decided to 'discontinue banking services' and therefore her consultancy. But she was still busy, remarking to a leading journalist: 'I'm very pleased about the way my CV is developing.' Mary's *alter ego* had emerged. As one profile writer noticed, there were 'hints of a Jeffreyish streak of self-promotion, of flamboyance and a hitherto undiscerned naffness'.[3]

Her new life outside academia demanded a new look. Although Mary had in the past professed to be uninterested in clothes, she had always been immaculately turned out. Her friend and holiday companion Lavinia Nourse says, 'I don't think I've ever seen her look a mess. She's got wonderful hair and she looks equally good with make-up or without it.' The former principal of Newnham College, Jean Floud, says Mary was always very elegant, and dressed well in an understated way. Jeffrey is the first to agree: 'I've never seen her not smart,' he says, although he used to urge her to spend more on new clothes, complaining that she kept wearing her old ones. 'The children and I have to say: "That is a shabby dress, burn it and go and buy a new one," and she's "Oh, I like this, no I like it; I've had it since schooldays" . . . she's been a lot better lately'.[4] Mary herself, in a style profile in which she posed in a variety of outfits, said she was a no-nonsense person. 'I've never dressed competitively. I like well-behaved clothes . . . my wardrobe is just like a filing cabinet. Something I no longer need, I chuck out.' She also thought it was better to live with the little signs of ageing, rather than try to cover them up with make-up. 'Although I have no religious objections to a facelift . . . If one thought it would do something useful with one's appearance . . . One would probably look better without bags.'[5] But the no-nonsense approach of the eighties – which saw Mary in mannish businesslike suits and classic 'Englishwoman' styles like crisp blouse and fullish skirt – was giving way to a more eye-catching, alluring – even dazzling – wardrobe. Mary was by now looking much more glamorous, partly thanks to the skills of a French dressmaker called Nicole Manier, who had made the red dress worn on the New Year's Eve television show. Mary had been introduced to the couturier by Lavinia Nourse, who was already a customer. 'Mary never wore designer things before, but became terribly glamorous. She has a wonderful figure: she's a perfect size 10. I made special occasion clothes for her,' says Nicole Manier. And Mary enjoyed parading her new image to the press: 'modelling' her clothes for *Tatler* and the *Daily Mail*. She swapped her Cambridge hairdresser for a top London salon, and bought designer shoes such as Maude Frizon and Ferragamo, whose elegant lines showed off her good legs. Her dresses became more shapely, emphasising her waist and petite figure. Mary wears a tasteful amount of expensive jewellery: always earrings, often a brooch and frequently pearls. And, following Mr Justice Caulfield's compliment about her fragrance, she has been asked many times which perfume she chooses: Caleche, by Hermes, although Jeffrey once bought her Fragonard's Soleil, for obvious reasons. Being Mary, her clothes are well looked after and always pressed and ready to go: 'I wouldn't put them away in the wardrobe if they weren't.'

Although Mary claims to have 'scruffy sweaters and jeans' there are few people who have seen her looking less than beautifully turned out. She once commented that once you have worn couturier clothes, it is very hard to return to off-the-peg. Mary is not the sort of woman who buys all her underwear at Marks & Spencer's, as Lady Thatcher was proud to do. She once told a reporter that she was 'very frugal and cautious about money', and, although this was said with a lack of irony, the journalist noted that most people would not call Gina shoes exactly frugal. She could, of course, afford the best clothes; after Nicole Manier, she bought Yves St Laurent, Valentino and Bruce Oldfield. Nevertheless, she likes value for money and says one of her favourite outfits is a black and white Valentino houndstooth silk suit which cost her £300 in a sale in Milan. 'It doesn't crease or ride up and show your thighs, which I wouldn't want at my age,' she said when aged fifty-two, although in fact her thighs were in good shape, as she has demonstrated by posing in squash, tennis and running clothes. As she allowed more sides of her personality to be on show, Mary seemed happy to reveal more of her figure; and if she was ever self-conscious about the 'flat chest' her son had once commented on, she might have been interested in an interview which was shown on breakfast television around the time she was showing her décolletage to the Lloyd's Council. An actress called Sally Farmiloe was speaking of the dangers of breast implants, of which she had experience. Sally, a former deb and proud member of Mensa, was to become Jeffrey's mistress four years later.

Along with Mary's sexy new image, *Tatler* reported there was a growing Mary Archer fan club, made up of men. A leading member is Kit Hesketh-Harvey, half of Kit and the Widow. 'She is prickly,' he explains, 'but in that lovely sort of way that makes you coo and squeal with pleasure, which any Englishman who has been brought up by a nanny instantly responds to. It's that tiny clink of ice . . . such a deliciously terrifying package when she's roused.' Another fan is Professor Michael Graetzel: 'I find her charming and not difficult to approach . . . she is very warm hearted and open . . . although a male chauvinist might have problems.' The former MP

Lord Woodrow Wyatt, clearly in the male chauvinist category, wrote that he found Mary 'very delicious'; and 'She is such a pretty girl . . . She has perked up no end since the great libel action . . . She also has very nice legs though her bottom is getting a tiny bit wider these days . . . She is much smarter than she ever used to be . . . really quite beautiful in a classical way. She has small soft hands and clear eyes and an oval face. Behind it she can be tough. Her skin is clear and pale.' In the scientific world, marginally less chauvinist, Mary's charms do not go unnoticed. A solar energy expert says: 'Certainly you would pay more attention to what she was saying because she's a good-looking woman.' And a French professor, Lionel Salem, who met Mary in the mid-seventies says, 'She was very beautiful, contrary to the vast majority of lady scientists . . . she had a sharp tongue and is very, very British in her manners and mannerisms.' Another long-standing friend and admirer, Dr Stephen Feldberg from New York, says, 'She is very bright, intelligent, certainly attractive. What's not to like?'

Many testify to Mary's coquetry and flirtatiousness, 'although it takes a few drinks,' says one. And Richard Cohen, Jeffrey's editor, says the only times he saw her unbend were her parties when surrounded by admiring senior male politicians 'and then she blossomed'. Another remembers a lunch when the Duke of Edinburgh visited Cambridge as University Chancellor and Mary 'kind of leaned into him and fluttered her eyelashes at him. Several people did comment on it and told the photographer to get a shot of it! She just lit up and radiated and was just gushing. And he kept sort of edging backwards . . .' The wife of an Addenbrooke's employee also describes her as 'an eyelash flutterer sort of woman', and a colleague says: 'She's soft and smiley with the male consultants, but prickly with me!' Several women who've worked with Mary agree that she is more of a man's woman than 'one of the girls'. Perhaps Mary's attitude is similar to that of many successful and ambitious female high-fliers, particularly those of a certain age who have had to prove themselves in a man's world. These women can appear cool, focused and calculating in professional situations, but are charming on a personal level, able to use their femininity to great effect. David McCall, the Anglia chief executive, describes this contrast as 'like turning on a light switch. She is very focused in business mode, and very animated out of it.' Another Anglia colleague, Patrick Sharman, agrees. 'We used to travel to meetings in Norwich together and I found her an extremely pleasant and interesting person.' Mary's friend Adrian Metcalfe says: 'She likes showing off, she likes pretty frocks, she likes looking pretty, she likes people looking at her knowing that she's beautiful . . . and she's quite flirtatious in a kind of old-fashioned coquettish sort of way . . . she's quite naughty really.'[6]

One of the Archers' regular guests, Sir Clive Sinclair, thinks he was cold-shouldered after bringing a much younger woman to one of the Grantchester parties. Mary herself likes to be seen with younger admirers; she partners a 'nice young man' at tennis, according to a Cambridge player. The designer Julian Dakowski – also several years younger – says he was once taken to Newnham for tea, feeling a bit 'wheeled out like a trophy'. He wishes he'd had an affair with Mary, and still goes weak at the knees thinking of an occasion when he was with her in Heal's furniture showroom when she noticed he was looking down her blouse. 'She carried on talking and just closed her blouse, and for me that was marvellous! She is fragrantly untouchable and there isn't a moment of overt sexuality.' His views are echoed by a business acquaintance who once saw her let her guard down to sing a snatch of musical comedy, swaying to the rhythm. 'She wasn't being provocative but it showed a sensual side to her, and she exuded sex appeal,' he says. 'She made my knees tremble. I think she knows how to play on a man's susceptibilities; she wants to be the academic, and she is. You want her to be the goddess who comes down from on high for you, and she does – for a moment. A lot of men find that combination pretty intoxicating because it makes them feel favoured.'

However, despite speculation in the press, there is no sign Mary has been unfaithful to Jeffrey. Years ago, Mary denied she had an 'open marriage'. In 2003 she admitted there was 'something sort of maternal now about the way my relationship with Jeffrey has evolved'.[7] Her brother David told a reporter that he would 'stake his life' on the fact that Mary had not cheated on Jeffrey. Mary collaborated on a book with her former colleague at the RI, Professor Jim Bolton; she sometimes visited him in Canada, and he stayed at Grantchester, but he says he found her rather 'cold'. He says, 'I want to make it clear my relationship with her was on a scientific level', and points out that his wife was invited along when he made trips to the Caribbean to work with Mary. Although the two scientists later fell out, Professor Bolton still has great admiration for some of Mary's professional qualities: 'Her lecturing abilities are amazing; she can present a superb lecture, with a degree of grace and decorum which is quite something to see.'

Mary finds her male confidants in the world of science, both in Cambridge and abroad. Stephen Feldberg has known Mary for more than thirty years, but he is reluctant to be drawn on whether there is a romantic relationship. 'It's not anybody's business,' he says. 'And she's married, so it's a dead end.' Modestly, he says he doesn't know if he's special to her. 'She's not about to leave Jeffrey. Why, I don't know. If she left Jeffrey I might ask her.' Feldberg, a keen fisherman and sailor, is a nice-looking sixty-eight-year-old, with a ready sense of humour. Friends have described him as charismatic and brilliant. Now retired from Brookhaven National Laboratory, he is an award-winning electrochemist, a visiting fellow of New College, Oxford, and has collaborated with Mary on a number of publications including an entry in a McGraw Hill encyclopedia of science.

More recently, at Addenbrooke's, Mary has had close professional contacts with another leading brain, Sir Keith Peters, the Regius professor of physic, said by one of her friends to be 'a great fan'. A Fellow of the Royal Society, and extremely sharp, Peters is a powerful figure. 'I would say he controls academic medicine in the UK,' says one colleague. 'He is a key mover, and makes sure he gets the right people in the job; he is highly skilled in medical politics. He knows how to get the best deal for Cambridge.' Called

'Regius' in Cambridge circles, the married Peters is a dapper, bearded Welshman; and said to be charming with women. Another acquaintance says, 'Like him or not, he just made the place buzz. He turned Cambridge round from a backwater into a major league player. And you don't do that by making enemies of people with money like the Archers.' His path has also crossed Mary's on the National Energy Foundation and at Lloyd's where, in 1992, he became a trustee of the Lloyd's Tercentenary Foundation which was set up to commemorate the first recorded reference to Lloyd's and to encourage and endow research in medicine, science, engineering and the environment. Mary had become a trustee three years earlier. 'I have great professional admiration of Dr Archer's contribution to Addenbrooke's NHS Trust,' Peters says, although unwilling to enlarge on this due to being busy with 'major national and international commitments'.

Apart from – unsurprisingly – enjoying the company of clever, amusing and powerful men, Mary is particularly attracted by rolled-up shirt-sleeves – something to do with hairy forearms, she supposes, plus the expectation that it heralds some sort of action. She once told an afternoon television audience that she found the Loire Valley a 'sensuous region', prompting the comment from her husband that he would obviously have to take her back there, but when the television programme *Love in the Afternoon* asked her, as part of its Celebrity Love Test, what would get him in the mood for love – a sexy film, a romantic song, or reading a biography – a highly amused Mary answered: 'None of the above!'[8] Ever since the libel trial, the press have been curious about Mary's fidelity. Once, when asked the direct question by a journalist: Have you had extra-curricular relationships? Mary did not deny she had, merely telling the questioner: 'That's an indiscreet question.'[9] Nevertheless, friends of the Archers see signs of affection between Jeffrey and Mary. Stephan Shakespeare wrote: 'you can see these two still find each other attractive, still delight in little touches that suggest a physical excitement. When he is standing next to her on formal occasions, you will sometimes see his hand brush against hers. Or she, catlike, will place her chin on his shoulder.' However, Richard Cohen, who worked with Jeffrey for fourteen years, says, 'I never saw Mary overtly, or covertly, make any gesture of warmth or loving-ness towards Jeffrey.'

Mary's increasingly extensive CV meant that she was spending more and more time on business matters, and there was still no sign of the book on photoconversion of solar energy that she was co-writing with Jim Bolton. Jeffrey, asked whether he would be reading his wife's work, replied, 'Yes, if I'm still alive.' In the twelve years since Mary had embarked on her opus, Jeffrey had turned out four novels, two short-story collections, and two plays, all of them successful. There was to be no such acclaim for Mary. In 1992, Jim Bolton's patience with Mary's perfectionism had run out, and he pulled the plug on the collaboration. He had written numerous scientific papers in the meantime, fifteen of them with Mary, and says he is proud of the work they did together. But he thought the book-writing project would never end. 'My interests had shifted to environmental photochemistry, so I decided to end the association unilaterally. Mary did not take it well and in fact was quite ugly about it; verbally ugly. However, it was the right decision for me; I felt that a yoke had been taken off my neck, and I could get on with the rest of my life.' The two corresponded briefly to finish off two papers in 1994 and 1996, but have not spoken since.

Professor Bolton's assessment of Mary as a scientist is one which is shared by many others: 'She is an excellent "reviewer and fixer-up". She can take a subject idea and "clean it up" so that the science is "very tidy". She is not noted for significant original ideas. I think she has the intelligence to be innovative, but she is blinded by her perfectionism. She cannot move on without every i being dotted and every t crossed.' He cites her tendency to want to rewrite over and over again. 'I remember one particular chapter, I would do a draft of it, and she would come back with all kinds of red marks all over it and come back again with another and another, and the irony was that after the fourth or fifth time we were back to what I had at the beginning. I think that was the straw that broke the camel's back.' Nevertheless, Bolton singles out two of the papers he wrote with Mary, which came directly out of the work they did on the book, as important. 'Those papers are elegant and I'm proud of working on them.'

Mary started work on another scientific book, the first of three volumes, in which she edited contributions from scientists around the world. She continued to give scientific lectures, and called on Jeffrey to help her with presentation to enliven the subject matter; he says he'd like to believe that her ability as a speaker had come from living with him for many years. For one lecture, called 'Hello Sunshine', he had arranged for special copies of the *Sun* newspaper to be printed with Mary on the front page so she could show them to the audience; at the same lecture, the actor Martin Jarvis read quotations from scientists. One member of the audience said Mary told him she practised it in front of Jeffrey. 'It was an outstanding lecture, beautifully paced, and it went down very well. She was wearing a fabulous diamond brooch she said she had borrowed from a friend.' Mary has lectured round the world for many years and is noted for her skills as an exponent: she is much more at home in front of a large audience than behind the scenes. A member of the Solar Energy Society says: 'When you run a society there's loads of stuff to be done, arranging meetings, standing at the door taking money, washing up the cups. I've never seen her do that; it's always this queenly presence; I've never seen her roll her sleeves up – perhaps they cost too much!'

Mary's presentation wasn't confined to lecture theatres; she also recorded an interview for Anglia television about more spiritual matters. The programme was called *Halfway to Heaven* and asked its guests to explain what they understood by 'heaven', with reference to people, places and art, and those who had been important to them in life. Mary chose the scientist Michael Faraday and said she was inspired by King's College Chapel in Cambridge and a sixteenth-century alabaster relief sculpture of the Adoration of the Magi in the Fitzwilliam. She also liked a poem by Sir Walter

Raleigh, 'What is our life? A play of passion', which compares life to a 'short comedy' on stage. She told the interviewer Richard Collier that 'if you are going to do good, you should start in the home and work outwards'.

But for now, there wasn't much chance to be at home, as a lot of her time was spent in one boardroom or another. In 1992, when she had been a director of Anglia Television for five years, there was a company development which would have interesting consequences. The Anglia board had adopted new rules on share transactions, in line with common practice for public companies. Directors were required to sign a copy of these rules which prevented them, their spouses, relations and associates from dealing in company equity during the 'close' period between the end of the company's financial year and the announcement of the annual results. And they had to tell their spouses officially, so Mary wrote to Jeffrey. In August, he replied on his new House of Lords writing paper:

> Dear Dr Archer, Thank you for your letter of 31 July. I acknowledge being your husband and I am aware of you from time to time. I have no Anglia shares and have no intention of buying any in the future. With best wishes Love, Weston-super-Mare X. I have long been an admirer.[10]

Having responded in this frivolous vein, Jeffrey forgot all about his letter, with disastrous consequences.

13

Needless Embarrassment

IN THE MID-NINETIES, during a time when the government was discussing cross-media ownership rules, Lord Astor, the parliamentary under-secretary at National Heritage (the department responsible) got a curious call. Lord Archer, a man he had never met, wanted to have a meeting with him. Astor was puzzled but, being a fellow Tory peer, agreed to meet Jeffrey in a room in the House of Lords, assuming it was a party rather than government matter. 'If he had come to my office, I would have had someone taking a note,' he says. When Astor arrived for the appointment, he found not Jeffrey but Mary, who said her husband would be late. Knowing that she had media connections, Astor told her: 'I'm very sorry we can't discuss anything that relates to our respective interests; we'll just have to sit here and wait.' The two sat in silence until Jeffrey turned up, saying in a jovial way: 'I'm sure you two have had an interesting conversation?' The meeting did not appear to be about anything specific, and still baffles Lord Astor. 'It might have been entirely innocent. But I haven't met either of them before or since,' he says.

This enigmatic episode took place during the time when Mary was involved in commercial radio and television in East Anglia, and, according to her colleague David Ball, had been lobbying for a relaxation in the rules on radio ownership, networking with ministers, MPs and media owners. But the managing director of Mid Anglia Radio, Stewart Francis, who was also chairman of the Association of Independent Radio Contractors, insists Mary had nothing to do with the easing of the rules, and that only the major groups had any impact. He says, in any event, the takeover of the Cambridge station by GWR in 1994 was possible under the existing rules. 'Mary's only involvement was at grass roots level,' he says. 'If she had been lobbying, it would have been ineffectual anyway.'

In November 1993, the National Heritage secretary, Peter Brooke, had announced that from the start of 1994, companies could own two major ITV franchises. Medium-sized ITV stations such as Anglia were suddenly prey for the larger ones, and there was frantic speculation and takeover activity. As a result, Anglia's future was thrown in doubt and its share price rose steadily. In December 1993, the Anglia board had received a tentative takeover proposal from MAI, the media and financial-services group run by the Labour peer Lord Hollick, whose company Meridian already held the ITV franchise for southern England. The Anglia directors had two meetings in early January and, following more negotiations with MAI, the directors were summoned to a further meeting on the morning of Sunday 16 January at Warburg's, the merchant bank, in London.

Four days before this emergency meeting, on the Thursday, Jeffrey telephoned a stockbroker (one he barely knew) to arrange the purchase of 25,000 Anglia shares and said he would be interested in buying more if they became available. The following day, his broker arranged a second purchase of 25,000 shares. Jeffrey asked that the deals should be in the name of B. Saib Esq, c/o himself at Alembic House. Broosk Saib was the friend who had accompanied him to Kurdistan in 1992; he was the son of wealthy and well-connected Kurdish Iraqi parents who had moved to Britain in about 1962. Saib owned properties in London and had been involved in several companies (including interior design) that went into liquidation, two of them with large debts. Despite the fact that Saib was accustomed to buying shares himself, the Anglia deal was arranged by Jeffrey, who asked for the shares to be bought for 'new time' so that the settlement could be delayed for two weeks, which meant no money need be paid straight away. It also strongly suggested he expected the shares to rise imminently, so he could sell them before having to settle his account.

On the Monday, the Anglia board of directors clinched the takeover deal, and it was announced early on Tuesday morning. Jeffrey immediately phoned his broker and instructed him to sell all Saib's stock, making an effortless £77,219. The deal looked suspiciously well-timed, and it wasn't long before the stockbrokers' directors were taking a closer look. They gathered to discuss the situation and suddenly realised the connection: Jeffrey's wife was a director of Anglia. 'My God,' said the brokers' managing director, David Howard, 'this is front-page stuff!' The Stock Exchange had also noticed the deals and, having received a report from the stockbroker, passed the matter to the Department of Trade and Industry which is responsible for policing share-dealing. In early February, the DTI appointed two outside inspectors: a leading accountant and a deputy High Court judge. Two days after they began their investigation, Broosk Saib deposited a cheque for £77,219.62 into his bank account.

For the next two months, the DTI inspectors conducted a rigorous and top-secret inquiry, summoning a long list of witnesses, including Jeffrey and Mary who were interviewed on separate days, and senior members of Anglia's board. One says, 'I called it the Star Chamber. We were told we mustn't breathe a word to anybody. You didn't know what the allegations were and they just fired questions at us.' Tony (now Lord) Grabiner, the barrister who represented Jeffrey, says it was 'one of the most memorable and eventful evenings of my career when we saw the inspectors'. Some questions were obvious. Had Mary told him about the takeover? Had he seen faxes or documents? Why had he ignored his promise to her not to buy Anglia shares? Why risk even the suspicion of insider-trading for what was, to him, a small amount? Why deal on behalf of Broosk Saib who could perfectly well buy his own shares? Why risk embarrassing his wife? More than a decade on, those answers are still known only to the inspectors, the DTI, and to Jeffrey, Mary and their lawyers. There has never been a convincing public explanation of this curious episode.

Unless prosecutions result, such inquiries may never be publicly known, and that would have been the case with the Anglia affair had not somebody tipped off a freelance financial journalist, Martin Tomkinson, that June. Tomkinson immediately investigated the story and took it to *The Times*. By 7 July, he had got confirmation from MAI and, unusually, from the DTI. The paper's City editor then rang Jeffrey, who flatly denied it. 'It is completely untrue. I did not buy any shares. I am not going to make a statement. That sort of accusation is libellous.' But it was true; he had bought shares; and the story was headline news the next day.

The chief executive of Anglia Television, David McCall, had just arrived for a relaxing round at the exclusive St George's golf club in Weybridge, when he was called to the phone at 8.45 a.m.; Jeffrey Archer wanted to speak to him. 'I had no mobile in those days, but I had a phone in the car, so I went back to ring him. The purpose of his call was to alert me to the fact that the story had got into the press. He didn't deny it – he said he'd done it for a friend who was hard up.' By coincidence, the very evening *The Times* was getting ready to run their scoop, Jeffrey was in the House of Lords for a debate on whether a court should be allowed to draw inferences from a suspect remaining silent. Jeffrey thought it should, a view which he revised some years later while standing in the dock.

The fact that the Anglia investigation was now public destroyed any chance, if there had been one, of Jeffrey getting a political job from John Major, which he so desperately craved. 'He was completely shattered,' said a friend (just as friends would say a few years later when Jeffrey got himself into the next scandal). The affair again illustrated Jeffrey's atrocious judgement, not to mention his lack of integrity. The share deal exposé also came at a time when stories about the conduct of Tory politicians were surfacing almost every week. Remarkably, these 'sleaze allegations' never tarnished John Major's reputation at the time, despite the fact that the biggest story of all was that Major had in the late eighties been having a passionate, adulterous affair with Edwina Currie, another minister.

At first, Jeffrey was treated sympathetically by the press and politicians, who fell for the line that his chances of a job had been scuppered by a dirty-tricks campaign. John Major gave him public support: ten days after the story broke he was a prominent guest at the Archers' annual garden party. Nevertheless, Major appointed the lightweight Jeremy Hanley as his new party chairman, the post which Jeffrey had particularly wanted. Shortly afterwards, the DTI inspectors' report – which had cost £215,000 – was on the desk of the secretary of state, Michael Heseltine, and for good measure being considered by an outside legal expert. All agreed: no further action would be taken against any of the parties concerned. Although the inspectors were deeply sceptical of Jeffrey's story, the deciding factor was the complete lack of evidence that any information passed from Mary to Jeffrey. Moreover, while insider-trading is usually motivated by money, the amount in question here was trifling to the Archers. There wasn't even a fifty-fifty chance of a successful prosecution.

Jeffrey and Mary seized on the decision not to prosecute, and gave it a typical Archer spin. 'I am grateful to have been exonerated,' said Jeffrey, although the DTI did not use that word and merely said there wasn't enough evidence to justify a prosecution. Neither inspector would comment, but, talking generally about DTI inquiries, one of them later remarked that, 'It is an inspector's job to produce a report. If the DTI with all its lawyers wants to let someone off it is up to them.'[1] The Anglia board made it plain they had supported Mary Archer, although the matter couldn't be discussed by the directors once the investigation had started, because people being interviewed were sworn to secrecy; and afterwards MAI didn't spend any time talking about what was effectively the previous board's business. But the general consensus at Anglia was that the fault did not lie with Mary. 'She was embarrassed by it, but didn't feel she was to blame. The board didn't think she had done anything wrong,' says David McCall. 'As a director, she was excellent: intelligent, lucid, very correct.' McCall says he does not believe such things can be kept from spouses anyway. 'If you are going out to a meeting in the City on a Sunday morning, it's apparent.' Another director agrees: 'Jeffrey didn't have to raid her briefcase; it was obvious. The papers were full of takeover talk, and then she tells him she's off to a meeting on Sunday morning.'

That summer, feeling exonerated, the Archers went off on a sailing holiday in Turkey. With them were a High Court judge and his wife, and the BBC's political editor, Robin Oakley, an old friend. Oakley, who was later censured by other journalists for being too close to Jeffrey, described the holiday line-up: 'When Jeffrey invited me and Carolyn [Oakley] that summer to join him on the luxurious *Taipan* for a cruise around the Turkish coast, the list of fellow guests was one no journalist would have turned down the chance to join. It included a senior former Cabinet minister [Kenneth Baker], an important figure on the American political scene and a distinguished judge.' A senior Whitehall mandarin had also been invited but did not come. Oakley summed up Jeffrey's attraction as 'an entertaining companion, a useful source of stories and a generous host of parties where you met a string of interesting people'. He said the August cruise was very enjoyable, 'even if each of us did have to give an after-dinner lecture on a subject unconnected with the day job'.[2] Kenneth Baker gave his on sleaze in the eighteenth century. The holiday was, by the sound of it, highly organised. Mary arranged a site visit somewhere in the morning, then there was time for swimming in the afternoon, followed by talks and dinner in the evening.

The luxurious yacht had been lent to the Archers by an American businessman called James Irwin who ran an Irish-American management consultancy called Impac, known on this side of the Atlantic for its annual fiction award in Dublin. In the early nineties, Jeffrey's pal Michael Stacpoole had gone to work for Irwin and introduced him to Jeffrey. The Archers and the Irwins began to see each other socially, but while their friendship flowered, Impac's relationship with Stacpoole deteriorated and he lost his job. Shortly afterwards, James Irwin negotiated a deal with Stacpoole in which Impac bought the story of his relationship with Jeffrey. The story was not published; in effect, Jeffrey, operating through Irwin, had tried to buy Stacpoole's silence. But he did not succeed, for in 1999 Stacpoole sold his story to the *Mail on Sunday* and this time it was printed, with details of Jeffrey's tax fiddle and dealings with prostitutes.

In the meantime, the press were trying to get to the bottom of the share deal story. Martin Tomkinson claimed that a firm of sleuths, Network Security, had been hired to investigate 'all aspects of my life' and that for months after the story, he received anonymous phone calls, even in the middle of the night. In the past, some newspaper editors had been sympathetic to Jeffrey – notably supportive were Stewart Steven of the *Mail on Sunday* and the *Cambridge Evening News*. But this was too big a story, and when the Archers returned home from Turkey, further damaging details about the Anglia deal had emerged. Far from merely 'giving advice' to his friend Broosk Saib, as the Archer camp had insisted, the extent of Jeffrey's involvement was clear. There were further detrimental headlines and more pressure on the Archers, as they faced criticism from all political parties and calls for the report to be sent to the Crown Prosecution Service. It was a difficult period for Mary as one Anglia director remembers: 'She was distressed at some of the allegations being made, which were wrong, and she suffered a lot of angst and looked as if she had been through the wringer. But their lawyer told her to keep her mouth shut.' Nevertheless, Mary's credibility in the City was damaged; as was the gravitas that is so important to her.

On 24 August, Jeffrey conceded publicly that, once again, he had made a serious mistake. His solicitor Lord Mishcon issued a statement which put a highly favourable gloss on the situation: 'The DTI . . . have decided that no further action be taken against anyone involved in the Inquiry. They can accordingly be taken to have concluded, as Lord Archer has maintained throughout, that this transaction was not carried out with the benefit of any insider information. He realises however that it was a grave error when his wife was a Director of Anglia to have allowed his name to be associated with the purchase and sale of shares in that company on behalf of a third party (and from which he in no way benefited) and indeed his deepest regret is the embarrassment needlessly caused to Lady Archer in this matter.'[3]

'This is legalese gone berserk,' said the reporter Martin Tomkinson. On what basis could it be said that the transaction was not carried out with the benefit of insider information? The DTI had not 'cleared' Jeffrey; the purpose of its report was to determine whether there was a case for a prosecution, and it decided there was not, although there was plenty of circumstantial evidence. And 'allowed his name to be associated' made it sound as though Jeffrey had absent-mindedly drifted into the deals. In fact, he had contacted the brokers, approved two share purchases, ordered the sale of the shares, specified that his flat be used as a mailing address, and given his reputation as a financial guarantee. Broosk Saib's only role was to cash the cheque and spend the money – which he did on a Mercedes car costing £76,000.

Oddly, Jeffrey seemed taken aback by Mishcon's statement, which he was shown by a member of the press during a promotional book tour in Australia. 'I didn't know there'd been a statement overnight,' he admitted to the crowd of reporters. Two years later, Jeffrey told a journalist that he had apologised to his wife 'because she asked me'. He claimed he had done nothing wrong, but 'she was getting the blame for something she wasn't involved in'.[4] Broosk Saib also made a statement saying he would love to speak out and clear his name 'but I dare not at this stage'. From Mary, however, there was no comment, although some years later she described it as 'very annoying and exasperating and embarrassing', and explained that Jeffrey made 'a recommendation' to a friend because he was 'kind and impulsive' just as he had been 'generous and foolish' over Monica Coghlan.[5] One commentator remarked that she 'evinced the moral superiority of a Victorian high ecclesiastic'. Many reporters have had the chance to ask her about Anglia, but only a handful have ever been brave enough to do so. The first was told his question was 'impertinent' and the most persistent, Michael Crick, was assaulted by Jeffrey's chauffeur for his pains five years later when Jeffrey was campaigning to be Mayor of London.

Anglia had now become a subsidiary of MAI, and there was a 'cull' of non-executives – two were kept on, Patrick Sharman and David Puttnam, but Lord Hollick wanted Mary out. She did not go immediately as it would not have looked good; however, she told David McCall that she wanted to leave the following February; she had anyway been on the board for nine years. Anglia was not her only interest that year; she had opened Corby power station and made a radio programme about the nuclear industry, which she said should be privatised. Assessing energy demand, she forecast road pricing in London and said that in her ideal future 'we would choose public transport and use smaller cars'.[6] (Mary uses trains and drives a BMW.) But despite her other work, it was Anglia that dominated. Mary had been embarrassed yet again by her husband, but this affair had damaged her name in the City and she would have to turn her talents elsewhere. The Tory party had been embarrassed too, and the Archers chose not to attend the party conference or hold their own Christmas parties that year. Mary did have another reason for this, as her mother had died in October from a brain haemorrhage at the age of eighty. She left her three children a net estate of £165,814, and her body to medical research. Although Mary said her father's death was one of the worst moments of her life, she did not speak publicly of her mother's, except to say that her mother was always 'there for her' during childhood and was the less strict parent.

Doreen Weeden's death had come just seven months after the

death of her younger brother, Stanley Cox. He had lived for many years in Cumbria (where his great-grandparents came from) where he worked as a technical representative for a roofing firm. Stanley and his wife, Christine, lived modestly and quietly in a pretty, rural cottage, and did not speak much about their famous relatives. When Stanley became ill, he went into a nursing home run by nuns, where he was described as 'a lovely gentleman'. A friend remembers Mary bringing her mother in a chauffeur-driven car to visit him at the home. Because Christine Cox was infirm, it was Mary's job to supervise Stanley's funeral arrangements, which she did with her customary attention to detail and organisation. 'She knew how she wanted it all,' said one of his friends.

To end a difficult year, there was another bad moment when the Archers and their sons were involved in a car accident. Their new BMW, with Jeffrey at the wheel, careered off the M25 in Hertfordshire just after Christmas as the family were travelling to Somerset to visit Jeffrey's mother, Lola. Jeffrey was unhurt, but Mary was thrown against the car window and suffered cuts under her eye and to her hand and arm. The family was taken to the casualty department at the nearby Mount Vernon hospital in Middlesex, and Mary was told she would need stitches. She opted to use her private health care policy and was transferred to a private hospital on the same site, Bishops Wood, to be treated by a consultant plastic surgeon, Douglas Harrison. Although very shocked, she left hospital the same day, and was said to be back at work soon after. Mary's decision to go private was immediately criticised by the *Daily Mirror*, which pointedly noted that 'the Archers learned at first-hand the realities of being an ordinary patient in the cash-conscious regime of the Tory NHS'.[7] A few days later there was more criticism from union leaders at Addenbrooke's NHS hospital in Cambridge, where Mary sat on the board. Calling on her to resign because of double standards, the Unison spokesman said: 'The NHS had been wonderful enough to provide her with emergency services to take her to the hospital. But as soon as she got there, and had to wait in line like other people, she wanted to go private. There is a massive conflict of interests here that need to be sorted out. How can she be involved in policy decisions at the hospital that affect thousands of people but won't affect her in the slightest?' The official also wrote to the *Cambridge Evening News*, but 'Dr Archer declined to comment'. Strangely the local paper made no reference in its news story to the fact that Mary was an Addenbrooke's director.[8]

The private hospital in Middlesex had been asked by the press whether Mary would suffer scarring as a result of the stitches. 'I wouldn't think so,' the spokesman replied. 'Dr Harrison is an excellent plastic surgeon.' In 1996, two years after the crash, Mary told a newspaper she still had scarring.[9] But it was not noticeable, and it may have been the skill of Dr Harrison's work which gave Mary the idea, and the confidence, to go ahead with plastic surgery for cosmetic reasons a few years later. But she carefully chose to have *that* private work done in America.

The Anglia affair had two postscripts. The first was the discovery that a female stockbroker called Karen Morgan Thomas – nicknamed Panda because of her eye make-up – had also made a large profit on dealing in Anglia shares. The interesting fact was that she was an acquaintance of Jeffrey's and had rung him twice during the crucial period, once to thank him for a small present. She had also made other calls to him, but her solicitor said there was no romantic attachment and the stockbroker herself vehemently denied she had discussed Anglia with Jeffrey. But so great was the concern in regulatory circles that the DTI inquiry was reopened, in August 1995, only to decide again against further action. The Anglia affair then went quiet until 1998, partly because Jeffrey was able to threaten journalists if the subject was raised, telling an interviewer 'the BBC would be frightened' to question him because he would sue immediately.[10] But eventually, during his campaign to be Mayor of London, he felt obliged to come up with a public explanation for the share deals. He now claimed that his friend Nick (now Sir Nicholas) Lloyd had suggested at a dinner party that the shares would be a good investment. This 'explanation' began to unravel within hours, as Lloyd angrily denied it and pointed out that the dinner party had been on the very day that Jeffrey *sold* the shares. Jeffrey himself rang Lloyd and asked: 'Are you sure it [the dinner party] couldn't be two weeks earlier?'[11] It was clear that Jeffrey had not given this explanation to the DTI inspectors, as they had never questioned Lloyd. It was also a story too far for Mary, who apologised to her furious former boyfriend, saying she was sorry he had been dragged into it. A year later, Jeffrey produced yet another rabbit out of his hat, this time in a statement through a new set of solicitors, Eversheds, who claimed their client had made the 'recommendation' to Saib based on reports in the *Daily Mail*. There had indeed been such a tip in the *Mail* but it is surprising if Jeffrey noticed it, as he was travelling in Kurdistan at the time. Once again, consideration was given to reopening the government investigation, but this came to nothing.

Broosk Saib is still unwilling to give his version of events, other than to say that he is a very good friend of the Archers, and thinks the Anglia affair was 'nothing but a muddle' in which he 'hardly had a role'. He says, '. . . it was a typical press thing to get at the Archers. Believe me, it was investigated by the right people. We had a whole government on our backs, and it was all left because there was no substance to it.' One explanation for Jeffrey arranging the deal is that Saib could not have afforded to gamble such a large sum, and his own broker would have known this. The deal also had to be done in a very short space of time, but this theory still leaves the question why he needed the favour from Jeffrey. Above all, why was Jeffrey so confident the shares would rise in value?

However, one dodgy deal that *could* be nailed involved Saib's friend James Archer. After leaving university James had joined a group of high-flying and publicity-conscious share brokers working for the investment bank Credit Suisse First Boston, who styled themselves The Flaming Ferraris after their favourite cocktail. It was reported they earned huge sums of money in the City; James, it was claimed, got a bonus of a quarter of a million pounds. At the end of 1998, James Archer orchestrated a series of deals on the Stockholm Stock Exchange which had been deliberately designed to reduce the level of the Swedish share indices. In effect, he arranged for the bank to trade with itself at a deviant price, but the deals were spotted by the Swedish authorities and the bank mounted an investigation. At first, Archer misled his employers about what he had done – even claiming his finger had slipped on the typewriter – and only admitted his share manipulation when confronted with information obtained at the Swedish end after an inquiry. Mary, the devoted mother, came to his defence, calling it 'a seven day wonder' and even blaming her son's employers. She said: 'He tumbled into that job very quickly and he had very little training from the bank. That team did some things they shouldn't have done, no question. But how grave was the offence; was it really a hanging offence? It's not for me to judge; I don't know all the details. But I am absolutely confident that he's a good boy at heart and he will go on and do well, and that's all that matters to me.'[12] It was a practised Archer response: make light of the offence, blame somebody else, acknowledge a little fault, and put forward your best side: the shameless approach which paves the way for a comeback.

14

Nobody's Perfect

IT WAS A BALMY SUMMER evening in Grantchester, champagne was being served in the garden before the guests drifted in for dinner. The marquee was fragrant with flowers, while the tables were decorated with glittering oyster shells and pebbles. This was July 1996: Jeffrey and Mary's thirtieth wedding anniversary – their Pearl celebration – and Mary was dressed for the part. Her couturier Nicole Manier had created a shimmering, tightly fitting gown of silvery lace, with a 'fish-tail' hem, worn with shoes made of the same expensive fabric. Mary wore three strings of pearls – a present from Jeffrey, together with pearl earrings. They had invited more than 330 friends, colleagues and neighbours – many of them celebrities and politicians – and made sure the occasion was professionally videoed and photographed. A faithful *Hello!* reporter was also on hand to note every flattering detail. Dinner was announced by the town crier for Weston-super-Mare; grace was said by Sir Martin Nourse who called Mary 'a pearl among pearls' and Jeffrey a lord among lords; Lord Wakeham proposed the toast. During the pudding course, soloists – the Three Trebles – from the Cambridgeshire Boys' Choir (of which Mary was patron) performed the duet from *The Pearl Fishers*; after dinner the Archers cut their four-tier cake which was displayed on a table specially commissioned from David Linley – Mary's anniversary present to Jeffrey – and then all assembled outside for a military tattoo by the band of the Royal Marines who emerged from a cloud of dry ice. Mary, being queen for the day, took the salute.

After a firework display came what *Hello!* described as the highlight of the evening, which 'became something of a karaoke night'. Mary took the microphone, looking every inch the showbiz professional, and began her cabaret act, accompanied by her son William. She sang a specially worded 'Well Did You Evah', working in the titles of Jeffrey's books, and her own version of 'Let's Do It'; then a 'money-themed medley specially written by her bank manager who used to be a crooner on the *QE2*' (according to *Hello!*), and ending with 'True Love', another song from *High Society*. Not all her guests appreciated her talents: one said 'she went on for hours and hours'. Others wanted to join in, including the songwriter Tim Rice, who performed a Rolling Stones hit, and Eddie Bell, executive chairman of HarperCollins, who sang 'Delilah'. 'It was tremendous fun and I am having severe withdrawal symptoms,' Mary said the following day. 'Our problem now is what do we do for our next party?'

Among the guests were Mary's PA, Jane Williams, who had done much of the organisation, and her architect boyfriend, with whom she had a stormy relationship. He had been employed by the Archers to do alteration work at the Old Vicarage in preparation for the event, and during the party began touting for work among the guests. To compound the *faux pas*, Williams supplied him with some of their addresses. Mary was very annoyed to discover this and wrote formally to Williams to say her action had been wholly unacceptable. It was one of a series of clashes between the two women that would ultimately destroy their relationship.

The guest list, which included many 'top' Tories, showed that Jeffrey had been forgiven for embarrassing the party over the Anglia share deal, and that they, like Mary, were prepared to overlook and excuse the dramas which 'befell' him. Jeffrey's grave errors and misjudgements were not to affect the gratitude which his party felt for him. 'Jeffrey Archer is my friend, has been my friend and will remain my friend,' insisted John Major loyally, reflecting the author's still huge popularity among grass-roots Conservatives. This indulgence persisted despite revelations the previous year about his character and unsuitability for public office. Jeffrey's blatant dishonesty was exposed in a 1995 biography, *Stranger Than Fiction*, written by the journalist Michael Crick, as was the astonishing news that he had a full brother called David Brown, and four half-sisters. (A later edition of the book revealed, even more amazingly, that one of these sisters had been an aristocratic high-society hostess in America, married first to a US presidential candidate and then to an ambassador – rather like a character from one of Jeffrey's novels, or Mary herself.)

The Archers' popularity with the media was also undiminished, and, following a lull while the fuss died down, both continued to give numerous interviews. Mary expounded on a wide range of topics: 'My Money' (PEPs, pension plan, academic pension, investments 'with back-up from our insurance agent'); 'Me and My God' ('I balk at the Virgin Birth'); her 'Fridge File' (juice, humous, bacon, cheese, leftovers, fruit and veg, Guinness and Coke); her two homes (works of art, beige marble, gilt chairs, glass coffee tables, red walls in London; and wood-burning stove, Bridgewater pottery, feline statuettes and cat radiator baskets in Grantchester); her health problems (depression, brittle nails, skin blotches, bony growth on heel, considering HRT); her cultural life, and even about what she wore in bed, and what was on her dressing table (cut-glass scent bottles, of course).[1]

A favourite theme for journalists and the public is the why-they-stay-together question, especially relevant after thirty years, and the Archers have their answers. Mary told a television programme that she had had an unusual marriage. 'First of all our careers are unusually different . . . and our tastes. But it has endured . . . through some extremely tough times and some much better ones and I think we've both of us taken a lot of pride in that.' She was unwilling to be drawn on Jeffrey's worst points:

'Goodness me, well nobody's perfect . . . I think it unfair to think of his bad points when I would rather, and do, think of his good points. I'm married to the man after all.' As for his good points, he was 'a tonic, always interested in what's going on, always got something to do. I thought when I met him, you know, this guy will be fun to be with and he is.'[2] Jeffrey thought the key to a successful marriage was 'to go on being interested in each other'. The fact that they didn't see that much of each other also helped.[3] Mary admitted that home without her busy husband had become the norm, but home without her cats would simply not be home. Her three animals were much more reliable than her spouse and she could be sure of finding at least one welcoming cat on the mat whenever she arrived home, although she couldn't be sure of finding her husband or children. (Comparing her cats to her menfolk, she once wrote of her slim, twin Abyssinians and her tubby silver tabby: 'I also have two sons and a husband, of roughly corresponding contours . . .') One interviewer asked the couple what they did *together*, and Mary answered: 'We sleep together for a start! We go to the theatre, listen to each other's speeches, manage two homes together. There is quite a lot of management.' Their son William was not so sure. 'I have no idea what keeps their marriage together. Lots of good luck probably. I wish I knew – if we did we could all be married for ever!'[4] Perhaps it is Jeffrey's ability to keep his wife by his side that made him an opponent of his party's bill to ease the divorce laws in 1996. He wanted more time for divorcing couples to think again, claiming that an extra six months' waiting time 'could save a few thousand marriages and a few thousand children'. Mary described herself in a television programme as 'a long distance runner in my affections' and her loyalty has been much admired, puzzled over, and analysed. So what is the driving force that ensures the loyalty is there? One theory is that it gives Mary, with her need to be in control – both of herself and of events – some sort of hold over her husband. While she gets a *frisson* from his outlandish behaviour, she also enjoys the power when he has to crawl back and apologise to her. 'It's the schoolmarmish impression she gives you,' says one observer who worked with Mary at Anglia.

The interviews ranged from the gushing ('Mary is restrained, poised and gracious . . . slim and elegant') to the spiky ('She is all clean lines and hospital corners, so much like one of those cut-out dolls that when she turns her back you expect to see two little tabs folded over her shoulders.') Mary had made a conscious decision to exploit her notoriety, rather than try to ignore it. Mostly, her celebrity was helpful to her and the organisations she supported. Although no longer on the Anglia board, and with her work on the Lloyd's hardship committee coming to an end, Mary still had an extensive portfolio of part-time jobs. She sat on a number of boards and committees which now included Copus, the newly formed Committee on the Public Understanding of Science, whose aim was to help explain science and scientific developments to the layman. She chaired the National Energy Foundation, was a trustee of the Science Museum, and had academic links to Imperial College, as well as Hertfordshire and de Montfort Universities. She was still president of the Guild of Church Musicians and was about to join the board of the Cambridge-based chamber orchestra the Britten Sinfonia, and become deputy chairman of the Fund for Addenbrooke's, the hospital's money-raising arm. She gave talks, opened buildings and attended school prize-givings, including one at her old school, Cheltenham Ladies' College, when she was asked to step in at very short notice. Sir Roger Young, a former chairman of the school's council, remembers Mary being rung up a day or two before the speech day, a big public occasion. 'There she was, looking absolutely magnificent in a marvellous huge hat, dressed up to the nines . . . she delivered a magnificent speech and it was quite a feat. She'd done prize-giving speeches before and had the basis of a good address, but she certainly adapted it very skilfully.'

Mary especially liked to take every opportunity to promote science education for women and girls, although she is not a member of the Association for Women in Science and Engineering. She told a conference that for girls to be scientifically illiterate was downright dangerous. 'Science is all about precision, accuracy and numeracy. The rest of life is about alcohol, cholesterol and protocol.' She was very willing to give time to spread the scientific word among young people. Dr Nicola Pearsall, an expert on photovoltaics, who had invited Mary to meet a group of Newcastle sixth-formers, remembers the trouble she took: 'Her flight was cancelled, but she went back into London and travelled up by train and we rearranged things; she wanted to talk to them.' However, women undergraduates were less impressed at a seminar at Imperial College when Mary was asked about the problem of sexual harrassment. 'She seemed to think it didn't exist and wouldn't even talk about it; it was distressing for the questioner and a lot of women felt it was a real problem,' said one of those present.

Mary had a huge network of influential and well-placed contacts, particularly in the Cambridge area, where she was highly prominent. When Mary first joined the board of Addenbrooke's, the appointments process was not as open as it is now; there was political patronage and people were simply approached. Mary was an obvious choice, with her links to the university, knowledge of science, and high profile locally. When she had first become a non-executive, the chairman was Dr John Bradfield, whom she had known at Trinity College. The next chairman was Tony Deakin, like Mary a staunch Conservative, and hoping to stand for the European parliament. It was just a matter of time before the board chose Mary as Deakin's deputy and she was heading for the chairmanship.

Although the chairmanship is a part-time and figure-head post, paying £20,240, it is an important position in Cambridgeshire, where Addenbrooke's is the biggest employer in the county with over 6,000 staff, and part of an internationally renowned centre of excellence in science and medicine. The city is a world leader in biomedical research, and Addenbrooke's claims this is largely due to its presence, and its important partnerships: with the University of Cambridge, the Clinical School, the Medical Research Council and the various research establishments which advance medical knowledge. Cambridge has also spawned a host of new organisations working 'at the leading edge' of new technologies. The explosion in biosciences and computer technology of recent years became known as The Cambridge Phenomenon, a title from a 1980s economic report which described the city as 'unique in Europe' in its wealth of science and technology-based expertise. The Trinity College-inspired Cambridge Science Park was founded in 1970, for commercial research, and now has more than sixty-six companies, while in 1999 the county was dubbed 'Silicon Fen' when the computer giant Microsoft announced that Cambridge would be its European headquarters. As the local writer Fulton Gillespie says in his booklet about the hospital: 'The magnet which has drawn these and many other organisations to Cambridge is the University and its various partners . . . [including] the Medical Research Council, Addenbrooke's Hospital and the big drug companies . . . just outside Cambridge, the Sanger Centre, founded in 1993 by the Wellcome Trust and the MRC, is sequencing a sizeable chunk of the . . . human genome, the blueprint of life itself.'[5] It is not surprising that someone as able and ambitious as Mary was keen to be identified publicly with one of the most important medical centres in the world.

She had also kept strong ties with the university chemistry department, which she regarded as 'home', although her scientific relationship with the department had ended in 1986 when she left Newnham and Trinity. She gave a sizeable donation to the refurbishment appeal and became a member of the Chemistry Appeal Advisory Board – yet another fundraising body – along with distinguished scientists such as Sir Alec Broers, the then university vice chancellor, Lord Butterfield (a former vice chancellor), and Professor David King (now the government's chief scientist) as well as with many leading members of industry including Sir Richard Sykes, former chairman of GlaxoSmithKline and now the rector of Imperial College, and BP's chief executive Lord John Browne. In 1996, she also became a trustee of the Cambridge Foundation.

Mary was taking on so many responsibilities that she would have been lost without her PA, Jane Williams. In a statement to a tribunal some years later, Williams said that her employer 'regularly admitted to being over committed, which Lord Archer and her sons would badger her to reduce. I sometimes tried to persuade her not to take on additional responsibilities and to take more leisure time in order to help balance her life. However . . . she always insisted that she preferred to be busy.' Williams had come second in the 1996 PA of the Year Award, but nevertheless found her employer increasingly difficult and demanding. She said that Mary would invariably be at her desk in her nightgown when she arrived at work, and also worked late into the evening and at weekends. Even on holiday she worked several hours a day, and whenever she was met at an airport, she wanted her PA to ensure a supply of work for her to do during the car journey home. Mary was a perfectionist: 'She was extremely particular about order, cleanliness and tidiness,' said Williams. 'She would, for example, edit and re-edit wording, timing and other fine details of everything she undertook. I recognised that, when dealing with scientific work, this was vital. However she would extend this practice to every other area she dealt with.'[6] Family and friends asked Williams to encourage Mary to take regular breaks, but without success. Jane Williams became more than just a secretary; she was working in the Archers' home and closely involved with most aspects of their lives. Her worst job, she said, was to take an old family cat to be put to sleep.[7] The PA also claims that she once had to stand in for Mary as dinner speaker at a Cambridge college, because Mary had preferred to accept a subsequent invitation to Glyndebourne. Williams says she was instructed to tell the dinner guests that Mary had been called to an urgent meeting at Lloyd's. In addition to Williams, Mary also employed a part-time secretary to work on the Archers' archives, and from time to time, research students helped her with her scientific writing.

'Mary never seems to lack the ability to find the time to do things which she regards as important,' says Sir Denis Rooke, the former chairman of British Gas, and one of her fellow Science Museum trustees. When he retired in 1996 after thirteen years on the museum board, he and his wife were 'stunned' during his retirement dinner to find that Mary had organised an 'entertainment' for him. Mary and another trustee, Leopold de Rothschild, joined in a duet to sing her adaptation of a Flanders and Swann song about thermodynamics, and songs about railways; she also asked other trustees to do 'turns'. Sir Denis says it was extremely well done, and very enjoyable. Mary told some of the trustees that she would have loved to have worked in cabaret. 'I am a wannabe cabaret artist,' she told Radio 3 listeners in 2003.

While Mary was too busy, Jeffrey was lacking a challenge and still hankered after a life in politics. Despite his complete unsuitability for public office, he wanted the excitement and the influence; he wanted to make a difference. Jeffrey quite openly said, 'I *love* danger.'[8] As so often in the past, he felt compelled to take the risk, to see if he could get away with it; and this time his goal was Mayor of London. 'Arguably the second most exciting job in England!' he asserted. 'The London mayor will receive more votes that any politician in the history of this nation . . . elected by millions . . . That will give him a unique authority and independence . . .' There had been talk of a London mayor (not to be confused with the Mayor of the City of London) for some years and it became last-minute Labour policy while Tony Blair was leader of the Opposition. Within days of Labour's election in 1997, Jeffrey was being mentioned, and touting himself, as a contender. His tactic was to go in very hard at the beginning and stay there, and his campaign effectively began in the summer of 1997; he had already been to meet mayors in America, Moscow and Jerusalem. He had huge advantages over potential rivals: fame, time and money, although later his spokesman said that he 'was not spending any of his own money' on the campaign. And in the aftermath of the Conservatives' election defeat, the question of the London mayor was the least of their concerns. The new leader, William Hague, was committed to ridding his party of sleaze and to giving members more say in party affairs; but these two aims conflicted in Jeffrey's case. He was the embodiment of sleaze, yet much of the Tory rank-and-file loved him. Jeffrey told the writer Gyles Brandreth that he sat down with Mary, James and William and said to them, 'If I go for it, we're all going to have to face the past.' To his shock, Mary backed him one hundred per cent. She told him: 'You're going to have to be very different. You're going to have to be serious . . . to show people you can do the job.'[9] Now that Jeffrey had hit upon a role for which she thought he was suited, she gave her blessing, saying it was 'a terrific ambition', a job he'd do extremely well and she very much hoped he'd make it; she knew he would give it all he'd got. For his part, Jeffrey said: 'I want to be able to face Mary and say: "That's what I did,"' and he wooed London voters with the promise that Mary would bring her 'immense intellect' to the job. There were plans for a 'two-for-one' act, with Jeffrey as the showman and Mary the brains; he wanted her as Commissioner for the Environment.[10] Mary's enthusiastic backing of the mayoral bid, given what she knew about her husband, seemed again to show surprising lack of judgement as she was well aware there would be huge media interest. One Lloyd's member commented in a forthright personal view: 'Mary certainly likes Jeffrey taking risks, and she found that exciting. I would say in some ways she had caused some of his misfortunes.'

Jeffrey began assembling an election team of more than a hundred. It was headed by Stephan Shakespeare, a former teacher and unsuccessful parliamentary candidate who became his campaign manager, and his treasurer was Greg Hutchings, the chief executive of the Tomkins Group, who was subsequently investigated by auditors for allegations of impropriety and 'corporate excesses' in his own company, although he settled out of court. Jeffrey's prodigious energy and enthusiasm came into its own. He began to lobby every conceivable organisation with an interest in London affairs; he set up a 'front organisation', the London Forum, which had a website and discussion meetings; he gave hundreds of interviews; he put huge emphasis on attracting ethnic minorities; he developed radical and imaginative policies; he began a rigorous keep-fit regime for himself in his personal gym in the London flat, employing a personal trainer called Karen, who was also used by Mary. When abroad, he stressed his contacts with important people, such as Diana, Princess of Wales, whose funeral he attended: 'Yes, I knew her very well. In fact, I was very flattered to be put just behind the family in the Abbey.' Incredibly for the man who liked to bully the media, he promised to run his mayoralty with openness and freedom of information, although his helpers did not register his own database with the data protection authorities – as required by law – until his campaign was in its third year, and Crick's biography *Stranger Than Fiction* was banned from a bookstall at the mayoral hustings.

It was incredible that Jeffrey – and Mary – thought he could run for mayor without ever explaining Anglia, given that one of the mayor's jobs would be to promote London's integrity as a world financial centre, but the polls suggested he had a good chance of winning. Even his son James's suspension – and eventual sacking – from his job, in February 1999, over the illicit share-rigging, did not seem to dent his popularity. By this time, many journalists had forgotten about the Anglia affair, and Jeffrey did not hesitate to threaten those who asked a few difficult questions with legal action. The Tories seemed incapable of stopping him, but the anti-Archer forces were gathering, among them the *Evening Standard*, whose editor, Max Hastings, was horrified at the prospect, believing that for a man with Jeffrey's history to become the public face of London would make it a laughing stock. He commissioned an article entitled 'Why this man is unfit to be Mayor' written by Paul Foot, who had first exposed Jeffrey's dishonesty in *Private Eye* thirty years before. Jeffrey retaliated by stressing, as he always does when under attack, his charity work and claimed that Hastings was waging a vicious campaign against him. 'People are sick of journalists asking about it [his past],' he said. 'I'm worth £50 million. I do more for charity than every single member of the *Evening Standard* put together and I challenge them. I've been to

152 functions in this city this year, raised £3.2 million and Max Hastings was not at one of them.'[11] Hastings, said Jeffrey, 'cares as much about London as Humpty bloody Dumpty'.

Even before the mayoral campaign got underway, Jeffrey spent a lot of his time attending charity functions, acting as auctioneer to raise money. It was at one of these events, the Two Cities Ball in November 1996, that he had met Sally Farmiloe, a determined and attractive go-getter and publicity seeker, but brasher than Mary and blonde. In her younger days, Farmiloe had once been photographed topless on a hang-glider and been an actress in the BBC series *Howards' Way*. She also had a beauty and showbiz website, and her writing paper proclaims her membership of Mensa. It was through Mensa that she had become friendly with the Archers' friend Clive Sinclair, who describes her as 'a super girl; very, very nice, terrific'. Like Jeffrey, she was an active Conservative and party fundraiser and claimed to 'hold the largest balls in London'. Soon she was Jeffrey's mistress. The couple often had sex at Jeffrey's flat but also, she claimed, in the Café Royal, in Jeffrey's mini and on the floor of an underground car park in Mayfair.[12] Farmiloe's pet name for Jeffrey was 'Wonderboy' – she says because he always got away with things.

Jeffrey's new mistress was no stranger to cosmetic surgery, having had breast implants;[13] and soon his wife decided that she, too, should improve her appearance. Although still a good-looking woman in her fifties, she undoubtedly had in mind the high profile she would have as Mayoress of London, should Jeffrey win. Mary had told interviewers in the past that she was unworried by ageing, and in 1992 had commented disparagingly about *The Golden Girls* in the TV programme, saying they looked 'nipped and tucked . . . and not remotely human'. But now that she was starting to lose the flawless looks for which she was famous, her views also changed. As was shortly to emerge, she travelled to America around the start of 1998 for cosmetic surgery. The fact of her facelift was known only to those closest to her. The secrecy is illogical, as it is usually perfectly obvious when someone has had cosmetic facial surgery. Mary's new look was hinted at in the press, and noticed by doctors at Addenbrooke's. 'It was abundantly obvious she'd had a facelift,' says one consultant, 'although I agree she looks very good.'

Equally amusing to the inhabitants of Grantchester was the cosmetic alteration to a piece of sculpture in bronze commissioned by Jeffrey for their garden. At an exhibition, Jeffrey had admired the original plasters of a flock of sheep and a naked man, all life-size. Local sculptor Chris Marvell said the figure was known as 'the shepherd with the big plonker'. He had just cast the bronzes when Mary told him she thought the shepherd was rather too well-endowed, and wanted him scaled down. 'Christopher, can't you just do me a little Greek number?' she delicately enquired. 'It was a bit surreal,' says Marvell, 'but we just chopped that one off and we remodelled another one. I've still got the piece I took off!' Mary declared herself pleased with the result; perhaps with the grim satisfaction of a woman used to a life surrounded by arrogant men.

In 1998 the Archers took another holiday on James Irwin's luxurious 152-foot yacht, this time up the east coast of America from New York to Cape Cod. They took a party of at least a dozen friends, including the judge Sir Martin Nourse and his wife, and the politician Malcolm Rifkind. When the group arrived in Cape Cod they stopped off to visit Professor Sir Hans Kornberg, the former Master of Christ's College, Cambridge, and his wife, Donna, who had been party guests at Grantchester. Lady Kornberg says, 'The yacht was enormous. It had a jacuzzi, a gym, private bathrooms, a grand piano in the sitting room. It was the most impressive thing I've ever seen on the water!' Sir Hans, twice winner of Mary's New Year's party quiz (prize: a box of cheeses; runner-up: Sir Martin Nourse) describes her as: 'intellectually restless. She doesn't feel that just sitting around and eating and exchanging small talk is a good way of spending an evening, while people are intellectually alive, which I applaud ... I was associated with the Marine Biological Laboratories in Woods Hole, which has the most complete manuscript library for ancient biological manuscripts on the eastern seaboard. Mary asked if she might look at those things, so a colleague of mine arranged for a curator to open up the library and special collection on the Saturday morning so the yacht party could go and have a look at it.' Lavinia Nourse says Mary was good fun on holiday. 'We did a play reading and she was by far and away the best; she's a very good actress. We read *Hay Fever* and she played Mrs Bliss, the author's wife. She's one of those irritating people; whatever she does, she does extremely well.'

In 1999 Mary was duly appointed vice chairman of Addenbrooke's NHS Trust, on an apparently unstoppable run to become chairman, although there were mutterings about her suitability for such a position, given her profile as Jeffrey's chief apologist. But Mary is highly able, experienced at board level, and knows a great many influential people in Cambridge, and her politics chimed with those throughout the county. Meanwhile, Jeffrey's campaign to be Mayor also looked unstoppable, despite one or two warnings from Conservatives who were sure he would get them into further trouble. But he had assiduously courted the right people as well as every constituency. He made endless speeches, and entertained lavishly. The party had a new Ethics and Integrity Committee but Jeffrey was not referred to it, despite a complaint from a fellow Tory, Sir Timothy Kitson. Instead, William Hague, who had set up the committee, was happy to accept Jeffrey's offer of the use of his private gym – another clever move by the peer. But Hague was not alone; Thatcher and Major supported Jeffrey and eight former ministers put their names to a letter endorsing him as the mayoral candidate: Howard, Rifkind, Fowler, Lamont, King, Mawhinny, Lilley, and Parkinson, although Lord Parkinson had not seen the letter and was never asked for his consent – though in fact he did support Jeffrey. Michael Ancram, the party chairman, did make one attempt to question Jeffrey: he asked for an assurance there was nothing further to emerge which might embarrass the party. No, Jeffrey reassured him; there was nothing. As one newspaper observed, if the police treated criminal suspects like that then our jails would be empty.

As well as giving her looks a makeover, Mary was trying out a new persona – acquiring some of what she thought of as Jeffrey's bouncy and cheerful 'Tigger-ish qualities'. (Jeffrey himself acquired a Tigger T-shirt – a gift from John Major.) She admitted to one interviewer that she might not have been touchy-feely enough when she headed the Lloyd's hardship fund: 'I'd never really dealt with people before, I'd always dealt with things. I'd dealt with students but students are a very special sub-category of people.'[14] She thought that she'd be a better campaigner now, and to the writer's surprise Mary kissed her and the photographer goodbye at the end of the interview. She also attended the hustings meetings which decided on who would be the Tory candidate for mayor and she was with her husband when the results of the final ballot were declared – Jeffrey had won by a large majority, the culmination of a brilliant campaign and his greatest political triumph.

The announcement was made at Conservative Central Office in October 1999, but as Jeffrey turned up with Mary for the result to be announced to the assembled media, there was none of his usual ebullience. Rather, he looked terrified. As the couple walked into the building, Michael Crick shouted a question about Anglia and was elbowed aside by Jeffrey's campaign manager (and City of London JP) Stephan Shakespeare, before being grabbed by Jeffrey's driver, and pulled violently away from the scrum. The driver was later given a police caution. The event descended into farce, with nervous party officials banning all questions from journalists, and taking Crick into a side room to try to prevent him entering the press conference. The party chairman, Michael Ancram, had vanished, and it was left to the hapless MP Shaun Woodward to announce the result.

The following week, Jeffrey and Mary were given an enthusiastic welcome at the party conference. Mary stood on the platform wearing a smart red suit and acknowledged the applause. William Hague welcomed his selection, describing Jeffrey as a man of probity and integrity. Hague later admitted that his own backing for Jeffrey was his biggest mistake as party leader, but in fairness to

Hague, he was saddled with the Archer phenomenon in the wake of John Major's reckless endorsement and the peerage he gave him. Within six weeks Jeffrey would no longer be the candidate for Mayor; within four months he would no longer be a party member; and within two years he would be in prison.

One person who did not want to see Jeffrey as Mayor of London was TV producer Ted Francis, an old acquaintance with a score to settle. He was still smarting about an episode ten years earlier when Jeffrey had misrepresented and insulted him in public. Ted Francis had some devastating ammunition: Jeffrey had asked him in 1987 for a false alibi for his libel court case (although Francis says he had not realised the reason at the time). Francis also had a useful contact, the publicist Max Clifford, who set to work. At the beginning of November, just as Mary was taking up her appointment as Addenbrooke's vice chairman, the *News of the World* (also with a score to settle) arranged for Francis to entrap Jeffrey into talking on the phone about the false alibi. This alibi had involved Francis writing twice to Jeffrey's lawyers saying he was having dinner with the novelist at an Italian restaurant on Tuesday 9 September 1986. Shortly afterwards, Jeffrey gave Francis £12,000 for a television project. In the taped call, thirteen years later, Jeffrey brushed off the dishonesty, explaining to Francis that the false alibi didn't matter because the court had not, in the end, needed it.

By Friday 19 November, the *News of the World* was ready to break the story, and its editor confronted Jeffrey, who immediately realised his campaign was sunk. Two years of hard work had been scuppered in a few minutes. Stephan Shakespeare and Jeffrey's other main aide, Nadhim Zahawi, tried to persuade him to stay on, but the Conservative party would not hear of it, and told Jeffrey he must resign. Mary knew nothing of this until late in the evening, although Jeffrey said she was the first person to be told all the details. Both she and Jeffrey had Friday evening engagements; he was giving a prize-giving speech in Surrey and she was at a fundraising event at Addenbrooke's. A guest at the dinner, Bob

Satchwell, says, 'Mary was full of beans because we'd raised so much money. The next day when the story blew she appeared in a TV report and I remarked on the difference in her body language. I cannot believe she knew on the Friday evening.' Caroline Lane, a member of the fundraising committee, also remembers Mary was 'as normal; she carried out her duties as professionally as always'. According to Stephan Shakespeare, who became his mouthpiece for the next eighteen months, Jeffrey drove to Grantchester late on Friday night for another of the 'free and frank' discussions with his wife which were now rather familiar. 'Not easy. Not easy,' he told Shakespeare. Mary later said she thought the alibi affair was 'trivial' but she immediately realised it would have catastrophic consequences. She felt bewildered and angry and the marriage was undoubtedly under strain. Later, she confessed on a radio programme she 'did think about' her loyalty.[15] Yet, in encouraging his bid, she had been hugely responsible. Common sense, let alone intelligence, should have told her that they were courting disaster. But as observers close to them have noted, she enjoys the excitement and danger that Jeffrey brings.

Jeffrey returned to London on Saturday with Mary and issued his resignation statement: 'Thirteen years ago, I asked a friend of mine, Ted Francis, to cover for me by saying that we were having dinner together, on the evening of September 9, 1987 [an error – he meant 1986] when in fact I was having dinner with a close female friend at a restaurant in Chelsea . . . Of course I should not have asked Ted to cover for me, even though it was beyond question that I was in the restaurant that night . . . I am unwilling to put my family or the Party through six months of sustained attack. I am grateful to be able to rely on the strong support of my wife and children as I withdraw my candidacy, and return to my writing career, my work in the House of Lords and my involvement with charities.' Jeffrey allowed the press to identify the 'close female friend' as Andrina Colquhoun. In fact, she had been on holiday in Greece at the time, and had nothing to do with the restaurant dinner, but Jeffrey had not spared her this unnecessary public exposure. To make matters worse, he even phoned her to let her know she was going to be involved when the story broke the next day, claiming he was sorry and had tried to keep her name out of it. Colquhoun was completely horrified. As always, she refused to comment publicly and her brother Alex spoke for her family. 'Jeffrey Archer is a pain in the ass and always was,' he said.[16]

The immediate consequences of the resignation, which over-shadowed the news that Tony Blair and his wife were going to have another baby, included enormous press coverage; hypocritical crit-icism from Conservatives; the hounding of Andy Colquhoun; Jeffrey's referral to the Tory party's Ethics Committee; and, most serious, the start of an investigation by Scotland Yard into whether Jeffrey and Ted Francis had committed perjury and perverted the course of justice. Two jurors even came forward to say they would have taken a different view had they known the truth, one saying she felt 'hoodwinked' about the state of the marriage.

Monica Coghlan, the prostitute vilified at the libel trial, also had her moment: 'Now we know this happy marriage was a sham. I told the truth; he ruined my life.' After some soul-searching and talking to people close to her, Mary made up her mind to put the best face on it, and, once again, came to Jeffrey's defence, promptly earning herself the headline: 'Is Mary Archer the new Hillary Clinton?' as she stood by her erring man. He had retreated to Grantchester and was said to be 'extremely upset, extremely sorry, destroyed, on the floor'. But within a week the rehabilitation process had begun. As Stephan Shakespeare remarked: 'Lying low in dignified defeat is not an option for a man of his peculiar char-acter.' Jeffrey began sending out handwritten letters of apology, and the couple called in a photographer to capture a stage-managed scene of domestic harmony. They were shown together at their kitchen table, with Mary's obliging and photogenic cat Stan nearly stealing the show. Mary issued a disingenuous statement saying she was 'cross with Jeffrey' but she had 'formed the judgement that he is a decent and generous spirited man over 35 years. And that will not change over one weekend or over any number of weekends.

We are all human and Jeffrey manages to be more human than most.' The cool control of this assertion was somewhat undermined by another from her brother, David. 'This has wounded Mary deeply,' he revealed. 'Inside she is very hurt and upset.' He added, 'The pity is that he didn't have enough faith to share the problem with her 13 years ago. There might have been a somewhat different outcome to this whole business if he had.'[17]

One of the many sympathetic letters sent to Jeffrey was from his friend and former Tory MP Gyles Brandreth, who had also written an article in which he said that Jeffrey had 'made fools of those of us who have defended him down the years'. Brandreth, who readily acknowledges he has benefited from Jeffrey's generosity, says he got a frosty reply: 'You can either hunt with the pack or sympathise with the prey. You cannot do both. Yours sincerely, Mary Archer.' Brandreth says his letter was heartfelt and he wrote back to Mary because he wanted her to know that, because Jeffrey had put his life in the public domain, he felt it was legitimate to write about him candidly in public as well as sympathise and understand privately. He heard no more from her.

But the hounds were unleashed and felt liberated from the threats of Jeffrey's writs. There was a string of stories about him, including damaging revelations from his former friend Michael Stacpoole that Jeffrey had paid him to go abroad during the libel trial so that he would not be called as a witness; allegations of business dishonesty, and deception at a charity auction; a claim from a new source that Jeffrey's main alibi witness in the libel trial, Terence Baker, had confessed to friends that he had told a pack of lies; and further details of how Jeffrey tried to get other witnesses to change their stories. The *Star* newspaper discovered the four-year affair between Jeffrey and Sally Farmiloe and its fashion expert was wheeled in to assess Farmiloe's sex appeal: 'Short skirts, high heels, stockings, lots of cleavage, perfect hair and make-up . . . Mrs [*sic*] Archer would probably rather die than be seen in a miniskirt . . . I suspect the only thing Mary Archer feels like doing with stockings is knotting them around her husband's neck and pulling very tight.' Mary had found out about Farmiloe in a distressing manner, Stephan Shakespeare related. 'When the Farmiloe story broke, Jeffrey thought Mary might not find out about it if the newspapers were kept away from her ... Obviously it made it worse when she did find out, via the shouts of reporters on her doorstep. If this marriage is going to break, I thought, it will be now. But it didn't.'

One of the most stinging articles was written by the feminist Beatrix Campbell of the *Independent on Sunday*, who said Mary was not merely tolerating a horrible husband, 'she has profited by him ... She harvests power and influence from the consequences of his alleged corruptions ...' Jeffrey didn't win that libel action, Campbell said – Mary did. 'The judge invented Mary Archer ... What she did not confess, however, was that they were also leading separate lives ... But Mary Archer's testimony and her unexpected tears in the witness-box were consummate propaganda. She was both sanctified and sexualised ... After the libel trial she instantly acquired a public persona that was swiftly rewarded by public positions. This was the kind of woman the men of the Establishment could do business with.' Writing of the Archer's kitchen photo-call, Campbell says: 'The *mise-en-scène* choreographed by Mary Archer is not just that of a woman standing by her man ... This cold, clever woman orchestrates the performance of loyalty as if she finds excitement in his abasement ... she is crucially connected to his degradation ... [She] has put herself and her skills at her husband's service. She basks in his risks ... when this self-defined "dispassionate" woman stands by her humbled husband, she is by no means abject. She is awesome.'[18]

More distressingly, Scotland Yard's Organized Crime Group began a thorough inquiry; and the *Star* newspaper demanded its money back from the 1987 libel trial. They claimed compensation of £3 million, made up of the original half-million pound damages, plus legal costs and interest. And the Tory party began an inquiry into whether Jeffrey had deceived the party chairman with his assurances; they eventually found that he had, and expelled him for five years, calling what he did 'dishonest and disreputable'. This was a grave blow to someone who had been associated with the party all his life, but Jeffrey soon managed to brush it off, even being allowed to resume his seat on the Tory benches in the Lords as if nothing had happened. Mary herself continued to be a party member and often attended local party events in Cambridgeshire.

The Archers cancelled their Christmas parties, but went ahead with a Millennium Eve party – although they abandoned plans to appear in fancy dress (Jeffrey as Dick Whittington and Mary in a black catsuit as his puss). About eighty guests turned up to the black tie evening, including Sir Malcom Rifkind, Lord Wakeham and Donald Sinden. Mary grandly called her event Feast for the Millennium and asked the composer Guy Wolfenden from the Royal Shakespeare Company to compile a selection of music from every century. Having ruled out instrumentalists as too expensive on Millennium Eve, Mary decided on songs and poetry, and seven men from King's College Cambridge, called Collegium Regale, agreed to perform. (Wolfenden merely asked for his expenses to be covered, a generous offer which Mary accepted.) Among the poems read by an actress was 'Warning' by Jenny Joseph: 'When I am an old woman I shall wear purple . . . I shall make up for the sobriety of my youth. I shall go out in my slippers in the rain And pick the flowers in other people's gardens. And learn to spit.' According to Stephan Shakespeare, Mary had planned twenty-three songs, but Jeffrey had cut this by half, and 'even then it was long'. The first part of the evening was about Time, and the second act, after dinner, was called Fairest Isle with folk songs chosen by Mary. At midnight, the guests went out on to the balcony of Peninsula Heights to watch the fireworks over the Thames. The evening was rounded off by Mary performing 'What's a Girl Like You Doing in a Place Like This?' and 'Come the Wild Weather', dedicated to Jeffrey – whose friends knew he was facing jail.

Despite his claims to be feeling broken, Jeffrey soon bounced back with a contrite interview on ITV, which Stephan Shakespeare had persuaded him to do against the advice of his lawyer, Lord

Mishcon. Shakespeare said he was able to get from ITV 'the best possible conditions' including 'a final veto over the whole interview'. Mary, 'steady and calm in a crisis', had also thought it a good idea, and pleaded unsuccessfully with Mishcon to change his mind. In the event, the interview went ahead, with Jeffrey admitting to Martin Bashir he made 'a mistake'. But Jeffrey always moves on, doesn't look back, has no regrets: 'I don't regret the past at all. What's the point of regretting? No, it's me sitting here . . . with £50 million in the bank, not you,' he had said in 1997. He 'dusted himself off' by signing a new book contract, and wrote another courtroom drama, called *The Accused*, which was based on a true story. It was breathtaking chutzpah. Like his previous play, it involves a man who is suspected of poisoning his wife, but this time the lead would be played by Jeffrey himself, who had somehow managed to stay an Equity member for twenty years. The play's audience would be asked to act as the jury in the case, and vote guilty or innocent at the end. The final scene reveals the 'truth' of the case – except that there were two different endings depending on which verdict the audience gave. Jeffrey's intention was to rally support among his many fans in the hope that they would 'acquit' him: he would be vindicated with a public endorsement that he was not guilty. A number of commentators were concerned that the play was mocking the criminal justice system and was in itself a contempt of court; even Mary's appearance on *Question Time* provoked comment. Others argued that an innocent man should be able to 'lobby' the media in his favour.

But soon life was imitating art, and on 7 April 2000, at a prearranged appointment at Mitcham police station in south London, Jeffrey Archer was arrested on suspicion of perjury. Mary found out from the press waiting at her gate. As was his right, Jeffrey refused to answer any police questions, but five months later, at 10.18 a.m. on 26 September 2000 – the very day his play *The Accused* opened in Windsor – Jeffrey was charged on five counts: two of perjury, two of perverting the course of justice, and one of using a false instrument, a diary.

A month or so before Jeffrey was charged, Mary had flown to Snowmass, Colorado, to attend an international solar energy conference, organised by her friend and fellow expert Dr Arthur Nozik. Her talent as a performer had already been demonstrated at a previous conference and she was asked to sing a cabaret as after-dinner entertainment for about 500 delegates at the conference banquet. Mary was naturally enthusiastic about the idea, researching in music shops for songs about the sun. 'It was an interminably long cabaret,' she recalls cheerily. 'I had a very fine sparkly dress and a very handsome young bass baritone called Gabriel.' Mary even made a CD of the performance for her fans, but it was not to be the start of a transatlantic career in musical entertainment. 'Nobody's asked me back since,' she said. 'I feel my talent is best suited to a smaller room.'[19]

15

For Better, For Worse

IN THE LATE 1980S, leading UK scientists were making plans for their part in one of the most important scientific projects of the twentieth century and beyond: the Human Genome Project, which would map the biological information of human life itself. Much of the UK work was done at the Laboratory of Molecular Biology (LMB) on the Addenbrooke's site – the place where the DNA scientists Crick and Watson had worked; and at the nearby Sanger Centre named after Fred Sanger, who developed protein sequencing methods. In 1986, Sydney Brenner of the LMB was instrumental in a bid made to the prime minister, Margaret Thatcher, for extra funds to launch a UK Human Genome Mapping Project. The bid had been prepared by Professor (now Sir) Keith Peters of her Advisory Committee on Science, later Regius Professor of Medicine at Cambridge. In 1993, a chemist called John Sulston moved from the LMB to become the director of the Sanger Centre, and was later awarded the Nobel prize for medicine for his work on the genetic map. Sulston was also instrumental in making the sequence information freely available to everyone.

In the summer of 2000, when he and the Genome Project were much in the news, Sulston received an email from Mary Archer, whom he scarcely knew. She told him she was going to be entertaining some important guests, including Denis and Margaret Thatcher, who had expressed an interest in the Genome Project. Mary wanted the future Nobel prize-winner to give them a pre-dinner talk about his work. Sulston, a firm believer in freedom of scientific information – and a helpful and modest man – agreed. He turned up at Grantchester in his old car, with his computer and projector, along with a colleague, Dr Richard Henderson, the director of the LMB. A makeshift screen, a sheet, had been rigged up above the Archers' mantelpiece, and the VIPs assembled in the sitting room. After the short talk, there were questions about genetic determinance and its social consequences although one of the guests, businessman Herman Hauser, was more interested in which companies he should invest in. An hour or so later, Margaret Thatcher was heard to remark: 'That was the best talk I've ever heard!'

The guests, who included Cambridge academics, were formally dressed in black tie and Sulston cut an incongruous figure in his casual clothes and sandals, but neither he nor his colleague – two of the country's most distinguished scientists – stayed for the meal. Richard Henderson says: 'We and our wives were invited to pre-dinner drinks, but not to dinner', although Sulston himself thinks he might have been asked, but anyway had another engagement. 'John was the cabaret,' says Henderson, 'and then we were sort of turfed out.' They drove off in their beaten-up old cars, which had been parked among the brand new limousines used by Thatcher's security team, and Jeffrey expressed astonishment that world-class scientists should be driving vehicles which were at least twelve years old. But as he says in his book about the Genome Project, *The Common Thread*, Sulston always felt there was more to life than money.

Several of that evening's guests had links to Lucy Cavendish College in Cambridge, which provides opportunities for women over 21 to study, and was founded by women determined to challenge the exclusivity of Cambridge. Lucy Cavendish was at that time looking for a new President, and Mary was very keen to get the job. Characteristically, she and Jeffrey were forward about using their contacts. 'To be frank, the dinner was part of a wooing campaign,' says one. The guests were being 'stroked' in the hope they would nominate Mary, but they were unwilling to be manipulated: 'I think in the end, she put her own name up,' says one of those present that evening.

Cambridge colleges are very coy about how they recruit people to the top jobs. Someone can express an interest, or be recommended, but are 'invited' in to meet the fellows before a shortlist is drawn up. In the case of Lucy Cavendish, several women professors at the university were approached, although Mary was seen, too. Quite apart from whether her academic credentials are good enough, Mary is a controversial figure to appoint, because she is seen to carry 'baggage': one Cambridge academic says: 'It's partly because of her husband and partly because of her own willingness to expose herself to the media, as if she were trying to become a celebrity in her own right. I think any college would have reservations about having a head of house who brought that sort of thing; it's very un-Cambridge. Colleges do not like hordes of press people outside their doors.'

Mary's name had already been linked (perhaps thanks to the Archer publicity machine) with another Cambridge College – Wolfson – in 1993; and a diary column close to Jeffrey predicted she would be appointed Provost of an Oxford college, Queen's, in 1998. Queen's swiftly denied she was even on the shortlist. There are many academics vastly more distinguished than Mary, and a college headship was not forthcoming by the millennium. She had an excellent chance, however, of success in another arena, and a very public one: Addenbrooke's Hospital. She eventually decided to put in an application to the NHS Appointments Commission for the job as chairman of the local NHS Trust. 'I do like running things, that's for sure,' she once admitted.[1] Her CV was becoming weightier than ever: she took on several more boardroom roles: chairman of the Chemistry Department steering committee; president of the National Energy Foundation; president of the UK branch of the Solar Energy Society, which she had helped found in the seventies; and had a visiting professorship at the Centre for Energy Policy at Imperial College. She also served on the council of the Foundation for Science and Technology, which provides a prestigious and neutral platform for policy debates and the exchange of views between senior scientists, businessmen and government officials. She was also employed several times as a 'facilitator' for events run by a company called The Corporate Theatre, which provides challenges to leading business people through artistic and theatrical experiences. Mary was an enthusiastic supporter of these aims, and highly paid, but some of the delegates thought her a bit too prescriptive, although 'her breadth of knowledge was appreciated'.

In February 2001, flooding affected much of the country, and Grantchester was no exception. Mary's ground-floor office in the folly near the river was especially vulnerable, and Jane Williams moved to temporary accommodation in the house as several inches of water lapped round the power points in the office. Mary, however, chose to stay in the folly, sitting at her computer on a garden chair, wearing Wellington boots and an anorak. Jane Williams thought this was bizarre behaviour, but Mary was proud of it, and took a snapshot of herself (partly for insurance purposes) which she gave both to her PA and to the chemistry department's newsletter *Chem@Cam*: '. . . as the picture shows, she didn't let little things like that stop her continuing her sterling work for the dept. Mary . . . has been instrumental in raising £1 million for the refurbishment of Lecture Theatre 1.' The newsletter's editor then was the award-winning science writer Dr John Emsley, who had first met Mary at Imperial College and later shared an office with her at the chemistry department. 'She used to give me news items and bits of gossip for the newsletter. We had some common ground because we were both involved with the media. It was her job to raise money from individuals and companies, and she went to the USA to do that.' Although *Chem@Cam* is an internal magazine, Mary gets plenty of publicity in it. There is an impression that the still largely male world of Cambridge chemistry appears to protect Mary as their 'glamour girl', just as the undergraduate male scientists of her Oxford days felt she was 'theirs'. One local observer says: 'She likes to be the star of the show, to be – like her friend Margaret Thatcher – a woman in the midst of a group of males. She would arrive for board meetings a couple of minutes late – to make an appearance.'

Among the news items that Mary gave Emsley was one about her being awarded the Melchett Medal by the Institute of Energy, which is given for 'outstanding professional activities in energy, the results of which have been made available to the community'. More controversially, she also supplied the newsletter with a spoof 'Hazardous Materials Data Sheet' composed for the joke element 'Woman'. Its list of Physical Properties included: 'boils at absolutely nothing, freezes for no apparent reason; melts if given special treatment; bitter if used incorrectly.' Its Chemical Properties included 'affinity to gold, silver, platinum and all precious stones; greatly increased activity when saturated with alcohol'; Tests on it showed: 'pure specimens turn bright pink when found in their natural state; turns green when placed alongside a superior specimen'; and its Hazards: 'highly dangerous except in experienced hands; illegal to possess more than one, although several can be maintained at different locations as long as specimens do not come in direct contact with each other'. This clever exercise (which can be found on the internet) cheered her up but did not go down well with feminists in the chemistry department who went to complain to the Head of Department. They were even more annoyed when they saw Mary's 'Data Sheet' reproduced in the *Daily Telegraph*.[2]

While Mary was photographing herself sitting in floodwater in Cambridge, another of Jeffrey's female 'specimens' was in her element in sunny South Africa. Fifty-one-year-old Nikki Kingdon, a leggy blonde, was photographed strolling along a beach near Capetown, hand in hand with the novelist. 'What'll Mary say?' screamed the paper's headline. A grim-faced Mary said nothing;

she might ignore the infidelities, but she doesn't like publicity about them. Two days later, it was revealed that the 'mystery blonde' was a Yorkshire-born, three-times married, glamorous wife of a plastic surgeon, who had met Jeffrey in the food hall of a Knightsbridge store. She cut short her holiday and flew home amid torrid publicity. This time, the media was losing sympathy for Mary: 'Yet again we're treated to pictures of the long-suffering, famously fragrant Holy Mary of Archer, stoically shuttling off to a tennis game in the face of yet another betrayal,' wrote Vanessa Feltz: 'Yet again we're invited to admire the woman's loyalty while feeling compassion for her heartbreak. Do me a favour. This is one tough old broad who knows exactly what the package is. There's only one fragrance in the Archer household and that's the smell of money. As Jeffrey himself tellingly said: "She has had a remarkable life with me, with remarkable privileges." . . . A business deal is a business deal.'[3] Geoffrey Levy in the *Daily Mail* noted that the cheated wife stayed cool and barely interrupted her routine, while the mistress was in a terrible flap. 'But,' Levy added, Mary 'does have crucial help . . . of close and good friends, people like fellow Cambridge academic and financial expert Viscount Runciman . . . to turn to for the kind of support and intellectual stimulus that even Jeffrey at his most solicitous cannot provide.'[4] Runciman, a distinguished social theorist, denies being a confidant, saying he hasn't kept in touch with her, while Jeffrey himself said it was not Mary's style to desert him – although she had every right – because she was so loyal. As one feature writer pointed out, Jeffrey must have nerves of steel to have the courage to pick up another mistress when he was already in deep trouble.

The trial date for Jeffrey's perjury case had been fixed for the middle of May, but his lawyers first tried to get it postponed on the peculiar grounds that it would be heard during a general election campaign. Delaying tactics were a hallmark of the defence, and the week preceding the trial was listed for legal argument, partly about whether Jeffrey could get a fair trial in the light of all the publicity about him – notwithstanding that much of it was self-engendered.

In the end, the trial did not begin until 30 May. Mary meanwhile had finally completed the first volume of her book *Clean Electricity from Photovoltaics* and threw a launch party in the rector's residence at Imperial College, which had published it. Jeffrey attended and the jolly gathering of scientists heard Mary thank her husband, 'but for whom my book would have been finished much sooner'. Among those acknowledged in the book's preface are her sons, her long-standing friend Stephen Feldberg, and Jane Williams. Contributors to the book, which is a compilation of chapters written by a number of specialists in the field, speak of Mary's insightful comments and meticulous editing, including the layout because the manuscript had to be submitted 'camera ready'. Dr Tim Coutts says he had never known an editor who paid the attention to detail that Mary did. 'After she had checked my manuscript, I received it back with all these traditional proof reading marks on it, in her handwriting – I had to consult a publication guide to translate!' The book's launch was a bright spot in an otherwise traumatic year for Mary. Hard on the heels of news of Jeffrey's latest infidelity came the preliminary results of the inquiry into her younger son's share dealing. A week later, an even bigger news story hit the headlines: Monica Coghlan had been killed in a car crash.

The circumstances of her death were startling; even more so given that she was the third person connected with the 1987 libel trial prosecution case to be involved in a serious road accident. Her Ford Fiesta had been hit head-on by a Jaguar driven by what the tabloids described as 'a doped-up gunman fleeing a robbery'. A local man, Gary Day – who later admitted manslaughter, had held up the owner of a chemist's shop, demanded drugs at gunpoint and fled in a stolen car. After crashing this vehicle, he flagged down and hijacked a passing Jaguar XK8; he drove along a single carriageway towards Rochdale, overtook on a blind bend and smashed into Monica Coghlan who was coming the other way. She was airlifted to hospital but died within hours. Mary Archer forebore to comment, although she posed for photographs outside her home, but Jeffrey's reaction was: 'How tragic; how ironic', adding unpleasantly: 'Was she involved in the crime?'

But the person who *was* involved in a crime was Jeffrey himself, and on Wednesday, 30 May 2001, he appeared in public in the dock of the Old Bailey to defend himself against very serious charges. Or rather, he allowed other people to defend him, because, remarkably, he exercised his option of remaining silent throughout the trial and never gave evidence in person.

Like the libel trial fourteen years earlier, there was intense public interest in the proceedings. The public gallery was packed and a queue formed an hour before the doors opened; photographers and camera crews crowded round the court entrance to see Jeffrey arrive with Mary at his side. As in the libel trial, Mary's appearance was of great interest to the tabloids who commented that she looked as if time had stood still: 'The intervening years only appear to have altered one thing – [her] taste in fashion.'[5] Lynda Lee-Potter said: 'She wore high heels with a short skirt showing off her stunning legs. She'd dressed for show and she acted for show. She posed deliberately for the photographers, looking at them with unsmiling hauteur. Her message was clear for all to see: "I'm not cowed, ashamed or hiding away . . . I don't want your sympathy or your pity."' The stage-managed air of Mary's arrivals with Jeffrey aroused curiosity, as did the fact that she only stayed in the building for a short time, before leaving by the back door.

Inside court 8, there were three legal teams, an impressive line up: Jeffrey's QC was Nicholas Purnell, a former chairman of the Criminal Bar Association, who had earlier refused to give reporters his name; solicitors from Mishcon's were headed by Anthony Morton-Hooper. The prosecuting QC was David Waters, who had recently successfully prosecuted Jonathan Aitken for perjury. Ted Francis's barrister was the equally eminent silk Roy Amlot, then chairman of the Bar Council. Presiding over the trial was Sir Humphrey Potts, a distinguished judge who had made legal history when he adjudicated in Britain's first war crimes trial. The Archer trial was his last before retirement.

Jeffrey faced a total of seven charges, two of them added at a late stage, but during the trial these were reduced to five counts: two of perjury and three of perverting the course of justice. His co-defendant, Ted Francis, who faced just one charge of perverting the course of justice, sat a few feet away from him in the dock, but the two men avoided looking at each another. Both pleaded not guilty to all the charges. The essence of the case was that Jeffrey Archer had instigated a false alibi for his 1987 libel trial, asking Ted Francis to lie for him in two letters to Mishcon's. (He had asked Francis to pretend the two of them were having dinner at the Sambuca restaurant on Tuesday 9 September, as a 'cover', he claimed, for the fact he was really dining with 'a female friend' which he said would have upset Mary.) In addition, Jeffrey had provided his secretary with a false diary – a blank A4 diary for 1986 – together with a list of entries to be written in it; and he had concealed the existence of the real diary, which was a smaller A5 *Dataday*. He then gave the fake A4 diary to his solicitors for use in the legal proceedings; swore an untrue affidavit in relation to the diary; and lied on oath about the diary at the libel trial. The 2001 case was therefore very complex: it concerned a previous trial; it had two defendants who were linked, although not for all the evidence (most evidence related to Jeffrey alone, some to just Francis); and a confusing number of diaries of several kinds were involved. The case against Ted Francis was that he had provided the alibi in the knowledge it might be used for the libel action, and not just to deceive Mary.

As with the libel trial, the huge publicity was an additional strain on all the participants. So extensive was the coverage about the first day in court that Jeffrey's barrister complained once more to the judge. He took particular exception to a piece written in *The Times* by Matthew Parris which referred to 'legal argy-bargy'. Parris's view, doubtless shared by most non-lawyers observing the case, was: '. . . as a new millennium begins, it becomes increasingly clear that what the legal profession needs is . . . a stick of dynamite up its *obiter dicta*'. Unamused, the judge threatened the press with 'serious consequences' saying: 'everybody in this case is straining every nerve to ensure that Lord Archer and Mr Francis get a fair trial'.

Parris noted that Jeffrey appeared to be riveted by the legal argy-bargy, and that during the prosecution's opening address, he opened a notebook and began to write, 'looking up from time to time like an exceptionally motivated student'. Beside him were rows of pens in several colours, and some Post-it notes. For much of the time, Jeffrey did write copiously, but often this appeared to be personal correspondence, or he doodled, or sometimes sighed loudly. Sometimes he would look exasperated; sometimes he nodded his head and said 'right'; he occasionally looked up at the public gallery above him as if to search for friendly faces. As the case unfolded, several familiar themes began to emerge: diaries, mistresses, methods used by the press, expenses fiddles, payments to potential witnesses, even bankruptcy.

The prosecution's main witness was Jeffrey's former PA Angela Peppiatt, whose evidence lasted six days. She told the court that Jeffrey paid her well and she was dependent on her job because she had been left by her husband, who had gone bankrupt, and she had no home and two children to support. She said that early in 1987, a few months before the libel trial, Jeffrey had given her a brand new diary for the previous year together with a handwritten list of engagements, which he asked her to put in the new diary for Monday 8th and Tuesday 9th September 1986, telling her the diary was needed by the lawyers for the trial. She did what he requested because she wanted to keep her job, but felt extremely concerned; Jeffrey reassured her with the excuse that his lawyers had said the real appointments diary, her own A5 diary, would be politically sensitive. Nevertheless, so worried was Peppiatt that before taking the diaries to Mishcon's, she took photocopies of the real diary entries, the list, and the new diary. She eventually put them away in 'a commercial storage place' for safekeeping and there they stayed until 1999 when the Ted Francis alibi came to light, and the police came to see her. What they discovered was explosive evidence.

During her testimony, Peppiatt was ambushed by Jeffrey's barrister, who had obtained details of her credit card account, which showed she had been buying meals and luxury items which were then charged to Jeffrey, sometimes double-charged. Peppiatt admitted she had claimed for things she shouldn't have and felt very ashamed, but she said Jeffrey had known 'full well' about it; it was part of the culture at that time, and in any case he liked her to use her credit card to buy presents for his girlfriends. She said Jeffrey or his accountants had approved all the expenses.[6] The barrister's surprise tactic was a risky one. Firstly, the judge was furious that Purnell had gone behind his back to get the authority to search bank accounts from the Recorder of London – whose offices were even along Potts's corridor. Secondly, Purnell's tactic led to further damaging claims by Peppiatt during cross-examination. She told the court that Jeffrey had paid Michael Stacpoole to go abroad during the libel trial, so that he could not give evidence; that Jeffrey had six or seven girlfriends, and was two-timing his mistress, Andrina Colquhoun, as well as his wife.[7]

Mary herself was quick to react to what she knew would be the next day's headlines – Jeffrey's affairs. She arrived for the second time with her husband, in what was clearly a publicity stunt: she was dressed for impact in an eye-catching low-cut red suit that showed off her cleavage. She stepped from her chauffeur-driven car, paused at the entrance to the Old Bailey, and ostentatiously straightened Jeffrey's tie in front of the photographers. She spent twenty minutes inside the building, and again left by the back door. The message seemed to be: 'It's not my fault if Jeffrey has affairs.'

Peppiatt's evidence continued, however, with claims that the affair with Colquhoun had still been going on at the time of the libel trial, despite the jury being told Jeffrey was a happily married man. She claimed the Archers led separate lives, that 'Andy really ran Alembic House', that she hardly saw Mary in London, and that when she did come, it caused a flurry. 'Andy would have taken down all Mary's photographs ... and we would have what we used to call 'hunt the photographs' to find Mary's photographs to

Mary was choirmistress at her local church in the eighties, and in 1992 made a CD of carols to raise money for charity. She is President of the Guild of Church Musicians.

The Archers with some of the sculptures in their Cambridgeshire garden. Mary had the life-sized shepherd scaled down because she thought he was too well endowed.

Mary and Jeffrey at home in Grantchester. It was Jeffrey who fell for the Old Vicarage first, and Mary grew to love it. 'It's just right for us' she said. 'It gives me a sense of security.' The Archers have allowed their home to be filmed and photographed many times.

Six days after Jeffrey withdrew in disgrace from the race to be Mayor of London, he and Mary stage-managed a scene of domestic harmony, complete with their obliging cat Stan. Twenty months later, Jeffrey was in prison.

'Home without the cats would simply not be home.' Mary in front of the house she loves with one of the cats she loves. She likes them because they are 'watchful, self-contained, inscrutable' – much like herself.

Mary flies the flag for Jeffrey in an eye-catching red designer outfit as they arrive at the Old Bailey in 2001 for his perjury trial. Mary gave evidence but her husband remained silent throughout.

A shocked Mary leaves the Old Bailey after hearing Jeffrey sentenced to four years' imprisonment for perjury and perverting the course of justice. Her elder son William became her escort in the months that followed.

Two days after Jeffrey's imprisonment, he was allowed out for his mother Lola's funeral, held amid huge publicity in Grantchester. The couple chose to walk from home to the church in full view of the media.

Mary and her son James visit Jeffrey in Lincoln Prison in October 2002. Mary had begun a campaign to clear his name and also helped him publicise his prison diaries – one volume of which is dedicated to her: 'The thousandth woman'.

The millionaire's wife,
after winning a powerful
injunction and damages
against her penniless
former PA, Jane Williams.
The gagging order
prevents Williams from
disclosing information
about her.

Jane Williams, Mary's
'right arm' for 13 years,
outside the High Court
in 2003. She is now
bankrupt, and has lost
her home.

Jeffrey attempts a welcome home kiss on the day he is released from prison in July 2003. His lips brushed her cheek as she turned her head away.

Top: Mary the fashion model. The silver lace mermaid-tail dress made by Nicole Manier for Mary's pearl wedding, as shown in a newspaper. Mary has appeared in several fashion shoots over the years.

Middle: Mary has always enjoyed the glitzy life Jeffrey has given her: in 2004, the couple attended a Christmas party along with the singer Shirley Bassey and the dancer Wayne Sleep.

Bottom: With their sons on the first night of Jeffrey's play *The Accused* which cocks a snook at the justice system. The lead was played by Jeffrey himself who asked the audience to vote on his guilt or innocence. A real-life jury unanimously found him guilty.

Lord and Lady Archer like to be seen at the 'right' parties. Here they arrive for dinner at Claridges to celebrate the former Prime Minister Margaret Thatcher's 70th birthday.

put them back up on the table or whatever . . . I mean, it used to be a joke actually.'[8] She revealed she had helped to dress Mary for court in 1987, advising her what outfit to wear, and she said Jeffrey had lied when he told Conservative officials in 1985 (when he was made deputy chairman) that he had ended the relationship. Peppiatt also had some damning detail about the false alibi Jeffrey had cooked up with Ted Francis: Jeffrey had asked her to research what programmes were on television so that he could say in his statement he had been at home watching television after the restaurant dinner and waiting for a phone call from Francis – all completely untrue. The implication was obvious: Jeffrey had corrupted a vulnerable employee with money and had been calling in the favours.

The next witness was the QC Michael Hill, who had prosecuted Jeffrey in the original libel case. He was asked about the two diaries shown in court at the time, one of them the fake A4 diary. Hill remembered that the diary pages had been obscured with brown paper, and bound in some way, either with sellotape or elastic bands. It meant nobody could see that most of the pages – apart from the relevant dates – were in fact blank. Hill said he had never believed the two diaries he saw were genuine, but he had been unable to probe further into their contents because of 'the rules'. Cross-examination is like fishing, he said, 'you can feel it before you can touch it'. The *Star*'s lawyers had assumed that someone from the other side had bound up the diaries and accepted them like that in good faith. Angie Peppiatt also recalled they were bound with something like packing tape.

Later that day, the court was diverted by an incident involving Max Clifford, the self-confident publicist who had brokered the Ted Francis alibi story for the *News of the World*. Clifford had been cooling his heels outside the court for several hours waiting to give evidence, and was now complaining that, if it meant cancelling another day's appointments, he might not turn up tomorrow. Mr Justice Potts was unimpressed. He called Clifford in and asked him whether he was going to come, as otherwise an order would be made compelling him to do so. Clifford was forced to admit that the administration of justice was 'of paramount importance' and that he would be attending after all. When he was eventually sworn in, what he said was interesting. His client, Francis, 'just wanted to make sure that the truth came out' and had asked only for £19,000 for his story – the price of a second-hand car plus a donation to charity – despite Clifford's own estimate that the scoop was worth £150,000. Clifford, by contrast, had been paid £30,000 by the paper.

The conduct of the press was again causing concern to Jeffrey's barrister, who objected to a headline in the *Evening Standard* which had referred to his client's 'mystery lover in Nigeria'. It was not evidence, Purnell said, but 'tittle-tattle'. The judge was sympathetic: 'It is often the case I find over the years that one sees something in the paper and one thinks "that is an interesting case to be in", and then one realises it is the one that one is doing! I think the jury may take the same view.' Purnell's concern must have been heightened by the fact that the next prosecution witness was Jeffrey's mistress, Andrina Colquhoun, one of the 'star attractions' of the trial. Wearing an expensive-looking black trouser-suit, white shirt and large ring, she spoke in a clear and confident voice to confirm that she had started working for him in 1982. She first demolished the notion that she had been having dinner with Jeffrey on the day of the false alibi; she had been in Greece on holiday with her husband. During her evidence, her former lover fiddled with his pens, putting them in a row, and occasionally looked intently at her. She had started an affair with Jeffrey in 1979, but five years later, she explained, when the chance of the deputy chairmanship came up, 'he thought it would be better if he tidied up his personal life'. The affair gradually faded away, though not completely; she was still seeing him until mid-1987. She occasionally stayed overnight, or dined with him privately.[9] She arranged flowers for the flat, and Jeffrey still gave her presents, but when she was cross-examined by Jeffrey's barrister about a list of credit card purchases claimed by Angela Peppiatt – such as designer shoes, and items at

Harrods and Asprey, she repeatedly answered: 'Nothing to do with me.' She denied she had been to the World Athletic Games in Rome with Jeffrey in 1987, as Angie Peppiatt had suggested, although the court later heard from another witness that she had been at the 1984 Los Angeles Olympic Games with him.[10]

It was apparent that Colquhoun was reluctant to be in court and that she had a lingering loyalty to Jeffrey; she was somewhat defensive about him. She revealed she had lunched with him at the Tate Gallery as recently as mid-1999, just six months before he resigned over the alibi. Asked by the prosecuting QC, David Waters, to explain the purpose of keeping their former relationship secret after Jeffrey became Deputy Chairman, she replied: 'I assume because Jeffrey wanted to show that he – I don't know; I'm sorry.' She did not recall him buying her jewellery, as alleged by Angie Peppiatt, nor could she remember hiding Mary's photographs. When shown a handwritten letter from herself to Jeffrey, she said airily: 'It appears I've addressed him by a nickname.' Colquhoun was sensitive about her subsequent marriage to Robert Waddington, and emphatically denied he had accompanied her to court. When she was asked when she met Waddington, she appealed to the judge: 'Do I have to answer that question?' The answer was 1985, when she was still seeing Jeffrey; they married in 1990.

Later that week, the jury were taken up the road to inspect court 13 at the Royal Courts of Justice, where the libel trial had taken place. The public gallery of the old Victorian courtroom had been specially dusted for the first time in years, so the press could sit and watch the visit. Two days later, Jeffrey's QC was given a shiny new document. It was an unexpected and belated statement from Mary Archer – made that day – saying that she remembered seeing an A4 office diary in use in 1986 as the main diary. It was now more than halfway through the trial and the obvious question was why she had not made a statement to this effect when she was first interviewed; it was clearly a vital bit of evidence to the defence case, which had been meticulously prepared without mentioning a main

A4 diary. Indeed, the defence had been arguing that if there *was* an A4 diary it was a forgery produced by Angela Peppiatt. Now Peppiatt had to be recalled and asked if she remembered it as the genuine diary. She absolutely did not.

More than three weeks into the trial, it was the turn of the defence to bring on their witnesses, and, with the press and public galleries full in anticipation of seeing the novelist testify, Purnell made an announcement which took onlookers by surprise: Jeffrey was not going to give evidence on his own behalf. Although the jury were entitled to draw inferences from this, Purnell explained that it meant they would have to concentrate on the prosecution's evidence, and its inconsistencies, rather than assessing Jeffrey's 'performance' in the witness-box. The central issue was: 'Is Lord Archer someone who has already lied upon oath?' and the prosecution had to make good that allegation. Instead of calling his client, Purnell summoned various character witnesses, who could have stepped straight from the pages of an Archer novel: there was a QC, a film producer, a political adviser and an Oxford academic. They spoke of Jeffrey's kind, generous and trusting nature, his loyalty and hard work. The academic, Michael Beloff (also a QC) said the characteristic he most admired was 'his capacity to raise one's enthusiasm and one's love of life, whenever one comes into contact with him'. Beloff faced just one question in cross-examination. 'I'm sure you would agree,' Roy Amlot said silkily, 'that anybody choosing to run as candidate for Mayor of London would have to be of the highest honesty and integrity?'

Next came Jeffrey's accountants, who were asked not only about their dealings with Angela Peppiatt and the expenses she submitted, but also about what had happened to the 1987 libel winnings, which the Archers always claimed went to charity but about which there were persistent question marks. The accountants could only vouch for part of the money – those donations which were covenanted for tax reasons – which left the matter rather up in the air, until the appearance of another witness who could shed more light: none other than Mary Archer herself.

There was a *frisson* in the court as Mary was called. Her friend, *The Times* sketch writer Valerie Grove, described the scene: 'We'd begun to snooze through interminable lists of dates and figures, [when] into the courtroom on neat black stiletto heels and encased in fine black stockings tripped the trim calves and ankles of Mary Archer . . . What an entrance, what a star.' Mary looked as immaculate as usual, in a black suit trimmed with purple, her hair neat and glossy. 'Her smooth rectangular face would have done credit to a woman 20 years younger,' noted another writer, 'the Ice Queen at her most regal.'[11] She gave a quick cool glance at her husband in the dock, as he and their sons William and James, now twenty-nine and twenty-seven looked on intently – the first time the whole family had been in court. Mary crisply asserted it was 'utter nonsense' that she and Jeffrey had been leading separate lives in the mid-eighties, but that it was true they were living 'a full life'. She launched into a detailed description of her circumstances as the sole breadwinner at the time, and was interrupted by the judge. 'I am just filling you in,' Mary responded sharply. 'You are certainly doing that!' replied Mr Justice Potts, amid laughter. 'We would all get on very much better if you listen to Mr Purnell's questions and answer them.' Later, Mary could not resist the temptation to give evidence for her husband, and was again rebuked by the judge. 'Please give evidence about matters that you know of . . . you are giving evidence, he is not.' It was clear by now that *this* trial judge was not enraptured by Mary's elegance and fragrance, nor her superior manner.

In a moment of theatrical drama, as befitted the wife of the author of *The Accused*, Mary then produced a set of jewellery from her handbag. Dangling the gems before the courtroom, she triumphantly announced there had indeed been a second necklace ordered by Jeffrey and it had been given to a lady who loomed rather large in his life – not Andrina Colquhoun, but Margaret Thatcher. Mary said the sets came from a South African jeweller, whereas Michael Stacpoole had alleged some years earlier that he saw Jeffrey buy a double set from Hatton Garden. Later, Mary was closely questioned about their donations to charity, and produced a list which she said showed that over the fourteen years since the libel award, they had paid out a total of £737,970. Asked to look for various individual entries, she sighed: 'It would be a lot quicker if I had my laptop and could search electronically.' Her schedule showed that tax relief (on an already tax-free award) was claimed on the larger donations covenanted over several years. The gifts included £50,000 to Brasenose College, Oxford (which has always maintained a lofty silence on Jeffrey's status there as a 'research graduate'); £30,000 to Magdalene College, Cambridge; £25,000 each to Ely Cathedral, *Cambridge Evening News* charities, Newnham College, the National Theatre and the Red Cross; and £10,000 to the Fitzwilliam; there were also 'masses and masses' of smaller ones, given to 'people who seemed in a small way deserving' as she put it.[12] At this point, some members of the jury began to snigger. 'This sum of money started our charitable giving habit if I may say so, which continues . . . to this day and will continue in the future,' pronounced Mary. Despite the clear statement made at the time of the libel award, she denied it had been their intention to distribute the money straight away, but rather 'as good causes came along'.[13] What Mary did not say, however, was that half a million pounds – even if dipped into regularly – can accrue a substantial amount of interest over fourteen years – well beyond £737,970. Indeed, the *Star* newspaper claimed the Archers now owed them £3 million.

As the hours wore on, there were further personal questions; was there strain in their marriage at the time of the libel trial? No, but 'I think we have explored the further reaches of "for better or for worse" more thoroughly than some other couples'. Was she aware of the affair with Andrina Colquhoun? 'He would hardly be the first aspiring politician to have had the odd fling.' Had she done her best to cover up for the fact of the relationship? 'Cover up, Mr Waters?' Mary demanded. 'Well maybe make light of it because at the time I discovered it, it was essentially in the past anyway. Wives are not necessarily the first to find out about these things.' Had the affair carried on in 1986 and 1987? 'You have heard more than I have heard.' Waters homed in on the impression given to the jury that Jeffrey was not a man who had affairs. 'Did you, when you heard that, have any sort of feeling of unease that perhaps the jury were being misled from what you knew?' 'I truly have no recollection of a reaction,' Mary replied, adding that it had been the prosecution's job to make such a suggestion.[14] (Two years later, Mary also told *Woman's Hour* that she had not, in 1987, volunteered any information about the affair because she had not been asked about it.[15]) Pressed on whether she knew the affair was continuing after she confronted Jeffrey about it, Mary said, 'To the best of my knowledge the affair stopped when I said it must.' Had she issued an ultimatum? 'I tend not to issue ultimata,' Mary replied with a wearily tolerant little smile. 'Let us say it was a fairly free and frank discussion.'[16]

David Waters also probed into Mary's sudden recollection that she had seen an A4 diary as the main office diary. Despite having said she regularly consulted Jeffrey's diary when she was at the flat, she claimed she could not recognise Angie Peppiatt's handwriting.[17] The exchanges became increasingly fractious, as Mary was given numerous chances to answer a question about the diary's contents. She became flustered when asked to recall its layout. Again, the judge intervened: 'You have to apply yourself, Dr Archer, to it.' In a moment of confusion about which diary was being referred to, Mary commented, 'I hope we are not about to discover another diary, are we?' 'That rather depends on you, I suspect,' replied David Waters smartly.[18]

There was huge media coverage of Mary's three hours of evidence. Nicholas Purnell later pointed out that it was perhaps an indictment on society's values that on the day the former Yugoslav president Slobodan Milosevic was returned to the International War Crimes Tribunal in the Hague, the lead story in every newspaper and on every television broadcast was Mary Archer's evidence at the trial. And her performance was scrutinised: unflinching self-discipline, thought *The Times*, but the *Mirror* disagreed: 'Mary's frosty exterior hid deep wells of bitterness, furi-ous whirlpools of anger and surging waves of hurt . . . For a proud woman like Mary Archer, it must have been an ordeal . . . [but] she was there, as she always has been.' But the tide was turning against her. She had come across as haughty and arrogant – ridiculous, even. One sketch writer noted that the jury looked unimpressed and that, at the end of it, 'Nicholas Purnell did something he didn't do at any other time during the trial. He sat down, popped two Alka Seltzer into a glass of water, knocked them back and gri-maced. The message was unmistakable: something had gone very wrong.'[19] Above all, why was she doing it? The pencils were already being sharpened for the end of the trial. It seemed to be a turning point; Mary was fast losing her fragrance, and the press would not be afraid to say so.

But there are many twists and turns in an Archer saga, and this one was no different. Three days before the jury retired, during the judge's summing up, came news that Jeffrey's mother had had a stroke and was likely to die. Jeffrey naturally wanted to go that morning to be with her. At first, the judge was not prepared to allow it. Although, he said, he wanted to reflect proper sympathy and understanding, he had a job to do, and there were certain rules. To let Jeffrey leave the dock, and to tell the jury why, would be 'a very exceptional course' and besides, there had been a similar scare about Lola's health earlier in the trial. He therefore suggested waiting until lunchtime, when he would consider an early finish. At this, James Archer stormed from court muttering, 'F***ing arse-hole.' By lunchtime, Lola's condition had worsened, and Jeffrey was allowed to go for the rest of the day, although the jury were not told why. He arrived at his mother's bedside an hour before she died; the papers knew that evening, but were prevented from pub-lishing because of contempt of court rules.

Mary, Jeffrey and their two sons arrived at court next day dressed in black; Mary sat dabbing her eyes. Mr Justice Potts argued with Jeffrey's counsel about whether the jury could be told – he was annoyed nobody had personally informed him of the death, and was not prepared to act on 'third hand' press reports. Purnell seemed taken aback. Eventually the judge explained to the jury, saying: 'I hope you will agree that the ordinary, civilised decencies prevail and everybody must, through me, express sympathy with Lord Archer because of his situation . . . I see you nod.' He told the jury that Lola Archer was eighty-eight or thereabouts, whereupon Mary, a stickler for accuracy at all times, called out from the back of the court, 'Eighty-seven!' The judge was not to be distracted from the job in hand: 'Your task,' he told the jurors, 'is to reach verdicts . . . and mine is to continue this summing up.' Among the key questions they had to decide was the conflicting evidence about the existence of an A4 working diary, in addition to the A5. Was it really credible that Angela Peppiatt was keeping two working diaries, not one? Or, on the other hand, had the A4 diary been Peppiatt's forgery, as Jeffrey's lawyers were suggesting, before they received the late statement from Mary? Mary claimed she first told her solicitors months earlier that the A4 was the genuine office diary, and yet until day 18 of the case, no such statement or reference had been included in a defence case 'prepared with enormous thoroughness'. The judge also said the jury must not be distracted by alleged affairs – 'Lord Archer is not charged with having affairs.'

The jury deliberated for more than three days; an agonising wait for the Archers. Mary, as she so often has done, found the distraction of work helpful. During the trial, she made a point of attending a prom performed by the Britten Sinfonia, of which she was a board member. 'It says much about her commitment and strength of character,' says the orchestra's chief executive, David Butcher. Two days after her mother-in-law's death, Mary (now wearing a white suit) travelled to Salisbury for the tenth anniversary celebration of the Cathedral Girl Choristers. And on the day of the sentence, she had been due to attend a meeting of a judges' panel for the Young Science Writer award, which she had supported for ten years. Roger Highfield, the science editor of the *Daily Telegraph*, which sponsors the competition, says, 'She was always very diligent in turning up, but this time she couldn't, but even so she sent in notes on the entries, which she had obviously gone through in detail.' Finally, the wait at the Old Bailey was over. The jury had been called back to be told they could reach majority verdicts, if necessary. Within an hour, they returned, having deliberated for a total of 23 hours and 31 minutes. They found Jeffrey guilty by unanimous verdicts on four charges (two of perjury and two of perverting the course of justice, namely forging the appointments diary and getting Ted Francis to lie for him). He was found not guilty on one count which related to perverting justice by making false entries into an *Economist* diary. Ted Francis was found not guilty.

Jeffrey was ordered to pay £175,000 in costs and he faced a maximum of seven years. Before the judge announced his sentence, Jeffrey's barrister, Nicholas Purnell, pleaded for his client. He said the offences were fourteen years old, and Jeffrey was now sixty-one and had given much of himself to charitable interests; he spoke of the unprecedented glare of publicity for the Archer family, with the death of Lola Archer adding to the tension: 'In 33 years at the Bar, I have never encountered a case which has taken place under quite such circumstances, in which the arrival and departure of the defendant from court each day, and every single aspect of the case, has been conducted under such stress and public attention.' Purnell told the judge that the past two years had been entirely blighted by the phone call with Ted Francis, and by the 'consequential shame', including disqualification from the Conservative party. 'My Lord,' continued Purnell, 'he has not, in the conduct of his case, compounded any untruth which was made 14 years ago by anything which was said to the police, by any evidence which he has given . . .' 'What about the evidence from Lady Archer?' interrupted Mr Justice Potts.[20] This electrifying question raised the possibility that Mary herself might now face a police investigation and perjury charges. Her evidence about remembering an A4 diary had been presented late to the court and had not changed the jury's mind.

Just before lunchtime, on Thursday, 19 July 2001, with his solemn family looking on, Jeffrey Archer heard his fate. 'I take into account everything that your counsel has said, but I am bound to tell you that I take the view . . . that these charges represent as serious an offence of perjury as I have had experience of, and as I have been able to find in the books.'[21] Not least, the judge said, Jeffrey had corrupted Ted Francis with money and he had drawn his PA Angela Peppiatt into corruption. At this point, Mary turned to her son William and remarked, 'That's outrageous.' The judge went on to recap that Jeffrey had also sworn an affidavit dishonestly and lied in court. Had the jury in 1987 known the facts, it was unlikely in the extreme that he would have won. 'Since then, I cannot overlook the fact that you have gone from strength to strength . . . You were ennobled . . . and that has to be taken into account in relation to the submission that this was a long time ago.' The judge said: 'Sentencing you, Lord Archer, gives me no pleasure at all, I can assure you. Very little in this case could be said to give any sensible person pleasure. It has been an extremely distasteful case.'[22]

Mary, wearing a large gold cross round her neck, sat with her hands folded as she heard the worst. Her husband was sentenced to four years' imprisonment; it would be two years before parole could be considered. She glanced at Jeffrey as he was led away; he did not look back at her. Mary, who thought she had learned to expect the unexpected, was in shock.

16

Prisoner's Wife

'JEFFREY ARCHER AND HIS family are shocked and disappointed . . . I can confirm that we shall be appealing . . . and the family will not be answering any questions,' said the Archers' solicitor Tony Morton-Hooper, as he faced a battery of cameras outside the Old Bailey. The handsome lawyer would find himself kept extremely busy during the next three years with legal work for not only Jeffrey but Mary, too. Inside the court, Jeffrey was getting advice from his barrister. 'Don't believe anything anyone tells you in prison, and never discuss your case or your appeal,' Nicholas Purnell told the convicted perjurer, just before he was put in a prison van bound for Belmarsh, the top security jail in south-east London. Within sixteen hours of arriving there, Jeffrey had taken a characteristic decision: he would do what he could to turn the experience to his advantage, and make money, by writing a book. At 6 a.m. the next morning, he rummaged around in his plastic bag of belongings, packed by his son William: 'Thank God for a son who had the foresight to include . . . an A4 pad and six felt-tip pens,' he thought. Two hours later he had completed the first draft of everything that had happened to him since he was sent to jail.

His supporters outside were also trying to turn the situation to advantage. Within hours of the sentence, 'agents' for the Archers were contacting national newspapers, touting Mary's story for a cool quarter of a million pounds.[1] They offered an exclusive interview with the family, and photographs of Mary, William and James; moreover, and more disturbingly, according to one Sunday paper, there was an offer of photographs from within Grantchester parish church where Jeffrey's mother's funeral was to take place just two days after the verdict. The tastelessness of this suggestion was compounded by the fact that it breached the Press Complaints Commission code of conduct, which says newspapers should not pay money to anyone convicted of a criminal offence or to their family. According to the *Mail on Sunday* and the *Sunday Mirror*, the agents responded to this difficulty by saying it was not a problem. The money would be secretly paid into a special bank account, and the name Archer would not figure in any way. Asked why the multimillionaire Archers should need the cash, one agent replied that the family had cash flow problems. The *Sunday Mirror* named one of the agents as Stephan Shakespeare – a JP who, together with a Wandsworth councillor, Nadhim Zahawi, was Jeffrey's main aide in the mayoral campaign. Both men had previously liaised with the media on his behalf, and been in businesses with him. (In 1999, Zahawi and Jeffrey had been referred to the DTI for investigation after the collapse of a company they, and James Archer, were involved in, and whose managing director accused Zahawi of forgery.[2] No charges were brought. Zahawi was also a contact of a senior journalist at the *Mail on Sunday*, as was revealed when he gave evidence to support Mary's privacy case against her PA.)[3]

There was once again enormous publicity following Jeffrey's sentence, with many papers running spreads over several pages about his life, his lies, his achievements, his court case, and, naturally, his wife. The publicity continued over the weekend, with the funeral of his mother, Lola Hayne, taking place in Cambridgeshire on the Saturday morning. Lola, the woman who in her youth dreamt of fame and fortune as a writer, was now to have one of the most public funerals imaginable for an elderly woman. Jeffrey was released on compassionate grounds to attend, but the way in which the occasion was turned into a photo opportunity was breathtaking and bizarre. 'Along with the grief,' wrote one journalist who observed the event, 'the extrovert instincts of a master showman were being shamelessly indulged . . .' Jeffrey was first taken by two prison officers in a white transit van to a crematorium north of Cambridge; following the short service, he was driven the few miles to his village, pursued by a fleet of cars and a television satellite van. Cambridgeshire police had expected he would be driven straight to the church at Grantchester, but instead, he jauntily walked into the Old Vicarage, where he spent an hour or so before the church service. Jeffrey had chocolate cake, milk and tea made by Mary's housekeeper, and took the opportunity to stroll in the garden with his wife and discuss his appeal; Mary outlined the mistakes she thought the trial judge had made, and told him she thought a re-trial might be possible. Outside were waiting dozens of photographers and even more reporters (at least sixty, estimates say), television crews, and twenty members of the Cambridge constabulary. Suddenly there was a cry of 'He's coming! On foot!' and to the astonishment of onlookers, Mary and Jeffrey and their sons led a procession of family and friends on towards the parish church. 'Keep it slow,' William was heard to say. First came James and his girlfriend, Talita; then William with Liz Tremaine (formerly Fullerton), Lola's foster daughter; then Mary and Jeffrey, closely followed by two plain-clothed officers. As they strolled the quarter of a mile to St Andrew's, with the traffic halted, the couple talked quietly to each other, Jeffrey telling her, 'Don't worry, everything's fine.' Mary wore a simple short-sleeved black dress and the gold bird brooch left to her by Lola. The service was conducted by Mary's friend the former Bishop of Ely Peter Walker with hymns, prayers and readings she had carefully chosen. Afterwards, the Archers retraced their steps, but for Jeffrey there was no more honey for tea in Grantchester; instructions from the prison governor were that he must not go back to the house. Jeffrey headed for the prison van parked in a lay-by, embraced his sons, kissed his wife and climbed aboard. As he sped off back to Belmarsh, Mary and her boys calmly walked back through the crowds to their house. The police officer in charge at Grantchester says they advised against the walk to the church, but did not want to have a confrontation in front of the world's media, and in any case the prison officers were relaxed about it. The Prison Service, however, say they were not to blame. Jeffrey himself claims a local police inspector, David Howell, who was a social acquaintance, made the suggestion; Howell himself says, 'it just sort of happened'. In any event, questions were later asked 'in high places' about it.

Jeffrey said he never wanted Mary to see him in Belmarsh, and she never did. She stuck to her plan to chair a summer school on solar energy at Strathclyde University and missed her chance to visit him, although her sons went. William accompanied his mother to Glasgow, but later flew back to London so he could join his brother for their first visit to their jailed father. Seeing the large number of journalists in the audience for her Strathclyde lecture, Mary joked: 'A special welcome to those of you who are new to the field of quantum solar energy conversion', but refused to answer questions other than to say she supported Jeffrey wholeheartedly. By the time she first visited him in jail, nearly a month later, he had been moved to Wayland, a medium security prison near Thetford in Norfolk, a forty-minute drive from her home. She made her first visit in the company of Jeffrey's agent and 'close friend' Jonathan Lloyd, who was there to discuss publication strategy for Jeffrey's prison diaries.

Six days after Lola's funeral came another headline: the ruling from the UK regulators about James Archer's share manipulation. They said he had taken part in an elaborate charade in breach of the Financial Services Act, and concluded he was the leading player in what one source called a 'cold, calculated operation – a premeditated strategy'. He had lied, prevaricated (allegedly so that he would get a cut of a reported £5 million bonus during the investigation), used 'persistence and guile' in his deception and tried to implicate his boss. The investigators rejected the suggestion that he had been inadequately trained and noted that 'his first reaction when questioned . . . was to lie.'[4] His misconduct was so grave he was banned indefinitely from being a trader, manager or director anywhere in the City. By now, twenty-seven-year-old James had already moved on, setting up a dot.com company called E-Phoenix which planned to provide meals and other services to desk-bound customers, but this failed. (Phoenix is also the name of a drug counselling service in New York where his former nanny, Liz Tremaine, works.) James's parents, as one would expect, backed him up, and Jeffrey even noted approvingly in his diary that James had now 'assumed the role of joint head of the household in charge of finance'. A week after the verdict, James and his brother, William, were dinner guests of great friends of their parents, Godfrey and Ann Barker. Unknown to their hosts, James took with him a tape-recorder and secretly bugged their conversation. He recorded the Barkers commenting about a previous dinner party in 1997 at which a guest was the judge Sir Humphrey Potts. Barker told the Archer sons that Potts had at that time given him an impression of 'generalised contempt for your father'. James gave the tape to his mother, who then tried to persuade Barker – and the 1997 dinner party guests – to make a witness statement for an appeal. They all refused; the Barkers felt betrayed and the thirty-two-year friendship between them and the Archers was at an end.

In 1988, shortly after the libel trial, Mary had written in an article for *Prep School* magazine: 'Happy is the family that adversity pulls together. You versus the rest of the world – that is a good feeling.' Now, after a second trial, and coping with Jeffrey's imprisonment, Mary relied heavily on her sons. William postponed his return to America where he was making documentary films in order to give her emotional support; James had returned from New York and was living from time to time at the London flat, and looking after his father's business. William had assumed the role of escorting his mother; he accompanied her on a working trip to Dresden, to the Proms, the Edinburgh Festival fringe and to television studios. Both helped her throw the usual Christmas party in

London. The Archer boys are a contrast to each other, and their father described James as having inherited 'all his barrow-boy instincts', and William as a 'missionary' by nature, having worked with Mother Teresa, and in Bosnia. Observers say both sons find it hard to cope with living in their father's shadow, and have reacted in different ways – William by moving away and keeping a low profile until recently, James by trying to make money. William, the older, is more artistic and, like his mother, has always enjoyed singing. He realised at Rugby school that he was not Oxbridge material and instead went to Georgetown, a good university in Washington D.C., to study art history – 'a very expensive option' said his mother – and he also speaks Italian well. In America he lived modestly, and spent several vacations doing voluntary work. He considered working for the Overseas Development Administration, tried directing plays and went into film-making. 'To be honest, I feel more of a Yank than I do a Brit,' he once said. Last autumn he publicised his debut film about his experiences of America's political system in an article in the *Mail on Sunday*. Allegedly, he insisted on copy and photo approval and a plug for his personal website. James, two years younger, is flamboyant and attention-seeking. He was captain of athletics at Eton (which was Mary's choice of school; Jeffrey had reservations about it because he had a chip on his shoulder about Old Etonians) and, like his father, a very good runner. He read chemistry, his mother's subject, at Brasenose College, Oxford, his father's old college. He flaunted his wealth at university and in 1994 a *Cherwell* reporter who visited his house found a wide range of electronic gadgets including a photocopier, satellite TV, an entertainment system, and IBM computer; James also made his life easier by employing a cleaner who did his laundry and provided breakfast, although these days he enjoys cooking. Mary said that after twenty years of her hastily prepared meals, described by one friend as 'awful', James did a Cordon Bleu course. James, like his parents, seems to enjoy the limelight and is frequently mentioned in gossip columns and 'society' pages, usually with a glamorous woman by his side. In the summer of 2004, he got engaged to Tara Bernerd, a divorced interior designer and daughter of the property developer Elliott Bernerd, donor to Newnham College and one of Britain's richest men – said to be worth £139 million. Mary said, 'We are thrilled at the prospect of adding Tara to our family.' James favours 'designer scruff' whereas William is more smartly dressed and rarely photographed with a woman in tow. William once said that describing his mother as fragrant had a wonderful ring of truth about it. 'Fragrance is the essence of Mum . . . I'm happy when she's happy, upset when she is. We're not especially physically affectionate, but I do hug and kiss her when I come home.' In 1994, William said, 'I think Mum's at her happiest when Jamie and I are around and she's quietly working somewhere. In fact, you could put her in jail for 20 years and she would probably be very happy. She'd miss the cats and Jamie and me, but she'd basically be fine.'[5]

The James Archer story was just one of many at the end of the perjury trial. Among the coverage, it was revealed Jeffrey had praised his mother's timing in dying just before he was sent to prison; Jeffrey's mistresses said they'd been told he had not had sex with his wife for twelve years;[6] politicians predicted that Jeffrey would lose his peerage; there was even an article by Dr Thomas Stuttaford, the medic lampooned in *Private Eye*, who said Jeffrey was suffering from a condition known as hypomania. (Stuttaford had known Jeffrey when they were both Tory MPs.) More seriously, there was news that Scotland Yard were considering the judge's comments about whether Mary had perjured herself with her evidence about the A4 diary.

One of the most important follow-up stories was raised by Baroness Emma Nicholson, a long-time supporter of Iraqi Kurds, who questioned Jeffrey's role in the 1991 Simple Truth fundraising campaign, a big factor in his getting a peerage. Within hours of Jeffrey's sentence, she told *Newsnight* there should be an investigation into what had happened to the £57 million he claimed had been raised; she said the Kurdish people had told her very little of the money had reached them. Jeffrey was not a likeable rogue, she said, but a 'guy who hurts other people . . . a brilliant conman'. Although questions about the £57 million had been raised before – as early as September 1991 – this time, with Jeffrey behind bars, the Red Cross and the police began investigating. Although it had not been Nicholson's intention to suggest Jeffrey had personally misappropriated any money, as a result of the investigation (which ultimately found no misappropriation or fraud), he was reclassified as a category C rather than D prisoner, which delayed his eventual move to an open prison. Mary was furious; she had already begun what would be a long, and most think misguided, campaign to clear her husband's name. Her anger and humiliation needed some release; rather than direct it against her husband, she put her energies into attacking her 'opponents'. And she clearly felt bitter. She had once commented of the earlier trial: 'Had we through some aberration not won [the libel case] then I might have been . . . permanently embittered.'[7]

Immediately after the sentence she had her say through her brother, David, who spoke on her behalf to his contact on the *Daily Mail*, Geoffrey Levy. She said the sentence was vindictive and the judge biased: 'Mary holds the view quite strongly that the judge's summing up was . . . unfairly sloped towards the value of the prosecution witnesses rather than the defence,' said David Weeden. 'She's terribly upset. Mary can take all the flak . . . but the truth is things are crowding in on her, and I think it showed in her face at the funeral.' She was also said to be furious at the possibility that Jeffrey would be stripped of his peerage, for his sake more than hers, although 'she will admit it has had its uses'. And, Mary had told her brother, she was 'angry at the very suggestion that she may have perjured herself . . . she found it deeply offensive that she might be thought to have lied . . . If there was anything incorrect in what she said, it would have been a mistake, nothing more.' For good measure, Weeden assured readers that Mary and Jeffrey slept in the same bed when they were together.[8]

In August, Jeffrey was moved from Belmarsh to Wayland prison in Norfolk, where he stayed until October, before being moved to

North Sea Camp (NSC) in Lincolnshire. The prison governor of NSC, Mike Lewis, was so taken with Jeffrey he gave him a small Christmas present (of a 1940 farthing) and Mary a birthday present (of a 1944 farthing) just before he retired – or so Jeffrey says. Jeffrey was also given plenty of top-notch advice – he supplemented his solicitors, Mishcon's, with help from friends such as the QCs Michael Beloff (an old friend who had given evidence for him at his trial) and John Nutting (the husband of one of Mary's fellow Anglia directors and now a judge). It was not long before his lawyers lodged an appeal. This was the signal for Mary to begin her media campaign in earnest, and she orchestrated it with skill. She popped up on so many programmes to defend her spouse that papers dubbed her the Avenger, and asked, 'Has she lost the plot?' raising questions about her judgement. At first, her media appearances were similar to her recent court demeanour: haughty and cool, with no concession to the style of the programme, but later, she softened her approach.

Mary's first interview was with John Humphrys of the *Today* programme, for which she had carefully prepared – she even managed to plug her book on solar energy. First, she got across her spurious message that the fundraising allegations against Jeffrey were 'entirely without foundation'. She said they had 'resulted in real harm to Jeffrey' and Emma Nicholson had 'smeared the Red Cross into the bargain . . . She is misled and misleading'. In fact, a former Red Cross official had already admitted that Jeffrey's figure of £57 million was misleading.[9] Humphrys then asked her how Jeffrey was bearing up. 'Do you know how he's spending his time?' he ventured, ignoring Mary's request that questions should not stray from the topic. 'I do indeed,' replied Mary, letting silence fall. 'And?' 'Private matter,' said Mary primly. Could she tell him about the basis of the appeal? 'No, of course I can't.' What about the possibility of charges against her? 'I would be amazed, astounded and outraged.' What about reports she had been offered money for her story – my life with Jeffrey? 'I'm not in the business of writing my story,' Mary responded. '"My Life with Jeffrey" –

that's not going to happen?' persisted Humphrys. 'That is not going to happen,' replied Mary firmly.[10] But she was soon in the business of making a television documentary called exactly that: *My Life with Jeffrey.*

As Mary knew, one interview leads to another, and a few months later she and William were sitting on a sofa in the incongruous setting of the *Richard and Judy* programme. Do you love your husband? Mary was asked. 'You're invading private territory,' was the guarded reply. 'I love all my family; perhaps I'll say that,' she continued carefully. Perhaps it had slipped her mind that seven years earlier she'd happily been telling *Love in the Afternoon* that France was the best place she'd ever made love, and that her nickname for Jeffrey was 'Beanie' (from 'runner bean'). Again, Mary attacked Nicholson, clearly angry that her husband was 'banged up 17 hours a day for ten weeks in a cell 7 paces by 3 paces, *on her allegation* . . . she blackened Jeffrey's character in an area where he's always worked tirelessly'. The possibility that Jeffrey was banged up for something *he* had done does not seem to have occurred to the Archers; once again, the blame had to be shifted elsewhere. William also went on the attack, saying he did not like the interviewer's tone. 'Why the dislike? What is there to dislike . . . it's a misunderstanding of his nature . . . he's not dishonest . . . We're here to protect [his reputation].'[11]

The Simple Truth figures were eventually analysed by the accountants KPMG, and Jeffrey's reputation for exaggeration was confirmed. Although there was no evidence of misappropriation or fraud, only £13.8 million had been raised by the British Red Cross Simple Truth Appeal in the UK. Other amounts, from corporate sources, could not be confirmed, and a figure of £31.5 million said to have been raised by Jeffrey from foreign governments was not supported by documentation and KPMG were unable to verify it. The British Red Cross 'had substantially relied upon Archer to provide the figure, however . . . he was unable to recall the breakdown . . .' The KPMG investigation also said that despite the shortcomings of 'presentation and verification', the appeal had generated widespread support and publicity for the Kurdish refugee crisis, and it praised Jeffrey for working hard to organise the concert.[12] Despite the Archers persisting in their claim that Jeffrey had raised £57 million Mary took legal steps against Emma Nicholson, seeking an apology. Eventually Nicholson issued a statement making it clear that she did not intend to suggest that Jeffrey had personally misappropriated the money. And Mary herself heard no more from the police about another contentious issue – her own trial evidence and her recollection of a 'main' A4 office diary. Mary said she had mentioned it at a meeting with Jeffrey's solicitor nearly a year before the trial, but Jeffrey's barrister, Nicholas Purnell, stated there had been no 'oversight' regarding her evidence. Mary's statement was not taken until the middle of the trial, he confirmed.[13] The police considered the judge's comments and took advice; they considered all the facts and the public interest. Ultimately, no criminal inquiry took place.

Mary's campaign was a double-edged sword, however. While she could easily get across the view that Jeffrey was an innocent victim of other people's malevolence, the very message itself was making her the object of derision. 'Her only claim to fame is that she is married to an unrelenting fibber, and is the mother of a con artist,' wrote one journalist. 'And yet, when she demands an apology, she gets one; when she sounds wounded, she garners a certain amount of support.' In February 2002, she was jeered during an edition of BBC TV's *Question Time*, in which *Private Eye*'s editor, Ian Hislop, mocked her for saying she saw the NHS 'in the round' because she was vice chairman of Addenbrooke's and the wife of a prison-hospital orderly. Later in the programme, she accused Hislop of taking a free kick when he mentioned the sleaze created by jailed Tories; to applause, he responded by saying she had put herself on a public programme and was most famous for being Jeffrey's wife. Mary glared at him icily. 'After the programme, she came straight over to me and harangued me for about twenty minutes,' says Hislop, 'asking what she had done to deserve such treatment. I told her she was a public figure and if she didn't want it she could stay at home. It's almost considered bad form to say anything – a very clever trick if you can get yourself in that position. She's been allowed to get away with it for years. In particular men don't want to challenge her; they don't want to challenge a pretty woman.' Mary's husband put it another way: 'Most men are frightened of her,' Jeffrey once told a newspaper.[14]

On *Midweek* Mary said Jeffrey had made mistakes in both his private and his public life, but did not feel remorseful about his crime. 'I think he feels, as we all do, that the whole process was very overblown and the result was ridiculous.'[15] She said he was chronicling his time in prison, which was an absorbing read: 'It is searing.' Later, in a programme called *My Favourite Hymns*, John Stapleton asked her, 'When you walk into that prison and see the man you married . . . what are your thoughts?' Generally, Mary replied breezily, 'Am I late? . . . Have I got the stuff he wants? Things like that, nothing more profound. Of course, the first time, it's a shock, but you have to cope.' And what are your feelings? Stapleton persisted. 'They're private,' Mary insisted. Interviewers usually ask why she stays loyal to Jeffrey, and Mary's replies were by now pat: Jeffrey was innocent; Jeffrey was unjustly treated; Jeffrey deserved her loyalty; leaving him was unthinkable after so long together.

Mary's serene appearance belied troubling times at home. In the months before the perjury trial, she and her PA, Jane Williams, had a bitter dispute which would lead to an employment tribunal and later see Mary in a high-profile court case for the third time in her life. The difficulties arose from a breakdown in relations between the two women, who had for many years got on well. Part of Mary's case was that she had become less reliant on her PA, as by the end of the 1990s she had given up nearly all of her commercial activities and 'refocused' on her scientific and Addenbrooke's work, where she had access to other secretarial support. Her social life was less busy, too, once Jeffrey was no longer in the running for

Mayor of London. Early in 2001, the two women had a meeting which Mary called 'very difficult'; she said Williams was tearful, rude and belligerent and wanted more money. Shortly afterwards, she found emails sent to and from Williams which were rude about her, and in one case, 'contained sexual content'. One of the emails compared Mary to the TV presenter Anne Robinson, whose screen persona is cold, rude and ruthless. Mary found the emails so offensive she called a disciplinary meeting about what she claimed was her PA's 'deteriorating performance and attitude'; she said 'it was clear to me I was not being accorded much respect from Jane'. Eventually, just as her husband's perjury trial was starting, she gave her a written warning, although she ended the letter by praising Williams's 'excellent work' and 'loyalty'. A couple of weeks later, Mary was called out of a meeting at Cambridge University to take a call from Mishcon's. The solicitor told her that Jane Williams had given a statement to the police which might be useful to the prosecution in Jeffrey's trial. In her statement, Williams said she knew that Jeffrey's driver had given inconsistent accounts of what happened to Jeffrey's diary from the original libel trial, one account being that someone had been asked to burn it. The driver had 'recounted differing versions of the destruction of the diary', Williams told the police.[16]

About a month after the trial, Mary asked her household staff, and other people working for her and her family, to sign confidentiality agreements. She even offered to pay Jane Williams £750 towards the cost of legal advice in relation to it. Williams refused to sign the agreement but she nevertheless returned to work and dealt with the letters which arrived after Jeffrey's trial. Mary had decided to review her staffing needs, and told Williams she could either work part time, or be made redundant. In November she gave her twelve weeks' notice, and asked for the return of her keys and filofax diaries. By this time, Mary was well aware of the significance of the diaries: 'I had paid for them, they had been created in the course of Jane's employment, they contained confidential information and I needed them back.' Mary also wanted to wipe the hard drive of her PA's computer, because it had previously been used by her son James (although she had already had it 'imaged' as a precaution). Williams refused, saying the diaries were hers, and there was an exchange of solicitors' letters: Mary was 'astounded' at the refusal, and legal action continued. Williams, like Jeffrey's secretary Angie Peppiatt, kept personal references – appointments and phone numbers – in her diaries and thought it was reasonable to hang on to them. In November 2001, Williams left her job after thirteen and a half years. There were no sad farewells, and the only reference Mary gave her PA, Williams claimed, was to describe her to a prospective employer as a liar and a thief.

On 24 February 2002, a front-page article was published in the *Sunday Mirror*. It disclosed that Mary had travelled to America for a facelift. Jane Williams was naturally suspected as being the source, and Mary immediately sought an injunction preventing any further disclosures. She was helped by Williams's former boyfriend, whom she approached for a statement. The man who had annoyed Mary by touting for business at one of her parties, and whom she knew had a difficult relationship with Williams, was now an ally. He claimed Williams had downloaded material from a computer belonging to Mary, with the intention of creating 'a pension fund' for herself by eventually selling the material. In March, Mary obtained a temporary order to gag her former PA, pending a trial. The judge, Mr Justice Stanley Burnton, said: 'Most ladies don't like it to be public information that they have had cosmetic surgery.' When the counsel for Jane Williams said it would be obvious to anyone who looked at Mary that she had been given a facelift, the judge retorted, 'It is odd that no one else has noticed it before now.' (In fact, it had been hinted at several times in the press.) Mary accused Williams of negotiating with a paper while still employed by her; Williams denied it. In any event, she had not sold the story; she had received no money from the press; and had herself been exploited by more sophisticated operators.

Fifteen years earlier, Mary said she could recommend taking a

High Court action as 'a sure-fire method of losing weight or stimulating a sluggish pulse'. Now she faced another one, to try to
obtain a permanent injunction against Williams. She also had to
deal with her PA's claim of unfair dismissal at an employment tribunal. And before both of those cases, there was Jeffrey's appeal,
which oddly enough was on the same day Mary had been called for
an interview with the NHS Appointments Commission for the post
of Addenbrooke's chairman. The interview was held in Cheapside,
not far from the Courts of Justice, at 1 p.m. Mary was not in court
for the 10.30 a.m. start of the hearing, when the judges took just a
couple of minutes to reject Jeffrey's appeal, but arrived for the
afternoon session in time to hear them rule on his sentence. The
three judges – who included Mr Justice Stanley Burnton, who had
dealt with Mary's injunction – said they had considered the length
of time over which the offences were committed, the involvement
of others including a vulnerable employee, the corruption by
money, the persistent dishonest conduct, and concluded that a four-
year sentence was not excessive. Mary was gravely disappointed.

On the bright side, she had done well in her job interview. The
three or four shortlisted candidates were seen by a more important
panel than usual, headed by the chairman of the Appointments
Commission, Sir William Wells. The others on the panel were an
independent assessor from outside the Cambridge area (whose
name is not made public); the Eastern Region commissioner, Rosie
Varley; and the chairman of the Strategic Health Authority for
Cambridge, Stewart Francis. Varley had worked with Mary over
the years because of her own NHS role, and Francis had known
her since their days in local radio, when she helped him raise
money for Mid Anglia Radio charities. Varley had asked for her
boss to sit on the panel because she felt it was important that they
were seen to be appointing on merit, especially since Mary was a
controversial person who excited public interest, and because
Addenbrooke's Trust was so significant nationally and internationally.

Mary duly impressed the commission, and within two days had

been offered the job. Jeffrey was delighted at the appointment, saying he wanted Mary to get the job more than he wanted to be released from jail: '. . . otherwise I would spend the rest of my life feeling that I was the reason she failed'. It was in some ways a curious appointment. Although Mary had been on the Addenbrooke's board for ten years, and had a very public profile, she was not particularly distinguished scientifically, especially in Cambridge, nor did she have significant business experience. The public are not allowed to know who the other candidates were for this important public job, nor whether the interview panel asked any probing questions about Mary's role as the wife of a convicted perjurer, particularly at a time when she was constantly in the news defending her husband; nor whether she was asked if she ever uses the NHS herself. She was, however, keenly aware that she must separate her role as Lady Archer from her NHS duties: Addenbrooke's hospital are quick to point out that Jeffrey is nothing to do with them. They deny there is an official ban on employees talking about Mary to the media – although the wall of silence in response to enquiries for this book suggests otherwise. Mary was 'the outstanding candidate,' says Rosie Varley. 'She had given a long period of extremely valuable and committed service to the NHS as a non-executive and deputy chairman, and she was appointed to the post against stiff competition entirely on her merits. People who speak to me who work with Mary have the highest regard for her ability.' Mary also charmed a security guard at the commission offices, who was 'entranced' after she had asked him where she could get a sandwich. The guard later checked to see if she had taken his advice and found her sitting right in the window of the sandwich bar.

Before Mary got to grips with the NHS, she went on holiday to Japan, where she was attending a conference. She hiked round the north island by herself before returning home to deal with yet more publicity, this time mostly as a result of Jeffrey's remarkable feat of creating self-serving headlines from inside prison, which was now North Sea Camp in Lincolnshire. First came an 'interview' in a Sunday newspaper for which Jeffrey passed on his views through his friend Chris Beetles. Then came stories that he was umpiring cricket matches, driving himself home on Sundays (even hosting a party) and signing a new multi-book deal with Macmillan, said to be worth over £10 million. Photographers seemed to be on hand at all the right moments. There was also news that Jeffrey was paying back the money to the newspapers he sued in 1987. He was still negotiating with the *Star* but agreed to pay the *News of the World* £362,000, made up of £50,000 in damages, £70,000 in costs and £242,000 in interest.

In August 2002, a highly controversial story broke: Jeffrey had started a day release job at Lincoln's Theatre Royal, and was filmed arriving in his BMW for his first morning. The job was actually part of a restorative justice project doing drama work with children, but caused an outcry about him enjoying a cushy life. Jeffrey, who loves attention, was in his element. He could easily have had discreet sandwich lunches but instead was seen out on long lunch breaks at several local restaurants. He even let himself be photographed (wearing a smart suit and tie) in a Lincoln café called The Old Magistrates' Tearoom. 'He acted without modesty or sensitivity,' says the then head of the Prison Service, Martin Narey. There was plenty of adverse comment about 'Lord Cushy' from locals and the media and a cartoon in the *Star* depicted Jeffrey getting into his BMW (with 'tax in the post' disc) dressed in a dinner jacket, being saluted by prison officers and saying: 'Don't wait up.'

The following month, Jeffrey was involved in what Mary called 'a technical infringement' of the prison rules. The couple had taken a 'detour' (of about 25 miles) to Norfolk one Sunday on the way back to the prison in order to attend a drinks party given by their friend Gillian Shephard, deputy chairman of the Tory party. Guests at the party were amazed to see Jeffrey turn up: 'It's not really a question of whether he kept within the rules,' said one, 'it's the propriety of doing it at all. It never seems to have occurred to either of them that it was inappropriate for him to be going out to parties with their friends. To say that jaws dropped to the floor when he arrived would be a classic understatement. What is it about Mary that makes her want to mother such a man? It's as though she is saying to the world, nobody touches my Jeffrey, and I'll go along with him.' It was also astonishing that Gillian Shephard, a magistrate, was entertaining in her home a prisoner only a quarter of the way through his sentence. But the Archers were once again making light of their situation; despite Jeffrey being a peer of the realm and law-maker, he was ridiculing justice. He had written *The Accused* which mocked the trial system, and had sent his friends 'Mr Toad' Christmas cards. Mary had called Jeffrey's crime of perverting justice 'trivial'[17] and had appeared disdainful of the court process, which she called 'overblown and ridiculous'.

The Shephard party was just one piece of 'a whole host of worrying information' reaching the ears of the Prison Service. It swiftly moved Jeffrey back to a closed prison pending an investigation into a 'serious breach of trust'. Prisoners were not allowed to go to parties; moreover, the extensive publicity was damaging the carefully thought-out policy of day release, which was vital in the rehabilitation of less advantaged inmates. Martin Narey, the head of the Prison Service, had to cut short a visit to prison and police officers in Leeds and travel back to London to deal with the media. Narey, who was obliged to spend many hours of his valuable time on the Archers and their antics, denied Jeffrey was getting special treatment and defended his decision to let him work at the theatre. The move to a higher category jail took the Archers aback and Mary was outraged on her husband's behalf, denying he drank alcohol, claiming he observed the rules 'punctiliously' and saying 'he wouldn't have dreamt of trying to get away with anything', but she did not help matters by adding: 'The locality of the lunch is essentially on the way back to the prison . . . prisoners are free to go out for picnics, or lunch or shopping.' She tried to contact Martin Narey, but he refused to take her call. 'They don't, of course, listen,' an irritated Mary told the television news, clearly having expected special attention. Narey, with 75,000 prisoners to consider, simply could not deal with calls from spouses unless, say, a death is involved, but he did ensure she was able to speak that day to the prison governor, Keith Beaumont.

Among the matters the Prison Service investigated was a suggestion that Jeffrey was entertaining women in a local hotel (this was found to be untrue); that he had been to the home of the prison medical officer for a meal; and that he had lunched in an Italian restaurant in Lincoln with an off-duty prison officer – who was in charge of security – along with an off-duty policewoman. The tabloids not only knew of this lunch, they had photographs of it. Narey says journalists suggested to him that Jeffrey himself had arranged for the press to be there. 'If this is true, he was prepared to sacrifice people's careers in the interests of self-publicity.' The prison officer, who had broken the rules, immediately offered his resignation. Mary, who took the view that her husband's behaviour was entirely reasonable, again sprang to Jeffrey's defence in numerous interviews saying she thought 'double standards' were operating. She was sorry the prison officer had lost his job. 'I think the Prison Service has gone into overdrive following the orchestration of another tabloid splash . . . Jeffrey acted no differently to any other prisoner . . . I will of course be looking to see whether they have followed proper procedures in all of this . . .'[18] She was asked if she felt betrayed that the party-going had been leaked. 'I've become very used to betrayal,' she said bitterly. But it was possible that any 'tabloid orchestration' had been contrived by her husband – known throughout Fleet Street as brilliant at feeding the papers – partly to provide a platform for his next headline grabber – the publication of his prison diaries.

The image that the Archers wanted to create was business as usual: Jeffrey was writing, making money, seeing friends, researching with contacts, lunching with 'an attractive blonde' (as he called the policewoman), spending weekends at home, partying with politicians. 'If there has been a technical infringement, he would have apologised,' said Mary. Business as usual.

Her pleas that Jeffrey should be treated like any other prisoner were somewhat at odds with her husband's extraordinary behaviour, and sounded all the more hypocritical when, a few days later, she was on the front page of the *Daily Mail* to promote Jeffrey's *A Prison Diary* (volume 1), which was published the following week. 'We meet in Jeffrey's Thames-side penthouse, a vast temple of stone, blonde wood and fine art,' gushed the *Mail*'s reporter. 'The room is museum tidy . . . a butler fetches coffee on a silver tray . . . [Mary] is rather queenly.' Mary told the *Mail* that she made a distinction between loyalty in the broad sense and sexual fidelity in the narrow one. But she refused to say, given that logic, whether *she* felt free to have an extra-marital affair. 'If I did, I would not be so indiscreet as to tell you.'[19]

This interview was useful to Mary in airing her allegation that the judge in the perjury trial had been critical of Jeffrey at a private dinner party some years beforehand. Describing it as a six-minute 'tirade', Mary said she thought 'a wise judge holding such strong views should have disqualified himself'. The *Mail* serialised Jeffrey's diary amid criticism that the peer was breaching the rules about payments to convicts, and making money from behind bars – he may not have been paid for serialisation but he was getting huge promotional publicity for the book. Once again, the prison authorities were obliged to spend taxpayers' money on an inquiry and legal advice; and once again Mary Archer tried to have it both ways, coming out with an astonishing plea: 'All we ask is that he is treated the same as any other prisoner in his category . . . I hope they will speedily conclude their investigation and return him to an open prison.' She also had a comment to make about another diary which had just been published: that of the former Tory minister, Edwina Currie, exposing her four-year affair with John Major. Mary remarked tartly that she was 'a little surprised, not at Mrs Currie's indiscretion, but at the temporary lapse in John Major's taste'. Pots and kettles, retorted Mrs Currie, herself a St Anne's scholar. 'Mary Archer wasn't nearly so posh at Oxford.'

Some papers were also scathing: 'Mary and Jeffrey Archer seem to think they live on a higher plane than the rest of us. Not for them the regulations and laws which govern the little people they look down on. Throughout his life Archer has lied, cheated and schemed his way to power and a fortune. Now, when he is supposed to be paying the price for getting caught out for perjury, he cannot resist trying to profit from his crime. And snooty Mary backs her husband to the hilt. The arrogance of the pair is breathtaking. They stand to make a fortune by tip-toeing through the rules with contempt for the prison system . . . The one thing missing from Archer's diary is remorse.'[20]

Martin Narey was very concerned about the damage all the publicity did to the reputation of the Prison Service. He had done his best to ensure scrupulously fair treatment for Jeffrey, but says 'it was a pretty sophisticated onslaught; it was extraordinary. It also damaged me personally and took a lot of my time. I've been with the Prison Service for 25 years and I like to think I'm remembered for insisting that prisoners are treated decently. But I was accused of abandoning my principles over Archer, and being put under pressure by the Home Secretary – that's absolute nonsense.' In the end, Jeffrey received a modest punishment for publishing the diaries: he was docked two weeks' pay (£24) and banned from buying canteen extras – all suspended for six months. The diaries themselves – relentlessly banal – were hailed at the best thing Jeffrey had written, but probably belong on the fiction shelves with his other books. They were full of what the Prison Service say are 'easily provable untruths' such as his claim that a 'child of seventeen' was locked up with murderers and rapists in Belmarsh. And there was nothing in the diaries to surprise anyone familiar with British prisons, despite Mary's claim they said important things about the penal system. They did, however, contain a menacing threat from a fellow convict: 'If you want that bitch of a secretary bumped off, I'd be happy to arrange it.' Angie Peppiatt, the perjury trial's main prosecution witness, was said to be petrified and afraid to answer her front door. It frightened Jane Williams, too. The cash Jeffrey earned from the book was swallowed up by the damages he eventually had to pay the *Star* newspaper.

The exact terms of the settlement in October 2002 are confidential, but Jeffrey had to pay back around £2.7 million, which comprised the half a million pound award plus interest, the original legal costs, and the cost of recovering the money. Part of the repayment had been made – though not announced – four months earlier: the original half a million plus £350,000 in costs from the libel trial. (The *Star*'s costs were estimated originally as £700,000.) There were then arguments over the amount of interest which had accrued over the fifteen years, and how it should be calculated. One method, calculating the compound interest, would have added up to nearly £4 million but the figure finally agreed was about £1.8 million, and that included the costs of getting it back. The new owner of Express Newspapers, Richard Desmond, got on well with James Archer who was the go-between in negotiations, and Desmond was clearly prepared to settle for less than the paper had previously been demanding – possibly to secure future Archer output, although this is denied by the company. Significantly, the Express papers gave the pay-back story less prominence than their earlier coverage, saying Jeffrey had paid 'a substantial part' of the legal costs and adding, 'as far as we are concerned, the matter is closed'. In 1999, they had been less conciliatory: 'We want our money back with interest. It's a small matter of £3 million. Not a penny more, not a penny less.' The settlement figure, let alone the original demand, was considerably more than the £738,000 which Mary said she and Jeffrey had given away, over fifteen years, as a result of the libel award.

Amid all the stress of dealing with her prisoner husband, Mary still maintained her professional life, although she did resign after just one year as patron of the British Society of Graduate Artists and Designers, which had been set up by a French businessman, Jean Bernardi, to support young artists. Among its members were a number of Royal Academicians who say that, after Jeffrey's imprisonment, some sponsors put pressure on Bernardi to get rid of Mary because her association was too damaging. Bernardi refuses to comment on whether there was such pressure, but says Mary was helpful and supportive. In any event, the Royal Academicians, who thought Mary should stay as patron, resigned and eventually the society folded. Mary herself gave pressure of work as her reason for standing down.

In addition to her membership of Addenbrooke's board, she had also joined the board of IPC – Independent Power Corporation – a small international power development company. IPC specialised in taking advantage of deregulation, and the move to privatise electricity, by acquiring and upgrading 'older generation assets' worldwide. Not long ago, according to a board member, it picked up about a third of the power generation of Bolivia. One of its directors was the former Tory energy minister Colin Moynihan, who, in 1991, had recruited Mary to a government advisory committee on renewable energy. Lord Moynihan is also a friend, with whom Mary attended a performance at Glyndebourne of *The Marriage of Figaro* during Jeffrey's trial. Moynihan, who at one time ran a company called Consort Resources, had links to Enron, the disgraced American energy corporation under investigation for large-scale accounting fraud, although there is no suggestion that he himself was involved in any wrongdoing. However, the role of another friend of the Archers, Lord Wakeham, a non-executive director of Enron, was called into question when Enron collapsed in 2001. Wakeham's professional conduct is still being investigated by the chartered accountancy's Joint Disciplinary Scheme in the UK.

The IPC/Enron connection came through Moynihan's energy consultancy, Colin Moynihan Associates (CMA). IPC was one of CMA's clients and, according to Moynihan's partner, the MP Philip Hammond, IPC had a collaboration agreement with Enron for the development of offshore wind-powered electricity generation projects. Moynihan, who says he left the IPC board in 1999, is now executive chairman of Clipper Windpower UK, developing wind turbines.[21] Mary's expertise in the field of renewable energy is valuable to IPC. According to another director, Sir Richard Morris (who also sat on the Foundation for Science and Technology with her), IPC's board meetings are usually held on Mondays to suit Mary's busy schedule. 'She never misses a meeting. She's charm itself once you get used to her.'

People who found Mary less charming were the local planners in Cambridgeshire, where Mary had applied for planning permission to build on a plot of land she owned next to the Old Vicarage. The plot had something of a history. Before the Archers bought the land, according to Robin Page, a local councillor, they had contacted him to object to outline permission (permission in principle) being renewed there on the grounds that it was important to have open spaces, and to preserve the area's literary heritage. The Archers couldn't object themselves because they had agreed with the landowner not to. Page did oppose it because he thought it was a bad place to build, but the District Council nevertheless renewed the permission. 'Jeffrey was using me,' Page says, 'because the next thing I heard, the Archers had bought the land. I was told by the planners that if they had been able to get it *without* the outline permission, it would have been much cheaper.' Some years later, when Page heard that Mary was applying to renew the planning permission, he thought it was hypocritical and tipped off a journalist friend on the *Mail on Sunday*. According to Page, Jeffrey refused to comment and instead contacted the paper's editor, his friend Stewart Steven, who forbade the reporter to write anything.

The outline permission was renewed several times over the years, despite repeated objections by Grantchester Parish Council, and in 2002 Mary wanted to renew it yet again. She tried, irregularly, to get the application heard in secret; she also issued a veiled threat of legal action for compensation, saying there would be substantial and irrecoverable loss in capital value should consent be refused. District Council officials pointed out this was not a relevant planning consideration; they thought the building would adversely affect the Grantchester Conservation Area, and Mary's application was refused. It was not the first time Mary had found herself at odds with local democracy. In 1996, at a time when her local authority was proposing to cut back the number of street lamps in the village to save money, she had put a special ornate lamppost with a cast-iron base outside her house in Grantchester. She suggested to the Parish Council that the lamps in three streets nearby should also be upgraded, at her own expense. Evidently unaware of the financial constraints faced by parishes, she also proposed that the Parish Council should contribute to this scheme. Grantchester councillors were worried about the potential cost of maintaining just *one* lamp of such a 'superior nature' and declined. 'Quite apart from the cost, what may look right outside an ancient vicarage would look daft on a housing estate,' commented one local.

Permission of a different sort led to another controversy in the village, this time involving the 'authorised' television documentary being made about her for Channel 4 by Fiona Sanderson. Sanderson and Mary had agreed that she should be filmed conducting the Grantchester church choir at the annual Christmas carol service, but the arrangement took villagers by surprise. Worshippers expecting to find a traditional candlelit service arrived to find the little church ablaze with light, and full of television lamps, cables and cameras. One churchgoer said: 'By ten o'clock in the evening, the poor vicar had got so many calls of such indignation that he had to spend Christmas apologising.' Mary herself said sorry to the choir and organist. The vicar himself later played down the episode, saying he was consulted, and that the production company made a donation to charity. But television viewers were denied the sight of Lady Archer in her choirmistress's robes – the scene ended up on the cutting-room floor.

17

Bitch!

THE PUBLIC FACE OF Mary Archer does not reveal anything about her emotions. Her sister, Janet, says they had been brought up not to show open emotion in public. 'Of course you do [feel it] but you don't push it on other people; that's bad manners.' Her brother, David, agrees: 'I suppose if you spent your formative years not showing emotional upset when under pressure, you tend to carry that into your adult life.' But in the months after Jeffrey's imprisonment, Mary was feeling under pressure: a very, very difficult and distressing time, she said. There was shock, humiliation, sadness, exhaustion, adjustment, and constant media attention – both sought and thrust on her. She had to carry on with an important and highly visible public position in the NHS; she was involved in an employment tribunal, and preparing for a privacy trial related to her injunction against Jane Williams. She had also faced the possibility of giving evidence in civil proceedings brought by the *Star*'s owners to recoup their money, as the Archers were fighting hard to reduce the amount of the settlement, despite having conceded liability. (The case was unique in that it was the first time a libel award had been overturned by civil fraud proceedings.) Despite all this, Mary continued to bat for Jeffrey. Those 'deep wells of bitterness and furious whirlpools of anger and hurt' needed a release but instead of being directed at her husband, where they belonged, her feelings seemed to be expressed towards those people Mary sees as her enemies, in particular those sections of the media who challenge her.

Early in 2002, she had done a congenial interview with ITN; in September, amid the furore over Gillian Shephard's party, ITN sent another of its reporters, Libby Wiener, to speak to her at home. Mary, who is normally treated with deference by interviewers, became increasingly annoyed at Wiener's pertinent questions, which reflected what the public – indeed, the home secretary – was asking. Wiener pressed her several times on the way Jeffrey appeared to be breaking the rules, especially by 'wining and dining', and 'making a mockery' of the justice system. Towards the end of the interview Mary raised her voice to deny Jeffrey was getting special treatment and told Wiener not to repeat the phrase 'wining and dining'. When the camera was finally switched off, Mary could contain herself no longer. 'If you say that one more time, I shall hit you,' she furiously told the reporter. 'Now please leave my house. Get out of my house! The others can stay but I want you out of my house, now!'

The Archers very much divide people into friends or foes, and Jeffrey's former editor Richard Cohen was no longer a friend. At the libel trial in 1987, Cohen had given evidence about Jeffrey's whereabouts on the night in question – though he was shocked when Jeffrey rang him during the trial to try to find out (unsuccessfully) what he was going to say. In 1995 Jeffrey invested £25,000 in Cohen's new publishing company, and over the years Cohen said very little about his famous author. He says by the time of the perjury trial, Jeffrey had stopped answering his letters and the relationship between them had cooled. A month after Jeffrey went to jail, Cohen wrote an article describing for the first time in detail his role as Jeffrey's editor for fourteen years. Some months later, Cohen was commissioned to write a scientific and cultural history of the sun. Thinking Mary would be interested, he wrote to tell her, asking if they might meet to discuss the subject. 'I got a vitriolic letter back, showing a degree of anger I've never seen her display, accusing me of being a traitor and making money from being disloyal. It was an abusive letter and she'd got her facts wrong about what I'd said to the press. She told me she would look forward to reviewing the book. And she copied the letter to Jeffrey.'

Someone else who had seen a different side of Mary was Jane Williams, who was by now involved in a prolonged, stressful and lonely dispute with the woman who had once called her 'my second skin'. The essence of Williams's case was that she had been victimised after Mary discovered she had made a statement to the police; she claimed Mary was 'dealing out retribution' and squeezing her out by reducing her work and thereby cutting her wages, and wrongly accusing her of cooperating with the press. Against the advice of one of her close friends, John de Bruyne – who was also on good terms with Mary – Jane Williams decided to bring a claim of unfair dismissal. De Bruyne advised her she would never succeed and even offered to apologise to Mary on Williams's behalf over the approach to Max Clifford, which he said was behaviour quite out of character. 'But she told me she wanted her day in court.' In the autumn, at a tribunal at Bury St Edmunds, Jane Williams detailed her side of the story of her relationship with Mary. Over the past five or so years, she said, Mary had become difficult, demanding, rude and hurtful, and insensitive over personal problems Williams was having with her ex-boyfriend. During this traumatic time, she also coped with a major operation and the death of her father; she had counselling, paid for through her job's private health policy but Mary was unhappy about the greatly increased premiums which she said she was not prepared to pay indefinitely, and passed on a £100 excess to her PA. Williams told the tribunal she had been upset by 'insulting and embarrassing gifts' from Mary, such as a gift-wrapped two-dollar 'made in China' Calvin Klein watch as part of a Christmas present, and on her birthday an inch of flat champagne left over from a photoshoot. Mary, who considered herself to be 'a fair and kind employer' thought she was being oversensitive, but did apologise for 'a clumsy attempt' to make up for forgetting the birthday, pointing out that she was given 'fairly expensive' toiletries at Christmas as well. (Mary keeps a record of gifts.)

As the tribunal noted, the relationship was by now distressed, and made worse by the critical emails Mary had discovered. (Although these had been deleted, Mary told a baffled tribunal that they were 'lodged in cyberspace' and she had recovered them with the help of a 'dead space resurrection program'.) On the one hand, Williams felt she was underpaid and undervalued; on the other, Mary was becoming increasingly concerned about confidentiality issues, and had sought the advice of a specialist lawyer. As was revealed in the tribunal ruling, she wrote to the lawyer: 'I feel it is appropriate that I write now to members of my domestic staff in both Cambridge and London to remind them of their general duty of confidentiality ... At the year end when I write to each member of staff a "re-engagement letter" I will add a "confidentiality clause".' She wanted to 'bind staff so far as it is possible to continuing confidentiality once they have left my service'. Mary also told the lawyer: 'I note that your fee is £250 per hour, so naturally hope this will not take too many hours' work.'[1] Jane Williams secretly kept copies of this correspondence because she was worried about the implications for her job. At the tribunal, Mary's lawyer accused Williams of 'salting away' documents, suggesting she would give them to the press; Williams maintained they were of no general interest and related only to concerns about her work. She said the 'offensive' emails were simply a light-hearted way to let off steam in a demanding job where she worked alone much of the time.

Crucially, Jane Williams said in her evidence she had maintained confidentiality during the years of working for the Archers, despite many approaches by the press. She was at the very heart of the Archer family and revealed that she had known since the start of her employment about Jeffrey's 'serial relationships' but when she mentioned them to Mary, she had seemed unmoved. 'I had to tell her that I knew all about Lord Archer taking Nikki Kingdon to

South Africa [because] I was involved with the difficulties of ensuring that her visit did not clash with [Mary's].' Mary's response had been, 'Well you know, I've never been bothered about all that.'[2] Williams said she had seen and heard things that she was very uncomfortable about, that she knew were wrong, and that eventually, despite her loyalty for many years, she felt 'there was a line over which I would not step'.[3]

The tribunal was told about events leading up to Williams contacting the police about Jeffrey. She had learned that his driver had made a statement to police, and she had concerns about his state of mind and thought he might perjure himself if he were called as a witness. Second, she had been asked to supply William Archer with a mobile phone number to contact a witness. This worried her, as the police had instructed Jeffrey not to attempt to contact or 'interfere with' any of the prosecution witnesses. Mary nevertheless told Jane Williams to give her son the phone number and he duly made contact.[4] Later, Mary claimed that it was not illegal for relatives of the accused to meet prosecution witnesses. It could, however, have been a breach of bail for a relative to act as agent for the defendant; in any case, if there was something which required contact, why not do it through a solicitor? During the next few weeks, Williams 'thought long and hard' about her loyalty to Mary, but also about the implications of withholding information. She decided to tell the police that the driver had told various inconsistent stories of what had happened to Jeffrey's diaries; she also told them about William Archer's contact. She realised that she was jeopardising her employment but thought it was her duty to speak.

When Mary found out about the statement she was 'shaken, surprised and upset'. After speaking to her lawyers, she took the precaution of telling her PA that she had acted quite properly and must cooperate with the police if necessary, although she must not work at the Old Vicarage for the duration of the trial. Within hours, she had turned up without warning at Williams's home and asked her to sign a letter which included words to the effect that the PA had been suffering from stress. Williams refused. Shortly afterwards, Mary confronted her with another allegation: the driver's wife had told Mary that Williams had had discussions with a journalist, possibly from the *Daily Telegraph*, earlier in the year, and had made her statement in order to 'drop a bombshell' on the trial and boost the value of her story. This was emphatically denied by Williams, who said it had never entered her mind. The tribunal later noted that the driver's wife appeared to be a confidante of both Jane Williams and Mary Archer and had 'no hesitation in saying to either of them whatever seemed to suit her at the time'.[5] In any event, Williams's statement to the police was not used in the trial.

To prevent any stories coming out of her own home, Mary insisted all her staff sign confidentiality agreements. She told her PA: 'You have not observed confidentiality, you have sent very rude emails about me which I would like to put in the past and accept that you were under stress at that time, but I must be assured that in the very, very difficult and distressing circumstances I find myself, and needing to carry on with all my usual professional commitments, to be sure of your, in particular, your confidentiality.'[6] Jane Williams again refused to sign, saying she did not see the need, and took legal advice, which was that the agreement was 'draconian'. It was alleged that another member of staff also refused to sign, but Mary refused to answer questions about this in open court. Mary admitted at the tribunal that she had made enquiries into the allegations that Williams had been talking to a journalist, but she told Williams that she 'would not be taking any further action regarding . . . contact with a journalist'. Just as she had been willing to enlist Williams's former boyfriend to her cause, Mary later tried – unsuccessfully – to get a journalist to cooperate with her case against Williams.

Mary also reviewed her staffing needs, claiming they were much reduced, despite the fact that she had as many engagements as the previous year; puzzlingly, she cited Lloyd's and Anglia even though these had ended some years earlier, and also that she was no longer being invited to school prize-givings following the scandal. 'Things go oddly quiet; people stop ringing,' she said. 'I was not less busy but the nature of what I was doing changed.' Williams was told she was in danger of being made redundant, and was offered a part-time job of fifteen hours a week on condition she signed the confidentiality agreement. Williams did not agree that the work-load had decreased, pointing out that Jeffrey's PA had kept her full-time job despite his being in prison; she also said she couldn't afford to live on two-fifths of her current salary. Numerous letters were exchanged, with Williams's lawyers accusing Mary of bully-ing and hectoring, and of using the process to further other aims. They suggested a settlement whereby Williams would agree to go for a sum equivalent to six years' pay, with a sum of £80,000 for-feited should she breach confidentiality. Her employer described the deal as 'extortion'. Finally, Williams was given notice and made redundant, though Mary wished her good luck in the letter. She said her last day at work was distressing: Mary spoke to her only about items of property she wanted returned and did not thank her for her work over the past thirteen and a half years. She says the final parting came when Mary simply walked out for an appoint-ment without a word.

At the hearing, Jane Williams was adamant that her police state-ment was the real reason for her dismissal. Her barrister at the tribunal said Mary would have been 'enraged' by it, and subse-quently 'tailored' her 'very carefully crafted' evidence to bolster her case.[7] But after six days of listening, the employment tribunal dis-agreed. They concluded that the principal reason for Jane Williams's dismissal was her refusal to enter into the confidential-ity agreement; they thought Mary was credible, honest and accurate, and had not unfairly dismissed her PA. Giving their rea-sons, they said Mary had a husband who was 'digging a deeper and deeper hole' and she was 'erecting higher and higher fences around it to try to protect her family from the increasing risk of media intrusion'. They called Mary 'fiercely protective of her family' and said she was perfectly entitled to do that in relation to the employee closest to her. They had been impressed by what Mary had said during cross-examination: 'I am not an organisation; I am a person, and the personal chemistry with the PA is important . . . If you entrust someone to learn your every secret, entrust them with the right to open your mail, however confidential and personal it may be, to read your emails, to take telephone calls and so on, then there has to be absolute trust.' The tribunal also pointed out that, in making Jane Williams redundant, Mary had chosen an expensive option. 'Lady Archer is a person who is careful about money, even with relatively small sums . . . Much evidence was put in front of us by [Jane Williams] about the extent to which she regarded Lady Archer as acting in a fairly stingy manner.' There was the flat champagne, the fake watch, the £100 insurance excess, the £200 Christmas bonus (about two days' pay), the way Williams always felt underpaid. 'Overall,' said the tribunal, 'the simple position was that [Mary] was prepared to pay what she regarded as an appropriate level of remuneration, but not a penny more.'[8] Later, Williams claimed that redundancy money she was owed was withheld for three months, during which time she was running up more debts.

The effect of the tribunal decision was to make life much harder for Jane Williams. She now had substantial legal costs, and losing her case of unfair dismissal was, as Mary would have foreseen, a disadvantage at the forthcoming privacy trial. She was still in dispute about the ownership of the diaries; she was jobless, and without a reference; and she felt extremely angry and upset about the way she had been 'bullied'. She decided to explore the possibility of cooperating with Paul Henderson of the *Mail on Sunday* who, along with a woman journalist, had contacted her after Jeffrey's trial. Then, she had reported their visits to Mary, suspecting a plan to trick her, and handed over their business cards. Now, she told Henderson, she might be willing to speak about her personal situation and her working relationship; however, she eventually rejected a deal, saying she was uneasy about what the paper wanted. Her solicitors then advised her to seek professional advice from the publicist Max Clifford about selling her story.

They rang him on her behalf and accompanied her when she went to see him. Clifford introduced Williams to Rob Kellaway, one of the *News of the World* reporters who had been involved in taping the conversation between Jeffrey and Ted Francis. The *News of the World* signed an undertaking with Williams that nothing would be published without first reaching a financial agreement with her. Clifford asked her to fax information, which she ill-advisedly did. The thirteen-page fax contained details of events, dates, flight numbers, and contact details, interspersed with unflattering comments about the Archers; they concentrated on particular items which the journalists had told her were of interest to the press. The *News of the World* lost interest, but Clifford then introduced her to the *Daily Mail*, and there were negotiations about terms, which were finally settled at £50,000. But before they could publish anything, word went round the Sunday papers that Max Clifford was touting a Mary Archer story; it appeared first in the *Sunday Mirror*, a paper Williams had not met.[9] Shortly afterwards, Mary began injunction proceedings against Jane Williams. The paper itself says the story did not come from Williams, and later Clifford denied he had sold the story to the *Sunday Mirror*. In any event, Jane Williams received no money.

As Mary prepared for yet another court appearance, due in the summer of 2003, she was also busy with the chairmanship of Addenbrooke's NHS Trust, a prestigious position. In November 2002, according to the ever-deferential *Cambridge Evening News*, more than twenty people had to be turned away from a talk on the trust which Mary gave at a local club lunch. 'Club members hung on her every word,' reported the *News*, and of course 'questions outside the business of hospital trusts were off the agenda' – particularly, no doubt, for *Cambridge Evening News* reporters. Things in Cambridge were rather different from her experience the previous January in Oxford, where there were so few takers for her talk at St Anne's College that the event was cancelled. Perhaps, with all the publicity surrounding Jeffrey's imprisonment, the senior members of St Anne's had heard enough from the Archers for the time being. But Mary's fans could look forward to her television documentary, shown a month before the privacy court case. As always, the media were interested in her comments on sexual fidelity. She thought life was about an awful lot more than sex and that faithfulness was not necessary to keep a couple together. But she agreed that it was 'certainly unhelpful' to see a partner's infidelity, especially when it was made public. What Mary did not say was whether her views on infidelity covered herself, as well as her husband. Her brother commented that it was a family difference: for his sister Janet and for him, infidelity would be a very major issue.

But the point of the documentary, as Mary candidly admitted, was to assist her campaign to clear Jeffrey's name, as well as to show that her life, and their life together, would go on despite everything. She repeated her claim that the trial judge's attitude had been hostile; she had hearsay of his 'strongly hostile opinions about Jeffrey's literary and political career . . .' She also took a free kick at the then home secretary David Blunkett who, she said, had sent 'an extremely intemperate communication' to [the head of the Prison Service] saying he was 'sick and tired of reading Jeffrey Archer stories . . . the freedom he's been given . . . to do whatever he likes and the snook that he is cocking at all of us'. In a *Radio Times* interview to promote the documentary, she also made a statement which appeared to further confuse the Archers' evidence about the diaries in the libel and perjury cases. 'The diaries that went to court were exactly the same as the one that Mrs Peppiatt produced,' Mary asserted. 'It was exactly the same in every detail.'[10] This was demonstrably untrue, as photocopies show, and the problem was that Mary's crusade was beginning to look absurd. She even told the programme, 'I don't think he lies more than most average people . . . Jeffrey likes colour, he's colourful.'[11] Mary made more allegations on *Woman's Hour*. 'Are you telling me that you still believe Jeffrey is innocent?' asked an incredulous Jenni Murray. 'I do indeed. I do indeed. I wouldn't try to defend the indefensible,' she replied, also hinting that her husband might try to re-enter some form of public life.

In gathering evidence for her campaign, Mary had been making extensive use of the Data Protection Act, which allows people to obtain information about themselves by making access requests from bodies which hold data. She had made requests to the Metropolitan and Cambridge police – as Jeffrey had to Emma Nicholson – and had encouraged her husband and sons to do the same. She claimed that she thus discovered her PA had been 'spying' on her and had tipped off the police about her investigation into Angela Peppiatt's credit card receipts. Mary said the tip-off was not disclosed to Jeffrey's legal team, which, she claimed, undermined their defence strategy. This is hard to square with the fact that the examination of Angela Peppiatt's credit card statements came as a complete surprise during the trial – even though it would have been obvious that Jeffrey would try in some way to discredit the main prosecution witness. Neither the prosecution nor the judge knew about the tactic, as it had not been revealed in the defence case statement, and because Jeffrey's barrister had gone to another judge for permission to obtain the bank statements. By contrast, the Crown had made all the appropriate disclosures, and had served Williams's statement on Jeffrey's legal team. Jane Williams, for her part, said the spying allegation was 'pure fiction'.

Just nine days before her High Court privacy battle, Mary gave Andrew Pierce of *The Times* a copy of a dossier, hundreds of pages long, which she had been compiling for two years since the perjury trial. The documents included a transcript of the secretly tape-recorded dinner party with her friends the Barkers, and copies of her private correspondence with Godfrey Barker. Naturally, it was front page news. In the ensuing coverage, Barker said he utterly dissociated himself from the suggestion the trial was not handled properly. 'I want to put several oceans distance between myself and Lady Archer,' he protested. *The Times* also got a statement from Sir Humphrey Potts, the trial judge, who was understandably exasperated. He said, 'I have remained silent about this matter until now, but there is a limit. I wish to emphasise that I am making this statement because I have been approached by *The Times* at my home in my retirement and I wish to put an end to this matter if at all possible ... To suggest that I engaged in abuse of Lord Archer ... is nonsense.' He also revealed that Ann Barker had written to him seeking help in gaining entrance to the courtroom during the perjury trial. Her letter 'contained no hint of reproach that I was the trial judge ...'[12] (Mary claimed it was because of Ann Barker's Parole Board links with Potts that she had put pressure on Godfrey Barker not to write a statement to help Mary's campaign.)

At the end of June 2003, Mary was back at the Royal Courts of Justice where sixteen years earlier she had smitten a judge with her radiance. She triumphed again, gaining a powerful and permanent injunction against Jane Williams; a serious infringement of press freedom, though one which the judge deemed necessary. She was also awarded £2,500 for 'hurt feelings' and £2,500 for breach of confidence, as well as £600 for issuing the injunction and her costs: around £170,000. Williams, who already owed large sums in legal bills run up before the trial, was ruined. Her former solicitors, Taylor Vinter of Cambridge, had taken a charge on her house for money owed to them, and as a result, she was initially forced to represent herself in the High Court proceedings. However, at the last minute, a firm of solicitors, Lyalls from Birmingham, and a pro-bono barrister, a human rights expert called Rambert de Mello, appeared on the scene. De Mello had taken the case only four days before it began, and, despite his skill, was at a distinct disadvantage against the carefully prepared Archer team.

For one thing, de Mello had no research back-up. He had no details of the recent Channel 4 documentary, nor of Mary's numerous other media appearances over decades. But his questioning certainly exposed hypocrisy. When asked about media interest in her appearance, Mary told him, 'One just tolerates it', failing to mention she had supplied the Channel 4 producer with photographs, video footage and press cuttings from her huge collection, or that she had been interviewed many times about her clothes and looks. De Mello asked if she had any objection to her PA telling the press about conversations that she might have had with visitors to Grantchester. 'Yes, I would,' said Mary. 'Visitors to my home . . . were entitled to think they were in a private place. They do not deserve to have themselves served up on a platter with a sauce of malice for the tabloid newspapers.'[13] Unlike the Barkers. She denied she had any plans to write a book; she was not questioned about the fact that 'agents' had touted her story. On the second day, Mary was wearing a gold necklace with a large emerald which Jeffrey originally claimed he had bought for her from inside prison through a deal with a Colombian drug runner, 'Sergio', and his brother.[14] Mary, who professes to have 'quite a strong ethical code' and was chairman of Addenbrooke's Clinical Ethics Committee, had been busy telling the media that Jeffrey was 'horrified by the drugs culture in prison'. By the time Jeffrey's book was published, the drug runner named in the book's advance serialisation had mysteriously become someone who was 'not involved in drugs'.[15]

The trial was essentially a conflict between privacy and freedom of expression. Jane Williams's barrister pointed out that Mary was in a position to present herself and her case through the media, as she had recently done on a radio programme accusing Williams of spying on her, thus removing the 'cloak of confidentiality'. If *she* could speak about what went on in her home, why did Jane Williams not have an equal right? And what about the publicity she had sought for her campaign for Jeffrey? 'I don't flatter myself that any TV programme could release my husband early,' Mary said, although her adroit and unremitting efforts belied that. But your principal objective was to gain public support for a second appeal? de Mello pressed her. To his surprise, the judge refused to allow this line of questioning, saying he did not think Jeffrey's appeal was relevant. De Mello protested: his case was that Mary was using the proceedings to bolster another appeal by her husband, partly based on the 'spying' claim, and Mary was trying to get public support through the media. Mary had put the accusation into the public domain and Jane Williams had a right to 'put the record straight' by defending herself in public and telling her side of the story. But the judge was not convinced: 'I direct there should be no cross-examination in respect of her husband's plans,' he said.

Mary told the judge the article about her facelift was a very great shock to her, particularly as it amounted to a betrayal. She had wanted to keep the surgery entirely private and had not even told her sister, let alone her staff, about her 'nip and tuck', and went to very great lengths to keep it secret – notwithstanding the obvious change in her appearance. She also thoroughly resented the disclosure of her friendship with the American academic Stephen Feldberg, with whom, it was said in court, she exchanged emails. Feldberg had been to stay at Grantchester and the court also heard there was a photograph of him and Mary at a party given by the chairman of Rolex watches in Geneva. The story of how the *Sunday Mirror* had contacted Stephen Feldberg was one of the high-spots of the trial. Feldberg, a keen fisherman, had been rung while on holiday in New Zealand to be told by the paper's editor, Tina Weaver, that she 'had a photograph of him holding his trout'. Unfazed, Feldberg declared Jeffrey was 'a jerk' for humiliating Mary. 'I'm very annoyed with him,' he said, and agreed that he found Mary very attractive, although he would not admit to any romantic attachment. 'I have a definite love affair with trout,' he volunteered. Once again, themes familiar to previous Archer trials surfaced: tape-recordings, Sunday newspapers, betrayal, and diaries – many of these stacked neatly at the judge's side in brown and white envelopes. And there were some light moments; the gallery was entertained with evidence about a baked bean birthday cake, floods in the folly, 'hot synching' of diaries, and legal references on privacy ranging from the Gary Flitcroft lap-dancing trial to the more obscure 'possum brush tail processing' case, not to mention 'the three limbs of the Coco test'. Mary bristled when a lawyer referred to 'Lord Archer's penthouse' – 'It is *our* penthouse,' she insisted.

Jane Williams argued that the leak to the *Sunday Mirror* was not her responsibility. Max Clifford, as her agent, was obliged not to authorise any publication without her consent. The judge acknowledged that she had asked her solicitors, Taylor Vinter, to advise her so that she was not in breach of duty to Mary Archer at any stage. Although the judge was attracted to this defence, he concluded that she had nevertheless embarked upon a high risk strategy. Max Clifford was using his contacts to find a buyer for the story and it would have been obvious to anyone that there was a substantial risk that, one way or another, the information would find its way into the newspapers. He also ruled that Mary was not a public figure, a view which must have surprised the people of Cambridge where she heads a public body that employs 6,000 of its citizens and where she had been a trustee of some of the nation's finest art treasures. And despite Mary's status as university lecturer, honorary professor, school governor, schools prize-giver and speaker, member of government committees, proponent of women in science, and choirmistress, the judge did not think she was a role model. 'If Mary Archer is not a public figure,' commented the *Guardian*, 'then her husband is Charles Dickens.'

Jane Williams had wanted to do what Jeffrey had done when faced with huge debts – dig her way out by writing, and said she saw nothing wrong with recounting 'amusing experiences and anecdotes' about her years with the Archers; she wanted to tell the press about Mary's spending, including her 'thrift and expenditures in relation to parties and clothing'. Not only that, she said it was in the public interest to show how the Archers had treated her, and the turmoil and anguish she had suffered. 'I thought they'd behaved illegally; they'd exposed me to situations that I did not choose to be exposed to – all four members of the family.'[16] She was questioned about the contents of her thirteen-page fax although the judge warned that details should not be revealed in open court. When Mary's barrister, referring to one item, accused her of spraying dirt about, Williams replied, 'That was a well-known fact.' Mary, sitting in the well of the court, fixed her with a contemptuous stare and hissed, 'Bitch!'

At the end of the case, Mr Justice Jackson called for an end to hostilities: 'Despite the confines of the injunction, Mrs Williams is still able to go on making hurtful public statements about Lady Archer. Furthermore, Lady Archer, armed with this judgement and the likely costs order, can greatly increase Mrs Williams's present acute financial difficulties ... I very much hope that in the aftermath of this trial they are both able to arrive at some form of truce.' That's a bit rich, exclaimed Mary. She was in no mood to be conciliatory, and immediately pressed for costs. (A few months later, however, Mary said she was saddened to see her former employee in 'such a distressing situation'.[17]) Outside court, she made a short statement to the press and went off to celebrate her victory at a garden party given by the television presenter David Frost. Somewhat reluctantly the judge ordered Jane Williams to pay all of Mary's costs despite acknowledging that Mary was 'a person of extreme wealth' and 'the defendant is, on all the evidence, penniless'. Mary's next move was to try to recoup her costs from Jane Williams's former solicitors, by getting a 'wasted costs order', for she knew her PA was broke. So yet another court appearance was in the offing, the fourth in three years, counting the tribunal.

Mary made a pre-emptive strike by sending a statement to the *Cambridge Evening News*. She told the paper she held Taylor Vinter responsible for a large portion of the costs. 'I wish to make it clear that the costs order I obtained [yesterday] was the automatic consequence of winning a comprehensive victory in this litigation. It has never been my intention to cause undue financial hardship to Jane Williams ... Her former lawyers have claimed substantial fees from Jane and have secured that debt by way of a charge on her house. I have today instructed my lawyers to contest Taylor Vinter's attempt to enforce their claim on Jane's home.' This statement, of course, put a spin on the situation, and it was headlined as Mary's 'dramatic bid to stop lawyers' claiming Jane Williams's home. For good measure, she was also pursuing a complaint of professional misconduct against Taylor Vinter. John de Bruyne, Williams's friend, also wrote to the paper, criticising Taylor

Vinter for making 'an error of professional judgement' in their handling of the case. 'Solicitors have a duty of care especially to a single unemployed woman without funds for speculative litigation . . .' he wrote. In addition, 'they forced Mary Archer to run up large legal bills just when she needed some peace and quiet . . . Should not the partners have the decency to waive their fee?'[18] De Bruyne, whose wife was responsible for some of the emails which Mary found so offensive, is still angry about Taylor Vinter. 'It was shocking for them to take instructions from her, and make her sell her house – I think it's wicked. Taylor Vinter is an enormously profitable firm.' Taylor Vinter say claims that they misled the other side are 'totally unfounded'. The firm's managing partner, Christine Berry, said they did not believe there was any basis on which Lady Archer was entitled to recover any costs from them.[19]

But a wasted costs case duly took place a few months later, with Mary claiming that Taylor Vinter had written abusive and strident letters, using phrases such as 'arrant nonsense' and 'bogus arguments'. They had resisted her 'meritorious claim' for an injunction, misled her solicitors, and pursued an 'improper objective' in that they tried to secure publication of Jane Williams's story so she could afford to pay their fees. But this time, Mary lost. The judge dismissed the claim, even though he agreed that some of the language in one letter 'overstepped the mark of courteous correspondence between solicitors engaged in an adversarial dispute'. The problem in deciding whether Taylor Vinter had wasted time and money (their bills are thought to have totalled £160,000) was that much of the relevant evidence was 'obscured from the court's view'. The judge said there was no way of knowing what advice they were giving to their client because she refused to waive privilege (reveal confidential matters discussed with lawyers). The fact that Mary was a successful litigant who was not able to enforce her costs order against Jane Williams was a 'powerful point', said the judge, but he also thought the wasted costs proceedings had become 'satellite litigation on an unacceptable scale' and the cost of it was already disproportionate to what Mary could hope to recover. Christine Berry of Taylor Vinter refuses to comment about the case; her response to enquiries for this book was to let Mary's lawyers know about the calls.

Several months later Williams faced the prospect of bankruptcy and applied for more time to challenge Mary's costs bill. Her application was refused, with the Costs Master saying it was a matter for the bankruptcy courts if Mary wanted to pursue it. The reason for Mary's persistence soon became clear. She wanted a lever to get Jane Williams to sign a 'peace deal' agreement – which would help in her Jeffrey-is-Innocent campaign and her complaint against Taylor Vinter. At this costs hearing, she offered to relieve her former PA of liability for the £170,000 High Court legal bill – and spare her from inevitable bankruptcy – in return for a confidential nine-point deal. Mary's solicitor, Tony Morton-Hooper, described it as 'an alternative to financial meltdown' but Jane Williams angrily rejected it, saying, 'It would involve me selling my soul to the devil. She is just persecuting me. I think they would be ashamed to relay the details to you . . . If she wants to bankrupt me, let her get on with it. I would prefer the axe to fall and get it over with.' So keen was Morton-Hooper to get the deal signed, he made a personal offer to pay for Williams to take independent legal advice on the proposal. What his client wanted was to get Jane Williams to waive her legal privilege over notes taken by her lawyers at meetings with the media.[20] Mary was annoyed that she did not know the full picture. She knew her PA had 'committed some of her thoughts to the keyboard' but there had been no disclosure of this information. As the *Daily Mail* said a few days later, only a handful of people knew 'the full details of what she told the police about the goings-on in the Archer household in the run-up to the perjury trial – information that could perhaps destroy Mary's determined efforts to help her husband win the right to a second appeal and prove his innocence'.

By this time, a beleaguered Jane Williams had already sold her home to settle her own legal bills and Mary's damages, and was 'running on empty', living with friends and working in temporary jobs. She says a private investigator video-ed her house, and that somebody tried to hack into her bank account and, just like Mary had in the past, Williams got stress-related skin problems and insomnia. In retrospect, she feels it was a big mistake to sue Mary for unfair dismissal. 'She is so powerful, I realise I didn't stand a chance.' Now fifty-two, she still faces an order for the costs of Mary's successful injunction. Mary Archer once said that grinding anxiety about money was the worst thing she had ever experienced. She said it made her sympathetic to those Lloyd's members she helped keep a roof over their heads. Fortunately for Mary, her husband is now worth an estimated £65 million. The woman who was her 'right arm' for thirteen years is bankrupt and has lost her home.

18

Portrait of a Lady

IN NOVEMBER 2003, shortly after starting work on this book, I received two strange phone calls. One of them was from a man calling himself Eric Walker. Eric wanted to meet me to discuss my writing a book for him about football: a very surprising request, given my antipathy to the game. But Eric had another agenda: he had heard about this book, and told me he knew Mary Archer very well and wanted to discuss her. Eric is a self-styled go-between for the Archers, and maybe he hoped that tempting me with a football book would dissuade me from writing about Mary. As the conversation progressed, I realised that he was actually Eric Vawser, one of Jeffrey's supporters, a former chairman of the Penistone Conservative Association in Yorkshire, and a garrulous con-man who made headlines in the early 1980s for duping numerous people and owing them money, and for an alleged relationship with the wife of the Earl of Wharncliffe. Vawser, like his friend Jeffrey, converses in a peculiar mixture of fact and fiction. He claimed to have been instrumental in Mary's campaign against Emma Nicholson, and involved in a lot more besides. 'We're talking mega, mega: it's a monumental success,' he boasted. He also hinted at the possibility of Mary taking legal action against me, saying, 'I'm surprised Jeffrey didn't sue your husband. She's very,

very skilful, more formidable. She is able to control males and females.' He said he had, at one time, spoken to Mary every day for two years. 'I'm pretty close; I've been her guest at livery company dinners in London.' Stringing Vawser along, I took his calls on numerous occasions, asking him for some proof that he knew Mary. All he supplied was a photograph of some ring-binders that he said were full of information about her but, more plausibly, he claimed to have been her guest at the tercentenary dinner of the chemistry department at Cambridge – an unlikely thing to have known about, unless he had been invited. Eventually, his bluff was called and he stopped ringing.

Shortly before getting Vawser's call, I was phoned out of the blue by a *Sunday Times* journalist, who is one of Vawser's contacts. This journalist was 'fishing' for information about why I had separated from my husband, Michael. The journalist had been told by 'friends' that we had disagreed about the way Michael had presented my research in his book; a gambit so preposterous it probably came from Vawser. When the journalist learned of my Mary biography, he said the Archers would be shocked and unsettled, as they had planned to approach me – having learned of my separation – to see if I would be willing to 'dig the dirt' on my husband. According to the journalist, this would have been part of their preparation for possible legal action over what they regarded as libellous claims in his biography of Jeffrey. So yet another of their 'enemies' was to be enticed to help the cause – first Jane Williams's boyfriend, then a reporter who had tried to get stories from Williams, next Jane Williams herself, and now the wife of the investigative journalist Jeffrey was said to be 'paranoid' about. This intriguing episode had Jeffrey's fingerprints all over it, but as yet the only evidence linking him and Mary to Vawser comes from the Yorkshireman himself.

After Jeffrey's conviction, Vawser wrote to the *Weston Mercury* in Jeffrey's home town to say: 'Jeffrey is not the villain that some people make him out to be . . . his sentence is massively excessive and I have serious doubts as to whether he is guilty.' A week after

Mary won an injunction against her former PA, Vawser popped up again, this time to attack Baroness Nicholson, whom he called 'a s***' for causing Jeffrey trouble over the Simple Truth affair. He claimed in the *Sunday Times* that he had known Jeffrey for more than thirty years, since his days as an MP, and wanted to help his old friend by mounting a possible legal action against Nicholson. The circumstances of the proposed lawsuit were complex, but centred on a South African man called Katiza Cebekhulu, a former bodyguard to Winnie Mandela, who had been rescued from prison by Nicholson. She brought him to England, paid for English lessons, and was said to be his legal guardian. Cebekhulu subsequently became the subject of a book about his life and Vawser claimed – untruthfully – that Nicholson owed the Zulu £60,000 in royalties. The tenuous connection between this story and the Archers was that it was all part of a scheme to discredit Emma Nicholson, and force her to pay legal costs defending herself. Mary confirmed that she had spoken to Vawser on the phone and 'may have said I would be interested to see what happened'.[1] Vawser also testified for Cebekhulu at a court case in March 2004 when he was convicted of stabbing a neighbour.

Meanwhile the Archers had themselves been feeding the press a series of stories, each of which proved nothing, but whose cumulative effect had been to sow doubt in the public mind about the safety of the conviction and the probity of the trial judge. Some weeks before his release, Jeffrey had used the data protection laws to see Emma Nicholson's files on her charity allegations; Mary had done the same thing to get Metropolitan Police and Home Office files on the perjury inquiry. It was part of a steady drip of innuendo. Godfrey and Ann Barker had been secretly taped; Mr Justice Potts had been smeared; the home secretary criticised as prejudiced; and Martin Narey, the head of the Prison Service, ticked off like a naughty schoolboy for being 'utterly wrong'. Jeffrey's friend, the art dealer Chris Beetles, was said to be investigating Angela Peppiatt, with the Archers' backing. A firm of private detectives had been hired to trawl through Peppiatt's finances, prompting her boss, the tycoon Peter Beckwith, to comment: 'This is the sort of bullyboy tactics Jeffrey has always employed. People like to think he's a likeable rogue but he's not. He's a thug.' Journalists had been approached and told that Mary 'would not rest until their foes were vanquished'. Reporters were told the couple had set up a £4 million war-chest to fund their pursuit of 'justice'; that more than seventy 'members of the Upper and Lower Houses' (peers and MPs) had visited him in jail; that he had received 'countless' letters of support; and that Jeffrey was taking legal action against the Prison Service for 'unfair and brutal treatment'. Dr Susan Edwards, an academic from the University of Buckingham, had completed a survey of perjury sentences and argued that Jeffrey's sentence was 'a significant departure from the principle of proportionality'[2] – in other words, did not fit the crime. Dr Edwards, a respected criminologist, is on first-name terms with Mary, and refuses to confirm whether the Archers had any input into her work. 'I would in principle be happy to help you,' she told me, 'but naturally I shall speak to Mary first.'

'I have been conducting something of a campaign,' Mary confirmed. 'I will carry on doing it until it is done.' It all showed how fanatical and obsessive the Archers had become, and it was the sort of bullying and intimidation only the rich and well connected can employ to give themselves influence well beyond what is justified. By now, they must have paid Mishcon's many hundreds of thousands in legal fees – with more to come, some of them incurred in fighting this book. What the Archers were conveniently overlooking was that it was a jury that found Jeffrey guilty; that his appeal was dismissed in minutes; and that three appeal court judges backed the four-year sentence. His crime was not simply lying on oath, it was an elaborate and calculated plan to pervert justice, bribe others and defraud two newspapers; as a result of the deception, he and his wife greatly benefited personally. If Jeffrey is so innocent, why wouldn't he answer police questions when they

arrested him, and why wouldn't he rebut the charges from the witness-box, instead of staying silent and sending in his wife to speak
on his behalf?

There had been suggestions, in the light of his extraordinary
behaviour, that Jeffrey might not get parole after two years, and in
the run-up to the Parole Board hearing, Mary's campaign got a lot
of suspiciously well-placed publicity. First, the former governor of
North Sea Camp, Mike Lewis (who Jeffrey said had given him farthings as a gift), wrote to a newspaper in Jeffrey's defence, saying
his early release 'has been seriously and unfairly undermined by the
Prison Service'.[3] There were stories that Jeffrey had a heart condition, and letters from his friends to a newspaper. Mary gave
interviews to the *Sunday Telegraph*, and *Woman's Hour*, in which
she made her assertion that the police had received secret information that undermined Jeffrey's defence. She accused 'a former
employee of mine' (obviously Jane Williams) of spying on her. This
was a well-timed accusation, coming just a month before the privacy case at the High Court, and at a time when Williams was
legally un-represented. Then came Mary's 'campaign platform'
documentary, with her comments on the 'injustice' meted out to
her husband. Next, Mary encouraged the *Sunday Mirror* to publish
an email purporting to come from a Home Office official, saying
Jeffrey should not be released yet; the email turned out to be a forgery.[4] A few days later, she passed to the *Spectator* copies of Home
Office memos which she and Jeffrey had acquired through access
requests, and an article headlined 'The plot to keep Jeffrey Archer
in jail' appeared, calling him a 'political prisoner'. Mary also gave
The Times her story about the taped dinner party conversation. On
18 June 2003, it was announced that Jeffrey had, after all, got
parole. Jeffrey's Parole Board papers were 'obtained' by the *Sunday
Telegraph*; they included appreciative extracts from reports by a
prison medical officer, Dr Walling, the former governor Mike
Lewis, and the director of the Theatre Royal in Lincoln, Chris
Moreno. Another report, by his probation officer, revealed that
Jeffrey had 'declined to comment upon his offence, conviction and

sentence, or any person who may have been considered to be a victim. He still maintains his innocence.'[5] Just before his release, the *Sunday Telegraph* commented of Mary: 'She has become spin doctor, campaigner and deal-broker. From her office . . . she has orchestrated a ferocious campaign to clear her husband's name and destroy their enemies. She has become a zealous news manager, on the phone to journalists, monitoring headlines, and assessing daily coverage with a rigour that would have bored her to tears in the halcyon days of the 1980s when it seemed the Archers could do what they liked.'

Despite his total lack of remorse or shame, Jeffrey was released from prison on 21 July, two years into his sentence. The media went into overdrive, one company even hiring a helicopter to track his journey back to Grantchester and into the arms of his wife – who chose for the occasion a red dress which was at least six years old. Dozens of cameras recorded the happy moment as Jeffrey emerged from his car, walked towards Mary to embrace her, puckered up for a kiss – and found his lips brushing her cheek as she turned her head away, smiling at her audience of photographers. Despite her unconvincing body language, she said she was delighted to have him home, and he would be joining her in the fight to clear his name. 'I will continue the campaign, though I expect Jeffrey to now share it with me. We will now do it together.' Except that they wouldn't actually be together; Jeffrey had decided to live at the penthouse in London rather than with his wife in Grantchester. Within a few hours, Jeffrey had his first meeting with a probation officer who was supervising his release on licence. With telling arrogance, William Archer parked his car on a red line outside the probation office.

Mary praised her boys for being absolute rocks. 'I salute them. It must have been very hard for them to watch their father go through that. Both of them in different ways have taken forward aspects of the fight for justice.' While the *Daily Mail* gave Mary a sympathetic platform, the *Guardian* took a different slant. Jeffrey intended to reinvent himself as a prison reformer, it said, as part of a confidence trick to make it look like his spell inside wasn't a punishment so much as a research project. Michael Gove of *The Times* had been even more scornful. 'The truth doesn't matter to the Archers. It never has. All that counts is coming out on top. And shamefully using the little people who get in your way ... The Archers have relished briefing the press that nemesis awaits all those who have stood against them. From Angie Peppiatt, who made the unforgivable mistake in the Archers' eyes of telling the truth in court, to Emma Nicholson, the Lib Dem peer who asked pertinent questions about the management of Jeffrey's charity efforts ... no one is to be spared ... No one who saw Mary's thin smile of triumph outside court after reducing this wretch [Jane Williams] to penury could doubt for a second that something dark runs in those veins. Mary, whose husband dealt profitably in Anglia Television shares while she was usefully employed as a director of that company, is no *ingénue*. Mary, whose curiously confused evidence ... was not quite what one would expect from the chairman of the ethics forum at Addenbrooke's Hospital, is quite a woman.'[6]

It was only a matter of weeks before Jeffrey was again making headlines, as a guest speaker at a conference organised by the Howard League for Penal Reform. He was somewhat pre-empted by his wife, who had already told the press that prison was 'a monumental waste of time', and that prison officers were lazy. This was quite a turnaround from ten years earlier, when Jeffrey had brought the Tory conference to its feet by urging the home secretary to be tougher on criminals, with stiffer penalties for white-collar crime. (As a result, his friend Michael Howard, then home secretary, changed the rules on the right-to-silence – to Jeffrey's detriment in 2001.) Jeffrey also made news in a novel role, that of Mary's running coach. She was taking part in a charity fun-run in Cambridge in aid of her hospital, and had to complete a 1.7 mile leg of the race, known as 'Chariots of Fire'. Ever the perfectionist, Mary had been in training for several months, particularly on breathing control, and had twice run the actual course to make sure she could do it. Shortly before the race, she and Jeffrey went to Scotland for a holiday, and limbered up by climbing Ben Nevis. According to her friend and former squash partner, Stephen Feldberg, she is a good athlete, but she found that running wasn't as easy as it looks; nevertheless she was clearly a very fit fifty-eight-year-old. Jeffrey himself, at sixty-four, was also in exceptional shape and a year after his release ran the 26-mile London marathon in 5 hours 26 minutes to raise money for charity. One of the people he had the nerve to ask for sponsorship was a former director of Anglia television.

In the summer of 2004, a year after his release from prison, Jeffrey was bouncing back once again. He was working on a screenplay about the mountaineer George Mallory; he was photographed at a party at the Kit Cat Club, meeting 'well-heeled ladies'; and his *Prison Diary: Hell* was put on as a play at the Edinburgh Festival fringe. In August, an intriguing news story hit the headlines, involving Jeffrey, his friend and oil-trader Ely Calil, and Mark Thatcher, son of Jeffrey and Mary's friend the former prime minister, Baroness Thatcher. The story concerned an attempted coup in the oil-rich African state of Equatorial Guinea, and one paper had documents which appeared to show that someone with the same surname and initials as Jeffrey had paid more than £74,000 to an offshore bank account belonging to the ex-SAS mercenary Simon Mann, who had led the ill-fated attempt. It was alleged the coup plot was financed by wealthy backers in Britain and South Africa, who were promised a share of the country's oil revenues. Jeffrey, using a new firm of solicitors in Sheffield, Irwin Mitchell, denied any involvement or 'prior knowledge' of the coup. His carefully worded statement had a familiar ring. It said: 'Our client strenuously denies any involvement in . . . events . . . We can confirm no further comment will be made by our client who considers the matter closed. Lord Archer has made his statement and it does not amount to an acceptance that the money was paid by Lord Archer into the account you mention . . . [he] will not hesitate to commence legal action should it be suggested that he was involved in any way.'[7] Ely Calil also issued a denial. His actor son George was quoted a few days later as saying he and James Archer were 'like brothers. Our families often spend Sundays together and we always have a real laugh when we go out.'

The story came around the time Mary travelled to New York, where she called on the president of this publisher's parent company to discuss this book. She was also having a break from her demanding responsibilities as chairman at Addenbooke's, which she somehow managed to fit in along with her campaign on Jeffrey's behalf. 'Fortunately, I can compartmentalise things,' she explained. 'It is important to me that the rest of my life goes on, and I'm very grateful to my friends and colleagues who have enabled that.' This is undoubtedly the case: as long as Mary separates her private life from her professional life, her colleagues – academic, NHS and business – seem willing to accept her for her outstanding abilities, and her fundraising acumen, and to turn a blind eye to her other *persona*. Mary even managed to give an interview about her medical treatment at Addenbrooke's – *A Bed to Remember* – without a mention in the article that she was the chairman. And 'unauthorised' media interest is rebuffed or ignored. Jeffrey is usually kept at arm's length, although he attends some social functions: 'We don't talk about him; she doesn't mention him; she is Doctor, not Lady, Archer here,' said one hospital employee. 'Her life with Jeffrey is a different world; it's not relevant,' says another. Scientists, too, say Mary is careful not to mix her personal life with her professional life. Although being 'Lady' Archer is very important to Mary, her 'Doctor' status is even more so. 'Call yourself Lady and they think you haven't got your O levels,' she once remarked. 'It's assumed you are a member of the Board of Visitors without a single O level to your name.'

Mary's supporters – those who would speak – praise her commitment and hard work, her knowledge of the issues, her focused agenda. She has no fear of medical professionals; she is used to dealing with scientists; she is good at detail and chairing meetings.

'The Trust has many irons in the fire, things it is trying to do politically, and locally with the council and so on,' says Dr Richard Henderson, head of the Laboratory of Molecular Biology. 'Mary is quite skilful in that area. For example, she hosted a seminar with business people about the rapid transit system that's proposed for the city.' As chairman, she is part of the Cambridge power base: 'Addenbrooke's is an enormous place in terms of kudos and clout,' says one observer. 'Major research bodies are involved, and captains of industry. She invites the right people to dinner and is a good front person.' Professor Stephen Smith, a former board member and now principal of medicine at Imperial College, says he was very impressed with Mary. 'The general feeling is that Addenbrooke's has been a success story . . . she's been extraordinarily positive and has every right to feel linked to its success.'

Mary does a great deal for the hospital, as she has with other institutions with which she has connections. 'She's a grafter for status,' says one NHS colleague. 'She takes a look round the room and goes for the most important person. She doesn't waste her time on lesser fry.' Her skills are a huge asset to the organisations she deals with; she is hardworking, conscientious and efficient. She gives her time, she helps with fundraising, donates to 'deserving' causes, lends her house for charity events, provides useful and important introductions through her extensive network of high-powered contacts, attends functions, opens fetes and gives prizes – she even launched a new type of sweet pea for charity. She has become 'a significant donor' to her old Oxford college, St Anne's, where alumnae from Mary's year set up a Year of 1962 bursary worth £25,000. She has done a lot to help fundraise for the refurbishment of the Cambridge University chemistry labs, a place she feels is home. 'Mary is in and out of the chemistry laboratory all the time,' says Dr Peter Richards, editor of an alumni magazine. 'She does a huge amount of unpaid and, outside the University, unpublicised work to support the place. She will cheerfully entertain you with mugs of tea in the rather seedy top-floor tea-room, and is on first-name terms with everyone, including the secretaries and lab technicians.' But there are dissenters. One leading chemist says, 'Unless she wants something, when she can be charming, she doesn't talk to people below her status.'

As with Jeffrey, many people are in her debt. Others are afraid of her – intimidated because she is clever, powerful, rich and litigious; even Jeffrey says that on occasion she frightens him.[8] Not everybody thinks the wife of a convicted perjurer should be holding a public office – especially one who is actively campaigning to re-varnish his reputation – but they dare not say so. Not even Labour party members or union officials in Cambridge will give their opinions publicly. Of the few who will talk about her most do not want to be named. Academics of both Oxford and Cambridge are also wary of upsetting the woman who has lent her glamorous flat for development fund meetings, helped find sponsors for their appeals, spent hours at committee meetings on their behalf, invited them to her parties. 'I would not want to offend Mary,' said one don. 'She would be a ruthless and tenacious opponent.'

Although they claim to separate her professional role from her private life, Mary's colleagues – particularly those in the public sector – are clearly embarrassed and defensive about working with someone who, however talented and useful, is so closely linked with a disreputable character like Jeffrey. One of Mary's supporters at the university admits that many people, including some hospital consultants, regard her as 'too tainted by association' for a public position and an inappropriate choice because she does not use NHS medicine. And a former NHS colleague says 'she likes to be surrounded by sycophants, by yes-men'. Researching this book, it was not surprising to get scant help from Cambridge University chemistry department, or from Addenbrooke's hospital. But it is significant, nevertheless, to find that not one member of the trust board, nor a number of past members, will comment. Two put the phone down and most simply ignored requests; hardly a cheerful endorsement of a well-respected colleague and somehow not quite in the new spirit of 'openness and transparency' which the health service is now supposed to embrace.

She has friends in high places. In March, I wrote to Sir William Wells, the head of the NHS Appointments Commission to check the accuracy of information I had been given about the way Mary had been selected. My source had told me that the Regius professor, Sir Keith Peters, had lobbied Wells, saying Mary was the right person for the job. In his reply to me, Wells – who knows Peters extremely well – denied such lobbying had occurred. Although our correspondence was marked 'private and confidential', shortly afterwards the content of our letters was apparently given to Mary as her solicitors referred to them in correspondence. Transparency seems to work one way, at least.

As Mary enters her sixties she can look back on a fantastic life of privilege and good fortune. She was born with a very good brain, and she has made the most of her opportunities through hard work, determination, ambition and careful presentation. 'She's a good lass; she's done us proud,' says her former Oxford tutor, Hazel Rossotti. But her fellow Oxford chemist Gillian Howarth says, 'I think she has had a very frustrating life for somebody so talented and with such a lot of opportunities. I can't believe she's given her heart to photovoltaic cells! She's never managed to achieve what she might have been anticipated to achieve . . . she hasn't really flowered in her own right, but there's still time.' Mary does indeed have plenty of time to do more; one must not confuse a biography with an obituary, as another of her admirers pointed out. Like Elizabeth, her devout Welsh grandmother, Mary has tried to do good in her community; and she does her duty, particularly to her husband, and uses her talents. Many people say she is helpful, generous with her time, efficient and reliable. A few mention private kindnesses that never reach the press. Members of her family say she is affectionate and supportive, turning up to christenings and weddings and handing down her and Jeffrey's expensive clothes to cousins. Socially, she can be more relaxed and light hearted than her public image suggests; an excellent hostess. She likes to lay on entertainments for her guests, and is famous for her New Year's Eve party quizzes which she carefully compiles herself, drawing on her wide-ranging knowledge.

Her friends think she is fun, charming and good company; 'she's certainly got a merry side to her,' says a musician who's worked with her. A school friend says, 'She probably comes over as a bit tougher and cooler than she really is.' Some, particularly men, find her friendly and sparkling; and a challenge. Always, she is poised, elegant and impeccable. 'Mary has a defensive shield,' says Sir Nicholas Bonsor. 'Underneath she is a deeply caring person with a warm personality.' 'If only she could lighten up and have real fun,' says an artistic friend. 'I think she's careful not to be seen to unbend unless she's very close to people.'

She remains, despite enormous publicity throughout her life, an enigma; partly because there are conflicting strands to her personality, but largely because she stays married to Jeffrey. 'We're a good team,' she thinks. It has been pointed out many times that Jeffrey and Mary are opposites: he's original, imaginative and inventive; Mary is guarded, painstaking and perfectionist. She is cautious; Jeffrey thrives on risk. He would like her to be more frivolous but he needs her to be a 'heavyweight' to give him ballast. Jeffrey can appear lightweight and trivial, whereas Mary says she finds serious things amusing. Their different and complementary personalities were what attracted them to each other, and probably still do, but the relationship is cemented by their many similarities.

The Archers are both workaholics who like to be permanently occupied; they are energetic, orderly and obsessively tidy. They were both good teachers: Jeffrey because he is enthusiastic and inspirational, Mary because she is good at precise and lucid explanations. Jeffrey is notoriously gaffe-prone; Mary is disarmingly frank when it suits her. They share political views, a love of the theatre and of art. They both like life in the fast lane; image, presentation and self-promotion are vitally important to them; like many famous people, they are both attention seeking and self-centred, and enjoy being interviewed about themselves. 'They are very good at taking the credit,' notes one acquaintance, 'that's a feature of the Archer publicity set-up.' They are both very careful with money and like a bargain, though are often hospitable to the press, and articles often mention this. Importantly, they are equals: 'This love, honour and obey is all very well,' said Jeffrey, 'but if you're married to someone as bright as Mary there's not much obeying going on . . .' On the other hand, he knows they are multi-millionaires because of his books, not her brains. Mary admits to being unemotional and, in a curious way, so is Jeffrey despite his bonhomie. There is a lack of engagement with other people, who often feel they are being used in some way to serve the Archers' own purposes: 'One couldn't make friends with them,' said a company director. 'It's all geared to some angle; there's a certain condescension involved in inviting you as one of their guests.' A woman who has sat on a board with Mary says, 'She makes very good use of her networks, and they've served her well. She uses them and drops them as and when required; but then we all do.' Jeffrey says he likes to think he gets the credit for Mary's 'ability to use contacts to get things done'. Although the Archers have many acquaintances, they appear to have few close friends. 'It's very hard to get a smile out of Mary,' one of her university contemporaries observes. 'She doesn't see the need to relate to someone. It's one of the startling things about her poise which makes her rather intimidating. She is very self-contained and enormously restrained.' A ruined Lloyd's Name is blunter: 'A bit of her is missing.' Mary herself puts it another way: 'You are the way you are . . . It suits me to preserve reserve when I am on display . . . if you keep your private thoughts private then that is exactly what they are and you are not visited by anyone you don't want around. If you let it all hang out, what is left for you?'

The defining characteristic of Mary is her control: her self-control, her emotional control, and the need to control her life as far as she can. She did what she could to try to obstruct this book, using all the powers at her disposal, from the petty (banning me from attending a lecture she gave; asking her photographer friend Billett Potter not to let me use any of his pictures for the book – pictures already seen by millions) to the obstructive (asking people not to speak to me and making unfounded accusations about me). She also used more direct methods (lawyers' letters and an appointment with the president of Simon & Schuster in New York) – and of course there was bullying from Jeffrey. She has controlled her looks, her publicity and her private life. Being married to Jeffrey has made this difficult, of course, but until recently Mary has managed somehow to control the damage – by giving him respectability, having a successful career of her own, rescuing him at the libel trial, glossing over his 'mistakes', fighting his corner and presenting him to the world as a victim. When faced with something she can't control, such as his imprisonment, her judgement seems to desert her. Hand in hand with the control is being in a position of power: power over her husband, power in her career, power over the audiences she tantalises with her performances in slinky dresses. The inevitable question is how much of her life has become a performance, to keep up the right appearances and protect the reality? Why the need for so much secrecy, for ever-present lawyers, for an injunction? Mary tries to have it both ways – media exposure *and* privacy. Yet the privacy case showed aspects of Mary that can't be concealed behind a confidentiality injunction. As the *Daily Express* said, 'Not even a Trappist silence from Ms Williams would have hidden the petty vanities that led Mary to undergo a facelift and then seek to conceal the fact. Had she not sued, the facelift would have remained an irritating rumour. By going into the witness-box, Mary was forced to admit both to the facelift and to the embarrassment at having had it . . . Had Mary failed to gag her assistant, what could Jane Williams have usefully added to our knowledge of the Archers?'[9]

The Channel 4 documentary in 2003 was also revealing. It showed that Mary came from a family where there were high parental expectations – essentially well meaning and caring, but short on emotional expression. She says she would rather die than discuss her emotions in public and is proud she was brought up in a household where 'you didn't go to the doctor unless you were on a stretcher; didn't complain of feeling cold and didn't give in to this, that or the other'. Her brother, David, spoke of Mary's formative years of 'not showing emotional upset when under pressure', and of how their father abhorred risk. David Weeden says it's a family thing: 'Mary and I are quite alike and my wife always says I am essentially emotionless.'[10] It is interesting that Janet, the eldest Weeden sibling who was a very successful example to Mary at school, became a secretary and the wife of an economist; that David married a motherly nurse who enjoyed being a housewife, but that Mary, who was 'such fun' as a little girl, rebelled by choosing a highly unconventional, ambitious and racy husband. Nevertheless, her father's opinion was important to her and she always valued his approval; twenty-five years after his death she said she wished she could see him and say, 'This is how I turned out – are you pleased?'

It has been said that Mary is like two people; indeed, she feels that way herself. She has a need for fun, showmanship, danger and unpredictability – which is why she married Jeffrey in the first place. 'She couldn't have stayed with him if she didn't have a sort of madness inside her somewhere,' says their friend Adrian Metcalfe. She can, through Jeffrey, enjoy a life quite different from what she expected, the sort of life she was brought up to regard with suspicion, and which was repressed until she became an undergraduate at a time of huge social change. She was once asked by her old college whether life had gone as she had hoped since she left St Anne's, and she replied: 'Certainly not as I expected, but all the better for that.' She also thinks that 'real life is so much more bizarre than fiction'. Perhaps she has had a scientific curiosity in Jeffrey and her marriage, staying with it like an experiment to see how it will turn out; he is a challenge which cannot be 'solved' by cool calculation. Perhaps the stress placed on academic achievements in her childhood was at the expense of another side of Mary, which has found its expression in her relationship with Jeffrey.

Some think it is a psychological co-dependence in which she enjoys the power over him when he has to ask for forgiveness. She was once asked if he ever had to forgive *her* for transgression. 'No, it's been a pretty one-way street,' she replied.

Mary's family say she is grateful for the life Jeffrey has given her. 'She has honoured the vows she made to stick with her husband through the good and some really bad times,' says her brother. And Gillian Howarth, who has known Mary since their under-graduate days, says, 'She's a very loyal person and I think she has very fine principles that she tries to stick to all the time. Through thick and thin, she'll stick.' Mary says leaving Jeffrey is 'an unthinkable thought' and her steadfast loyalty has been much admired, although in recent years it has been interpreted as a kind of arrogance, a refusal to accept that she has made a mistake. Her school friend Lisa Jardine suspects that Mary is 'crucified' that Jeffrey wasn't 'the great success' and that an enormous amount of what she does is 'a personal attempt to rescue that situation. Because "we" never lose at anything, and it won't do for that to have gone wrong.' Another classmate agrees: 'If she left him, it would reflect on her, and if she allowed it all to be true, she would have to face a lot about herself and I think she would find that dif-ficult.' Yet another school friend says, 'I don't think Jeffrey could live without her. I think he needs her; she protects him.' Or maybe she needs him. Elliott Bernard, the property developer whose daughter Tara is now engaged to James Archer says, 'She stays with Jeffrey because of loyalty and love.' And staying is also a practical option; it is simply easier than divorce, and better for their sons. She enjoys the high-life with Jeffrey which she would be unlikely to have as ex-Lady Archer: 'Mary Archer is the Posh Spice of the middle-aged,' says the former *Sun* editor Kelvin Mackenzie.

Her celebrity status means she can sing cabaret songs with prime ministers at her feet. She doesn't need to stay for the money, as divorce would leave her wealthy, 'a much richer woman than remaining married', she has already calculated,[11] and providing she did not remarry she would still be able to call herself Lady

Archer. She doesn't need to go off to lead her own life, as she already has one. And quite apart from the difficulty of finding eligible and available men of a suitable age, a new relationship would be a gamble. Mary has spoken, with intriguing insight, of her apprehension of walking away into the unknown: 'In the first flush of some new love, of course you imagine that a new relationship or a new marriage will put right everything that went wrong in your previous life, but nothing, nothing could be more unlikely or untrue . . .'[12] Mary's view is that striving after happiness is often deceptive, because no life is perfect. 'It would take great optimism to suppose that the next one would do any better, wouldn't it? . . . Striving after happiness, it's so often illusory . . . Life is imperfect. You change everything, your new life will also have imperfections in it.'

When Jeffrey was released from prison, several PR experts were asked for their views on revamping his image. 'He should be hosting a new game show called *What's My Lie?*,' said Max Clifford. 'Mary is his biggest problem; she's become increasingly unpopular in the past few years. She could host a programme on cosmetic surgery. But there's no way that they'll follow this advice. They can't see the reality. How can you change their image if they themselves can't see the problem?'[13]

Some who know Mary speak of her high principles, but there are areas where she displays an amorality which is striking. She has spoken of sexual infidelity as being relatively unimportant, objectively, and she has brushed off wrongdoing (dishonesty, perjury, share manipulation) by her husband and her son as trivial 'mistakes'. This is one reason people are distrustful of her, particularly in terms of holding public office. On the day Jeffrey was sent to prison, the journalist and former Tory MP Matthew Parris said sympathy for her was 'out of place and always has been . . . I have no doubt that Mary Archer found out a very long time ago the kind of man she married. Each of them understands each other very well. I've a pretty good idea she'd have known quite a lot of what was going on, though perhaps not all. And she's come to

321

terms with that marriage to that man and with that partnership . . . she's a pretty grown-up person who has not been taken in.'[14]

Maybe Mary shares the view, held by some of Jeffrey's friends, that he is a person who doesn't know he is dishonest – he is simply a fantasist for whom fact and fiction are hopelessly muddled. Mary says to *her*, he is not a criminal. She loves him, although is not 'in love'. 'There are many aspects of love,' she said some years ago, 'and the tenderness which grows from long familiarity is under-valued . . . I'm immensely fond of him and I defy any wife of 30 years to do better than that.' Mary has been with Jeffrey since she was nineteen and her reasons for staying with him have remained constant: 'Because I want to . . . Because I like it here. I like the place I'm in . . . This is my life, too. I don't want to walk out of my life.' Jeffrey's explanation is that it's 'chemistry, a subject that's always been a mystery to me. I simply adore her.'

In 1995, Mary was asked to write for the *Sunday Times* about a book which had affected her in her youth. She chose Henry James's novel *The Portrait of a Lady*, and with characteristic thoroughness, before writing her article she went to see an English don at Newnham to rehearse her thoughts about the book, even though she had a clear idea of what she wanted to say. Mary, in her early twenties, had identified herself with the young heroine in the novel, who is called Isabel Archer. Isabel is innocent, curious, clever, and with everything a girl could want: 'Kindness, admiration, bon-bons, bouquets, the sense of exclusion from none of the privileges of the world she lived in, abundant opportunity for dancing, plenty of new dresses, the London *Spectator*, the latest publications . . .' Mary thinks of Henry James's story as a fairy-tale in reverse; the reader is not allowed to know what happens to Isabel Archer in the end, except that she is not happily married. And here, as with so much in the Archers' life, fact and fiction are blurred. We can only speculate about what will happen to Mary Archer and *her* marriage. She says she wants to be remembered – although not just yet – as 'someone who did good and not mischief'; as a scientist 'who made a useful contribution'. But she's not ready to be *remembered* for anything; she's still thinking about what she can usefully do next. When she's an old lady she wants to learn to play the organ.

In the meantime, she is clearly proud of the achievement for which she is best known, and always will be known: 'Whatever happens,' she says, 'I know that I have done my best for Jeffrey.'

ENDNOTES

Prologue

1 *The Archers: Not an Everyday Story of Country Folk*, BBC2, 18 August 1987
2 *Sunday Times*, 14 June 1998
3 *Daily Mail*, 19 September 1996
4 *Sunday Telegraph*, 18 May 2003
5 Martyn Lewis, *Reflections on Success*, Lennard Publishing, 1997, p. 32

Chapter 1

1 *Daily Mail*, 25 July 1987
2 *Evening Standard*, 31 October 1995
3 *Eureka: Conversations with Scientists*, BBC Radio 4, 13 March 1995; *My Favourite Hymns*, Granada TV, 19 May 2002
4 *Daily Telegraph: Weekend*, 19 December 1998
5 *Desert Island Discs*, BBC Radio 4, 17 April 1988
6 Chairman's Notes, Epsom Cine Society, 15 January 1953
7 *My Favourite Hymns*, Granada TV, 19 May 2002

Chapter 2

1 *Sunday Times*, 29 December 1991
2 *Eureka: Conversations with Scientists*, BBC Radio 4, 13 March 1995
3 *My Favourite Hymns*, Granada TV, 19 May 2002
4 *Tatler*, November 1992
5 *Cheltenham Ladies' College Magazine*, 1957
6 Lisa Jardine interview [quoted in *Jeffrey Archer: Stranger Than Fiction*, Fourth Estate, 2000]; *My Life With Jeffrey*, Channel 4 TV, 19 May 2003
7 *Evening Standard*, 31 October 1995
8 *My Favourite Hymns*, Granada TV, 19 May 2002
9 *Daily Telegraph*, 6 December 2003

10 *My Life With Jeffrey*, Channel 4 TV, 19 May 2003
11 *Cherwell*, 26 February 1964
12 *Mail on Sunday: You* magazine, 4 July 1999
13 *Mail on Sunday: You* magazine, 4 July 1999
14 *Smart to be Smart*, BBC Radio, 25 March 1997

Chapter 3

1 *My Life With Jeffrey*, Channel 4 TV, 19 May 2003
2 *Desert Island Discs*, BBC Radio 4, 17 April 1988
3 *Omnibus*, BBC TV, 13 May 1998
4 *Omnibus*, BBC TV, 13 May 1998
5 *Independent on Sunday*, 14 February 1993
6 *Smart to be Smart*, BBC Radio, 25 March 1997
7 *Evening Standard*, 20 October 1993
8 *My Life With Jeffrey*, Channel 4 TV, 19 May 2003
9 *My Favourite Hymns*; *Desert Island Discs*
10 Interview with Oxfam official
11 *My Favourite Hymns*, Granada TV, 19 May 2002
12 *This Is Your Life*, Thames TV, 14 January 1981
13 *My Life With Jeffrey*, Channel 4 TV, 19 May 2003
14 *Omnibus* rushes, BBC TV, 13 May 1998

Chapter 4

1 Letter, N. Hall to J.D. Walters, 23 February 1966, NBT/N6/1/1
2 Letter, Archer to H.J. Heinz & Co., 14 November 1966, NBT/N6/7/1
3 H. Berkeley, interview with Michael Crick
4 *Evening Standard*, 27 September 1967
5 *Daily Mail*, 17 June 1968
6 *Evening Standard*, 20 October 1993
7 *Daily Telegraph*, 15 January 1986
8 *Daily Mail*, 8 October 1969
9 Louth Conservatives' campaign leaflet, 1969
10 *Desert Island Discs*, BBC Radio 4, 17 April 1988
11 *Sun*, 11 December 1969
12 *Sun*, 11 December 1969
13 *Daily Express*, 26 February 1970
14 *Daily Mail*, 3 November 1970

Chapter 5

1 *Mail on Sunday: You* magazine, 4 July 1999

2 *Daily Mail*, 6 January 1994
3 *The Archers: Not an Everyday Story of Country Folk*, BBC2, 18 August 1987; *Independent*, 21 May 1990
4 *Daily Mail*, 6 January 1994; *Independent*, 21 May 1990
5 *Daily Mail*, 14 December 1972
6 *Daily Telegraph*, 10 May 1974
7 *Daily Mirror*, 29 August 1975
8 *Daily Telegraph*, 10 May 1974
9 *Woman's Own*, 7 June 1986
10 *Grimsby Evening Telegraph*, 23 August 1974; *Daily Mirror*, 24 August 1974

Chapter 6

1 *London Evening News*, 23 August 1974
2 *London Evening News*, 23 August 1974
3 *The Archers: Not an Everyday Story of Country Folk*, BBC2, 18 August 1987
4 *My Life With Jeffrey*, Channel 4 TV, 19 May 2003
5 *Sunday Express*, 25 March 1984
6 *Daily Mail*, 6 January 1994
7 *Sunday Times*, 10 July 1994
8 *Cambridge Evening News*, 24 March 1980
9 *Daily Express*, 9 December 1977
10 *Daily Express*, 9 December 1977
11 *Daily Mail*, 9 December 1977
12 *Sunday Times*, 4 July 1982

Chapter 7

1 *Woman's Own*, 7 June 1986
2 *Woman's Own*, 7 June 1986
3 *Woman's Own*, 8 November 1980
4 *Woman's Own*, 8 November 1980
5 *My Favourite Hymns*, Granada TV, 19 May 2002
6 *Daily Telegraph*, 15 January 1986
7 *Private Eye*, 16 July 1982
8 *Sunday Times*, 4 July 1982
9 Perjury Trial Transcript, Day 15, 19 June 2001, p. 22
10 *Daily Express*, 4 September 1985
11 *Daily Mail*, 17 February 1984
12 *Daily Telegraph*, 15 January 1986
13 *Daily Mail*, 10 October 1985

14 *Daily Mail*, 14 October 1985
15 *About Anglia*, Anglia Television, 1981
16 *Daily Mail*, 6 January 1994
17 *Cambridge Cats*, ed. Tony Jedrej, Duckworth, 1994, Foreword
18 *Woman*, 10 October 1987

Chapter 8

1 *Daily Telegraph*, 18 August 1990
2 *Mail on Sunday: You* magazine, 4 July 1999
3 *Woman's Own*, 7 June 1986
4 *Sunday Times*, 1 November 1987
5 Libel Trial Transcript, Day 5, 10 July 1987, pp. 4–5
6 *Prep School* magazine, Spring 1988
7 *Sunday Times*, 1 November 1987
8 *Family Wealth* magazine, April 1987
9 *Apollo* magazine, December 1991
10 *Sunday Telegraph*, 13 May 2001; 27 May 2001

Chapter 9

1 Perjury Trial Transcript, Day 12, 14 June 2001, p. 65
2 *Home on Sunday*, BBC TV, 17 July 1988
3 *Desert Island Discs*, BBC Radio 4, 17 April 1988
4 *Desert Island Discs*, BBC Radio 4, 17 April 1988
5 Libel Trial Transcript, Day 1, 6 July 1987, p. 75
6 LTT, Day 2, 7 July 1987, p. 66
7 *Daily Express*, 28 October 1986
8 LTT, Day 12, 22 July 1987, p. 12
9 Perjury Trial Transcript, Day 21, 29 June 2001, p. 84
10 LTT, Day 4, 9 July 1987, pp. 73–4
11 *Daily Mail*, 27 July 1987
12 *Sunday Times*, 29 December 1991
13 LTT, Day 5, 10 July 1987, p. 2
14 LTT, Day 5, 10 July 1987, p. 8
15 LTT, Day 5, 10 July 1987, p. 1
16 *Woman's Hour*, BBC Radio 4, 19 May 2003
17 LTT, Day 8, 15 July 1987, p. 3
18 ITN news interview, 10 July 1987
19 *Independent*, 24 October 1994
20 LTT, Day 13, 23 July 1987, pp. 2–3
21 *Sunday Times*, 1 November 1987
22 *Mail on Sunday*, 26 July 1987

23 *Mail on Sunday*, 26 July 1987
24 *Daily Mirror*, 29 July 1987
25 *News of the World*, 26 July 1987
26 *The Listener*, 28 July 1988
27 Woodrow Wyatt, *The Journals of Woodrow Wyatt*, Vol. 1, Macmillan, 1998, p. 395
28 *The Economist*, 27 November 1999
29 Michael Crick, *Jeffrey Archer: Stranger Than Fiction*, Fourth Estate, 2000, pp. 296–312

Chapter 10

1 Perjury Trial Transcript, Day 21, 29 June 2001, p. 56
2 *The Mirror*, 25 November 1999
3 *Sunday Times*, 26 July 1987
4 PTT, Day 21, 29 June 2001, p. 54
5 PTT, Day 21, 29 June 2001, p. 65
6 *Daily Mail*, 23 November 1999 and 24 November 1999; *Daily Mirror*, 13 November 1987
7 Martyn Lewis, *Reflections on Success*, Lennard Publishing, 1997, p. 36
8 *Sunday Telegraph*, 31 January 1988
9 *Mail on Sunday*, 22 May 1988
10 *The Archers: Not an Everyday Story of Country Folk*, BBC2, 18 August 1987
11 *Sunday Times*, 10 July 1994

Chapter 11

1 *Guardian*, 11 January 1989
2 *Daily Mail*, 17 November 1988
3 *Evening Standard*, 3 January 1989
4 *Guardian*, 11 January 1989
5 Adam Raphael, *Ultimate Risk*, Corgi, 1995, p. 24 [quoting the Neill Committee 1987]
6 Cathy Gunn, *Nightmare on Lime Street*, Smith Gryphon, 1992, p. 30
7 Cathy Gunn, *Nightmare on Lime Street*, Smith Gryphon, 1992, p. 31
8 Julian Barnes, article reproduced in *Letters from London*, Picador, 1995, p. 226; *Mail on Sunday*, *Night and Day*, 10 October 1993
9 *Daily Express*, 10 July 1996
10 *Sunday Telegraph*, 25 August 1996
11 *Hansard*, 13 July 1994, Members' Interests debate, pp. 1122–30
12 *Country Living*, February 1994; *Sunday Times*, 15 November 1992
13 *Daily Telegraph*, 22 August 2001

Endnotes

Chapter 12

1 Michael Crick, *Jeffrey Archer: Stranger Than Fiction*, Fourth Estate, 2000, p. 367
2 *The Ashdown Diaries*, Vol. 1, Allen Lane, 2000, p. 116
3 *Independent on Sunday*, 20 December 1992
4 *Omnibus* rushes, BBC TV, 13 May 1998
5 *Sunday Express*, 20 March 1988
6 *My Life With Jeffrey*, Channel 4 TV, 19 May 2003
7 *Woman's Hour*, BBC Radio 4, 19 May 2003
8 *Love in the Afternoon*, Channel 4 TV, 13 November 1995
9 *Radio Times*, 17 May 2003
10 Letter, J. Archer to M. Archer, 10 August 1992

Chapter 13

1 *Sunday Times*, 11 September 1994
2 Robin Oakley, *Inside Track*, Bantam, 2001, pp. 345–8
3 Mishcon statement for J. Archer, 24 August 1994
4 *Observer*, 19 May 1996
5 *Sunday Times*, 14 June 1998
6 *Opinion: Light at the End of the Tunnel*, BBC Radio, 29 September 1994
7 *Daily Mirror*, 28 December 1994
8 *Cambridge Evening News*, 28 and 29 December 1994; 12 January 1995
9 *Daily Mail*, 19 September 1996
10 J. Archer interview with P. Donovan, 1996
11 *Liquid Assets* rushes, BBC3 TV, April 2003
12 *Mail on Sunday, You* magazine, 4 July 1999

Chapter 14

1 *Daily Express*, 10 July 1996; *Sunday Telegraph*, 31 August 1997; *Daily Express*, 12 April 1997; *House and Garden*, February 1995; *Evening Standard*, 31 October 1995; *Guardian*, 4 July 1997; *Daily Mail*, 19 September 1996
2 *Omnibus*, BBC1 TV, 13 May 1998
3 *Hello!*, 20 July 1996
4 *Hello!*, 20 July 1996
5 Fulton Gillespie, *About Addenbrooke's*, July 2000
6 J. Williams, Statement to Employment Tribunal, Bury St Edmunds, 29 August 2002, para 31
7 *Times*, 18 February 1998

8 *Hello!*, 21 March 1998
9 Gyles Brandreth, *Brief Encounters: Meetings with Remarkable People*, Politico's, 2001
10 *Mail on Sunday*, 13 August 2000
11 *Evening Standard*, 3 April 1998
12 *Rich and Famous*, Carlton TV, 29 November 2001; *What Makes Jeffrey Tick?*, Channel 5, 28 November 2001; *Jeffrey Archer*, ITN production, 28 January 2005
13 *BBC Breakfast*, BBC1, 7 January 1992
14 *Mail on Sunday: You* magazine, 4 July 1999
15 *Midweek*, BBC Radio 4, 23 January 2002; *Mail on Sunday*, 13 August 2000
16 *Mail on Sunday*, 21 November 1999
17 *Daily Mail*, 29 November 1999
18 *Independent on Sunday*, 28 November 1999
19 *Cocktails with Kit and the Widow*, BBC Radio 3, 8 November 2003

Chapter 15

1 *Sunday Times*, 1 May 1994
2 *Chem@Cam*, Issue 13, Winter 2002; *Daily Telegraph*, 6 February 2002
3 *OK!*, *Daily Express*, 20 February 2001
4 *Daily Mail*, 24 February 2001
5 *Mirror*, 31 May 2001
6 A. Peppiatt's solicitor quoted in *Daily Mail*, 20 July 2001; Perjury Trial Transcript, Day 7, 7 June 2001, p. 39
7 PTT, Day 10, 12 June 2001, p. 53; Day 7, 7 June 2001, p. 29
8 PTT, Day 10, 12 June 2001, pp. 53–4
9 PTT, Day 15, 19 June 2001, pp. 44, 47–9
10 PTT, Day 19, 27 June 2001, p. 135
11 *Mirror*, 30 June 2001
12 PTT, Day 21, 29 June 2001, p. 56
13 PTT, Day 21, 29 June 2001, p. 65
14 PTT, Day 21, 29 June 2001, p. 84
15 *Woman's Hour*, BBC Radio 4, 19 May 2003
16 PTT, Day 21, 29 June 2001, p. 107
17 PTT, Day 21, 29 June 2001, p. 91
18 PTT, Day 21, 29 June 2001, p. 101
19 *Sunday Telegraph*, 22 July 2001
20 PTT, Day 34, 19 July 2001, p. 29
21 PTT, Day 34, 19 July 2001, p. 33
22 PTT, Day 34, 19 July 2001, p. 34

Endnotes

Chapter 16

1 *Sunday Mirror, Mail on Sunday*, 22 July 2001; *Guardian*, 23 July 2001
2 *Sunday Times*, 28 November 1999; *Evening Standard*, 1 July 2004
3 Injunction case, Day 1, 30 June 2003
4 Securities and Futures Authority, Board Notice 594, 27 July 2001, p. 5
5 *Daily Mail*, 6 January 1994
6 *Daily Mail*, 23 July 2001
7 *Sunday Telegraph*, 29 November 1992
8 *Daily Mail*, 23 July 2001
9 P. Healey letter to *Guardian*, 23 July 2001
10 *Today*, BBC Radio 4, 16 August 2001
11 *Richard and Judy*, Channel 4 TV, 29 January 2002
12 KPMG Report: *Investigation into the 1991 Simple Truth Appeal*, 19 November 2001
13 Perjury Trial Transcript, Day 21, 29 June 2001, p. 86; Day 34, 19 July 2001, p. 31
14 *Daily Telegraph*, 27 February 1999
15 *Midweek*, BBC Radio 4, 23 January 2002
16 J. Williams, Statement to Employment Tribunal, Bury St Edmunds, 29 August 2002, para. 82
17 PTT, Day 21, 29 June 2001, p. 77
18 *Today*, BBC Radio 4, 28 September 2002
19 *Daily Mail*, 5 October 2002
20 *Daily Mirror,* 7 October 2002
21 House of Commons Register of Members' Interests, 2000; Lords Register of Interests 2004; C. Moynihan letter to MC

Chapter 17

1 Decision of Employment Tribunal, Bury St Edmunds, 13 November 2002
2 J. Williams statement to Employment Tribunal, 29 August 2002, para. 68
3 *Look East* BBC1, 25 July 2003
4 J. Williams statement to Employment Tribunal, 29 August 2002, para. 86
5 Decision of Employment Tribunal, Bury St Edmunds, 13 November 2002
6 Decision of Employment Tribunal, Bury St Edmunds, 13 November 2002
7 Employment Tribunal, Legal submissions on behalf of J. Williams, para. 34

8 Decision of Employment Tribunal, Bury St Edmunds, 13 November 2002
9 Injunction case judgement, 3 July 2003, para. 28
10 *Radio Times*, 17 May 2003
11 *My Life With Jeffrey*, Channel 4 TV, 19 May 2003
12 *Times*, 21 June 2003
13 Injunction case, Day 1, 30 June 2003
14 *Daily Mail*, 21 July 2003
15 J. Archer, *A Prison Diary, Volume 2*, Macmillan, 2003, p. 89
16 Injunction case, Day 2, 1 July 2003
17 *Guardian*, 2 October 2004
18 J. de Bruyne letter to *Cambridge Evening News*, 15 July 2003
19 *Cambridge Evening News*, 4 July 2003
20 Injunction case, Day 2, 1 July 2003

Chapter 18

1 *Sunday Times*, 6 July 2003
2 *Sentencing and Society* conference, Strathclyde University, 27 June 2002; *Criminal Law Review*, August 2003
3 *Sunday Telegraph*, 11 May 2003
4 *Sunday Mirror*, 1 June 2003
5 *Sunday Telegraph*, 13 July 2003
6 *Times*, 22 July 2003
7 *Mail on Sunday*, 8 August 2004
8 *Hello!*, 20 July 1996
9 *Daily Express*, 4 July 2003
10 *Daily Mail*, 20 July 2001
11 *Daily Mail*, 5 October 2002
12 *Woman's Hour*, BBC Radio 4, 19 May 2003
13 *Independent*, 16 July 2003
14 *Newsnight*, BBC2, 19 July 2001

INDEX

333

at Cambridge 89–95, 97, 104, 105,
121–4
car accident involving, 211
cats liked by, 10, 115, 116, 218
Caulfield's eulogy to, 148
CD made by, 237
charity fun run entered by 310–11
at Cheltenham Ladies' College,
19–24
chemistry first won by 27–8
choirmistress's post taken by,
116–17
Clause 28 criticised by, 158
clothes and, 31, 64, 66, 75, 93,
141, 143, 192–4, 215, 245,
248
Coghlan affair and 127–32, 150
(*see also* Coghlan, Monica)
Colquhoun affair and, 110–12
cosmetic surgery on, 212, 226–7,
272, 298, 318
Desert Island Discs appearance of,
14, 45, 157, 159
Dewar fellowship awarded to, 89
early life of, 9, 10, 13–14, 17–24
energy-saving measures installed by,
181
Farmiloe and, 234
Grantchester book written by, 116
Guild of Church Musicians joined
by, 117
at Imperial College, 51
Imperial College visiting
professorship of, 186, 241
interviewed about marriage,
217–18
James's share dealing and, 214
Jeffrey's appeal and, 268
Jeffrey's libel action and, 139–49
passim, 164
Jeffrey's Louth selection and, 61–3
Jeffrey's mayoral bid backed by,
224
Jeffrey meets, 34–5
Jeffrey's perjury trial and, 245, 248,
251, 252–9
Jeffrey proposes to, 37–8
Jeffrey's trial and, 2, 4
Jeffrey visited in prison by, 263
limerick competition won by, 118
Lloyd's and, 98, 161, 167–80
passim, 185–6, 198

LP made by, 187, 191
lyric-writing skills of, 118–19
Mann-Craven Junior Research
Fellowship held by, 59–60
marriage of, 39, 48
media campaign conducted by, 5
Melchett Medal awarded to 242
memberships held by, 3–4
Millennium Eve party given by, 235
Newnham bye-fellowship of, 162
Newnham fellowship of, 89–90
Nuffield scholarship won by, 24
at Oxford, 24–39
piano exam passed by, 24
pregnancies of, 71, 72–3, 81
public positions of, 2
short-story competition won by,
70–1
singing of, 1, 3, 26, 58, 67, 70, 109,
118, 185–6, 186–7, 216
solar-energy expertise of, 69, 72,
77–9, 95
sought after following libel case,
157–8
Sparks Memorial Prize won by, 23
sponsored swim undertaken by, 65
television approaches to, 79–80
thirtieth wedding anniversary of,
215–17
This Island Now contribution by,
79
twenty-first wedding anniversary of,
156
Who's Who entry of, 183
William born to, 73
Williams's legal battles with, 271–4,
287–93, 296–303
Archer, William (Jeffrey's father),
39–41
Archer, William (son), 72–3, 75, 80,
82, 94, 103–4, 105, 147, 187,
216, 260, 264–6, 289, 309
car accident involving, 211
Coghlan affair and, 128–9, 130
at grandmother's funeral, 262
Jeffrey visited in prison by, 263
in nativity play, 117
999 wheeze committed by 90–1
on parents' fame, 114
at perjury trial, 253
schooling of, 87, 161
TV appearances by 114, 269